Complete
Canadian
Curriculum

Grade **5**

Revised *and* **Updated!**

Math
English
Social Studies
Science

Credits

Photos (Cover "boy" Sergey Novikov/123RF.com, "polar bear" Buchachon Petthanya/123RF.com, "Inuksuk" pilens/123RF.com, "Chateau Frontenac" citylights/123RF.com)

Copyright © 2015 Popular Book Company (Canada) Limited

Printed in China

ISBN: 978-1-77149-033-7

Contents Grade 5

Mathematics

English

ISBN: 978-1-77149-033-7

Social Studies

**Heritage and Identity:
First Nations and Europeans in
New France and Early Canada**

**People and Environments:
The Role of Government and
Responsible Citizenship**

Science

Answers

ISBN: 978-1-77149-033-7

MATHEMATICS

* The Canadian penny is no longer in circulation. It is used in the units to show money amounts to the cent.

ISBN: 978-1-77149-033-7

Numbers to 100 000 (1)

I have ninety-nine thousand nine hundred ninety-nine blocks.

- Write, compare, and order whole numbers to 100 000.
- Write numbers in expanded form and in words.
- Identify the value of a digit in a 5-digit whole number.

Count and write the numbers. Then write the 5-digit numbers in the blocks.

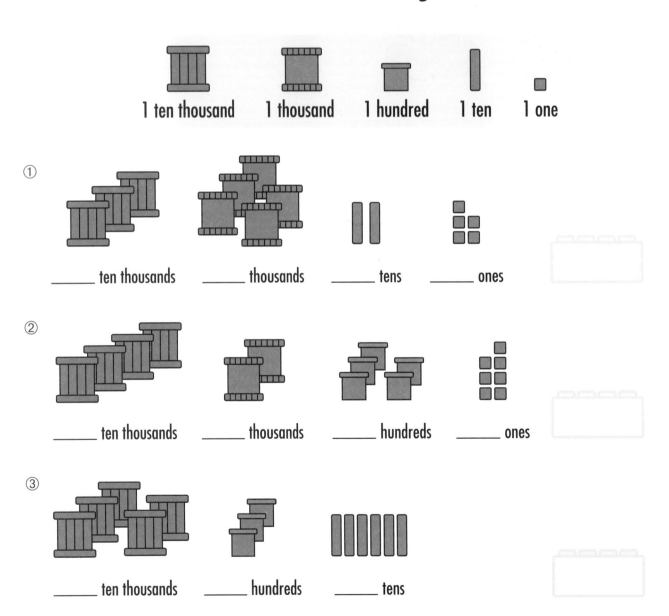

1 ten thousand   1 thousand   1 hundred   1 ten   1 one

① _____ ten thousands   _____ thousands   _____ tens   _____ ones

② _____ ten thousands   _____ thousands   _____ hundreds   _____ ones

③ _____ ten thousands   _____ hundreds   _____ tens

5-digit Numbers:

Forty-three thousand six hundred ninety-two

Standard form
43 692

Expanded form:
40 000 + 3000 + 600 + 90 + 2

Write the numbers in words.

④   36 453   _____

⑤   64 078   _____

⑥   90 156   _____

⑦   28 714   _____

⑧   59 203   _____

Write each number in expanded or standard form.

⑨   34 785 = _____

⑩   76 059 = _____

⑪   52 306 = _____

⑫   80 548 = _____

⑬   _____ = 20 000 + 5000 + 200 + 60 + 7

⑭   _____ = 40 000 + 1000 + 50 + 8

⑮   _____ = 30 000 + 70 + 4

⑯   _____ = 50 000 + 8000 + 900 + 60 + 2

ISBN: 978-1-77149-033-7   Complete Canadian Curriculum • **Grade 5**

Place Value Chart:

56 293

Ten Thousand	Thousand	Hundred	Ten	One
5	6	2	9	3

5 means 50 000;
6 means 6000;
2 means 200;
9 means 90;
3 means 3.

Write the meaning of each digit.

⑰ 27 854

2 means _____ .

7 means _____ .

8 means _____ .

5 means _____ .

4 means _____ .

⑱ 36 819

3 means _____ .

6 means _____ .

8 means _____ .

1 means _____ .

9 means _____ .

⑲ 65 923

6 means _____ .

5 means _____ .

9 means _____ .

2 means _____ .

3 means _____ .

⑳ 75 196

7 means _____ .

5 means _____ .

1 means _____ .

9 means _____ .

6 means _____ .

Write the numbers.

㉑ Write two 5-digit numbers which

a. have a 5 in its ten thousands place. _____

b. have a 9 in its hundreds place. _____

㉒ Write two 5-digit numbers which have a 7 in its thousands place and are greater than 60 000. _____

   ISBN: 978-1-77149-033-7

Comparing 5-digit numbers:

e.g. 27 869 28 113

Compare • 2 7 8 6 9 • 2 7 8 6 9
           2 8 1 1 3   2 8 1 1 3
              ↑   ↑
            same   8 > 7

Compare the digits in the ten thousands place. If they are the same, compare the digits in the thousands place and so on. The number with the greater digit is greater.

27 869 ⊙< 28 113

Put ">" or "<" in the circle.

㉓ 45 273 ◯ 74 511   ㉔ 28 593 ◯ 21 499

㉕ 30 639 ◯ 36 930   ㉖ 68 847 ◯ 68 874

㉗ 53 276 ◯ 35 276   ㉘ 40 083 ◯ 40 003

㉙ 50 600 ◯ 60 500   ㉚ 31 233 ◯ 31 332

Put the numbers in order.

㉛

from least to greatest   37 254   73 524   75 324   32 754

_____

㉜

from greatest to least   40 068   40 680   48 060   48 680

_____

Use the digits on the balls to form different 5-digit numbers. Then put the numbers in order from least to greatest and write them on the lines.

㉝ _____

_____

Numbers to 100 000 (2)

37 596 fish →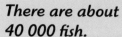

There are about 40 000 fish.

- Follow patterns to find the missing numbers.
- Develop a better understanding of place value of 5-digit numbers.
- Round 5-digit numbers.
- Solve problems involving numbers.

Fill in the missing numbers.

① 68 050 — 68 100 — 68 150 — ____ — ____ — 68 300

② 40 005 — 50 005 — ____ — ____ — 80 005 — ____

③ 78 250 — 79 250 — ____ — ____ — ____ — 83 250

④

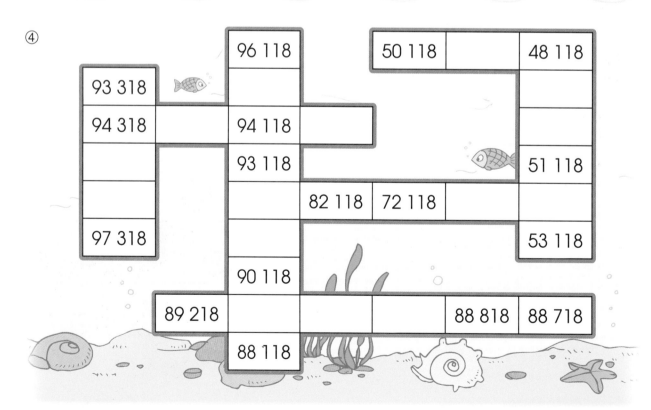

ISBN: 978-1-77149-033-7

Write the numbers.

⑤ a number 3000 more than 45 888 _____

⑥ a number 20 000 more than 73 645 _____

⑦ a number 500 less than 67 833 _____

⑧ a number 20 less than 58 624 _____

⑨

How many numbers are there between 79 997 and 80 004? What are they?

_____ ; _____

⑩

What number is 44 444 more than eleven thousand one hundred eleven? Write the answer in standard form and in words.

_____ ; _____

Write three sentences to describe the relationships between any two numbers in each group.

37 808 is 80 less than 37 888.

⑪

36 888
37 808   37 888
36 088

_____

_____

_____

⑫

59 650
60 650   70 650
59 550

_____

_____

_____

Rounding to the nearest ten thousand:

e.g. 38 625 —round up→ **40 000**

1st Look at the digit in the thousands place.

8 > 5

2nd If it is 5 or greater, round the number up; otherwise, round the number down.

84 173 → **80 000**

4 < 5

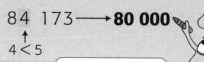

round down

Round each number to the nearest ten thousand.

⑬ 46 534 _____

⑭ 17 225 _____

⑮ 93 108 _____

⑯ 88 622 _____

⑰ 77 655 _____

⑱ 60 213 _____

⑲ 35 271 _____

⑳ 44 306 _____

Round each number to the nearest thousand.

㉑ 37 246 _____

㉒ 46 850 _____

㉓ 62 109 _____

㉔ 98 764 _____

㉕ 53 324 _____

㉖ 73 052 _____

㉗ 44 623 _____

㉘ 11 088 _____

㉙

36 450 cm

14 375 mL

12 225 g

$40 860

a. The height of the building is about _____ cm.

b. The capacity of the cooler is about _____ mL.

c. The bag of potatoes weighs about _____ g.

d. The ring costs about $ _____ .

ISBN: 978-1-77149-033-7

Help David write each number in numerals and round it to the nearest thousand.

...thirty-six thousand four hundred eighteen dollars were collected in the fundraising campaign...

...ABC Company has sold eighty-nine thousand seven hundred five packs of chocolate...

...twenty-one thousand five hundred sixteen men and seventeen thousand three hundred two women were asked about their favourite songs...

...there were twelve thousand two hundred seven people who visited Shark Land last week and seventeen thousand six hundred people this week...

③⓪

Exact: $ _____

About: $ _____

③①

Exact: _____ packs

About: _____ packs

③②

Exact: _____

About: _____

Exact: _____

About: _____

③③ **Shark Land**

a.

	Last Week	This Week
Exact	visitors	visitors
About	visitors	visitors

b.

About how many people in all visited me in these two weeks?

about _____ people

ISBN: 978-1-77149-033-7

Addition and Subtraction of 4-Digit Numbers

$$\begin{array}{r} 9988 \\ -\ 4695 \\ \hline 5293 \end{array}$$

- Add or subtract 4-digit numbers.
- Estimate or check the answers.
- Solve word problems.

$9988

$4695

I cost $5293 more than you.

Find out the number of toy cars a factory produced last year. Do the addition. Then circle the correct answers.

①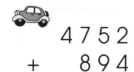
$$\begin{array}{r} 4752 \\ +\ \ \ \ 894 \\ \hline \end{array}$$

②
$$\begin{array}{r} 2563 \\ +\ 1309 \\ \hline \end{array}$$

③
$$\begin{array}{r} 5114 \\ +\ 2637 \\ \hline \end{array}$$

④
$$\begin{array}{r} 884 \\ +\ 5676 \\ \hline \end{array}$$

⑤
$$\begin{array}{r} 4060 \\ +\ 1947 \\ \hline \end{array}$$

⑥
$$\begin{array}{r} 3805 \\ +\ 1698 \\ \hline \end{array}$$

⑦ 2562 + 1768 = _____

⑧ 594 + 2677 = _____

⑨ 3815 + 3815 = _____

⑩ 1890 + 3274 = _____

⑪ 4206 + 189 = _____

⑫ 3105 + 2916 = _____

⑬ Which toy cars were produced the most?

⑭ How many and were produced in all?

523   8267   7267

Do the subtraction.

⑮
```
  6 2 4 3
- 1 5 9 6
```

⑯
```
  2 7 5 4
- 1 8 8 6
```

⑰
```
  5 0 0 4
- 3 6 9 7
```

⑱
```
  4 0 8 1
- 3 6 5 4
```

⑲
```
  3 3 0 6
- 2 5 1 7
```

⑳
```
  5 1 1 6
-   9 2 5
```

㉑ 2603 – 1564 = _____

㉒ 5077 – 4653 = _____

㉓ 9468 – 7430 = _____

㉔ 2566 – 888 = _____

Find the difference between the items.

㉕  − _____

The difference is _____ .

㉖

The difference is _____ .

㉗

The difference is _____ .

㉘

The difference is _____ .

㉙

Tickets Sold	
Mon	3682
Tue	4723

The difference is _____ .

㉚ **Eggs**

White: 2764

Brown: 5657

The difference is _____ .

ISBN: 978-1-77149-033-7

Round each number to the nearest thousand to do the estimate. Then find the exact answer.

㉛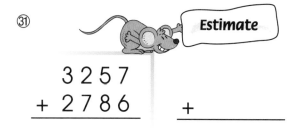

$$\begin{array}{r} 3\ 2\ 5\ 7 \\ +\ 2\ 7\ 8\ 6 \\ \hline \end{array}$$

+ _____

㉜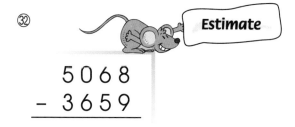

$$\begin{array}{r} 5\ 0\ 6\ 8 \\ -\ 3\ 6\ 5\ 9 \\ \hline \end{array}$$

㉝

$$\begin{array}{r} 1\ 9\ 2\ 4 \\ +\ 3\ 1\ 6\ 9 \\ \hline \end{array}$$

㉞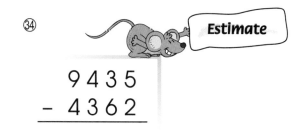

$$\begin{array}{r} 9\ 4\ 3\ 5 \\ -\ 4\ 3\ 6\ 2 \\ \hline \end{array}$$

Check the answer of each question. Put a check mark in the space provided if the answer is correct; otherwise, put a cross and find the correct answer.

㉟

A $3257 + 1464 =$ _4721_

B $8016 - 477 =$ _8539_

C $1594 + 2806 =$ _4410_

D $5253 - 2478 =$ _2775_

E $7000 - 2885 =$ _4115_

F $946 + 4193 =$ _5039_

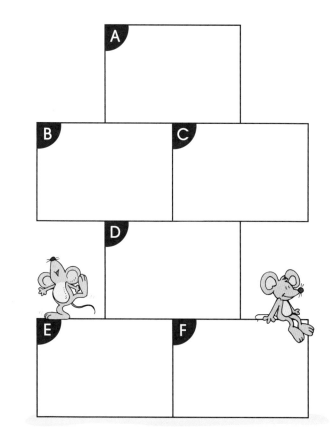

ISBN: 978-1-77149-033-7

Read what the children say. Help them solve the problems.

There were 4262 men and 3788 women who visited the library last week.

765 books and 432 audio items were delivered to homebound users last year.

There are 4663 hardcover and 982 paperback storybooks in the children's section.

㊱   How many people visited the library last week?

_____ = _____   _____

㊲   How many more men than women visited the library last week?

_____ = _____   _____

㊳   How many storybooks are there in the children's section?

_____ = _____   _____

㊴   If 3405 children storybooks are borrowed, how many storybooks will be left in the library?

_____ = _____   _____

㊵

I'm responsible for the library delivery service. How many items in all did I deliver to homebound users last year?

_____ = _____

_____

4

Multiplication

- Multiply 2-digit numbers by 2-digit numbers.
- Solve problems involving multiplication.

> I have 13 necklaces. I have 156 beads in all.

Fill in the missing numbers to complete the steps to do multiplication. Then find the answers.

① **Multiply by the ones.** ⟶ **Multiply by the tens.** ⟶

```
  3                3
  3 4            3 4
x 2 8          x 2 8
               2 2
```

```
  3 4            3 4            3 4
x 2 8          x 2 8          x 2 8
2 7 2          2 7 2          2 7 2
    0            8 0          6 8 0
```

34 x 28 = _____

② **Multiply by the ones.** ⟶ **Multiply by the tens.** ⟶

```
  2                2
  6 9            6 9
x 5 3          x 5 3
                 7
```

```
  4                4              
  6 9            6 9            6 9
x 5 3          x 5 3          x 5 3
2 0 7          2 0 7          2 0 7
    0            5 0          3 4 5 0
```

69 x 53 = _____

ISBN: 978-1-77149-033-7

Do the multiplication.

③
```
      2 7
  x   1 4
```

④
```
      3 8
  x   2 9
```

⑤
```
      4 7
  x   3 9
```

⑥
```
      3 4
  x   2 2
```

⑦
```
      5 3
  x   3 2
```

⑧
```
      6 8
  x   4 5
```

⑨ 42 x 16 = _____

⑩ 37 x 13 = _____

⑪ 61 x 45 = _____

⑫ 55 x 34 = _____

⑬ 73 x 23 = _____

⑭ 18 x 26 = _____

⑮ 52 x 19 = _____

⑯ 49 x 49 = _____

⑰ 18 x 67 = _____

⑱ 53 x 24 = _____

⑲ 35 x 48 = _____

⑳ 27 x 82 = _____

Fill in the missing numbers.

㉑
```
      3 _
  x   _ 6
    2 0 _
      8 _
    _____
    8 _ 4
```

㉒
```
        9 _
  x     _ 4
      4 1 3
    2 3 _
    _____
      _ 7 _
```

Look at the pictures. Complete the tables. Then answer the questions.

㉓

No. of Boxes	Chicken Burgers		Detergent	
	No. of Burgers	Cost	No. of Loads	Cost
15				
29				
47				
58				

㉔

No. of Bags	Candies		Balloons	
	No. of Candies	Cost	No. of Balloons	Cost
18				
26				
34				
85				

㉕ Mrs. Green buys 16 boxes of detergent. How many loads are there in all?

_____ = _____   _____

㉖ Aunt Lucy buys 42 bags of balloons for her company. How many balloons are there in all?

_____ = _____   _____

ISBN: 978-1-77149-033-7

Solve the problems.

㉗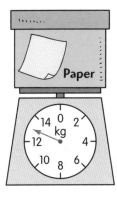

What is the total weight of 36 boxes of paper?

The total weight is _____ .

㉘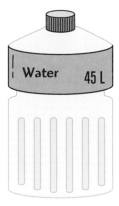

How much water do 28 bottles hold in all?

_____

㉙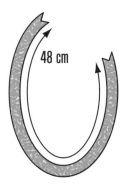

What is the total length of 33 ribbons?

_____

㉚ *How many pieces of dog treats are there in 22 boxes?*

_____

ISBN: 978-1-77149-033-7

5

I put 486 candies equally into 3 baskets. Each basket holds 162 candies.

Division (1)

- Divide 3-digit numbers by 1-digit numbers with no zero in the quotient.
- Use multiplication and addition to check answers.
- Solve problems involving division.

Do the division.

①

$$4 \overline{)736}$$

②

$$7 \overline{)847}$$

③

$$6 \overline{)744}$$

④ 351 ÷ 3 = _____

⑤ 856 ÷ 4 = _____

⑥ 632 ÷ 2 = _____

⑦ 585 ÷ 5 = _____

⑧ 938 ÷ 7 = _____

⑨ 768 ÷ 6 = _____

⑩ 976 ÷ 8 = _____

⑪ 765 ÷ 3 = _____

⑫

a. 3 girls share a box of beads equally. Each girl has _____ beads.

b. A pack has 6 sheets of stickers. There are _____ stickers on each sheet.

ISBN: 978-1-77149-033-7

Fill in the missing numbers.

⑬
```
        7 2 R 4
    ┌─────────
  5 │ 5 0
      4 9
    ─────────
          8
          1
    ─────────
```

⑭
```
      2     R
    ┌─────────
    │ 8 3
      6
    ─────────
      2 4
      2
    ─────────
        2
```

⑮
```
      1     R
    ┌─────────
  6 │ 5 1
    ─────────
        1
        2
    ─────────
        3
        0
    ─────────
```

Check the answer of each division sentence. Put a check mark in the space provided if it is correct; otherwise, put a cross and write the correct answer.

⑯ 475 ÷ 3

= _158 R 1_

Check 1st _____ X _____ = _____
                  quotient   divisor

2nd _____ + _____ = _____
     the answer above   remainder

⑰ 716 ÷ 5

= _144 R 4_

Check 1st _____ X ____ = _____

2nd _____ + ____ = _____

⑱ 647 ÷ 4

= _161 R 3_

Check 1st _____ X ____ = _____

2nd _____ + ____ = _____

⑲ 927 ÷ 6

= _153 R 5_

Check 1st _____ X ____ = _____

2nd _____ + ____ = _____

Steps to do division:

4) 3 2 8 ← 3 < 4; consider 1 more digit

```
      8 2
4 ) 3 2 8  ← There are 8 4's
    3 2        in 32.
    ───
      8
      8
```

328 ÷ 4 = **82**

Divide the things equally. Show your work. Then fill in the blanks.

⑳ **525** cm – **7** pieces

Each: _____ cm

 364 g – **4** bowls

Each: _____ g

 753 mL – **8** glasses

Each: _____ mL

Juice left: _____ mL

 466 blocks – **9** towers

Each: _____ blocks

Blocks left: _____

Do the division.

㉑   394 ÷ 5 = _____   ㉒   627 ÷ 8 = _____

㉓   564 ÷ 9 = _____   ㉔   463 ÷ 7 = _____

㉕   165 ÷ 6 = _____   ㉖   274 ÷ 4 = _____

㉗   583 ÷ 7 = _____   ㉘   391 ÷ 8 = _____

ISBN: 978-1-77149-033-7

Solve the problems.

㉙

488 children

a. 3 children in a group
- _____ groups
- _____ children left

b. 7 children in a group
- _____ groups
- _____ children left

㉚

755 flowers

a. 4 flowers in a vase
- _____ vases
- _____ flowers left

b. 6 flowers in a vase
- _____ vases
- _____ flowers left

㉛ Judy, Marco, and Tiffany share a box of 413 chocolate eggs equally. How many chocolate eggs does each child have? How many chocolate eggs are left?

_____ = _____

Each child has _____ chocolate eggs. _____ chocolate eggs are left.

㉜ Each bag has 8 gumballs. If Jason wants to give 178 gumballs to his friends, how many bags of gumballs does he need to buy?

_____ = _____

_____

㉝

This jumbo lollipop is on sale now. Its sale price is $2 less. If Mrs. White pays $125 for lollipops, how many lollipops can she get? What is her change?

_____ = _____

_____

6

Division (2)

My dress has 3 layers! There are 104 flowers on each layer.

- Divide 3-digit numbers by 1-digit numbers with zeros in the quotient.
- Solve problems involving division.

Complete the long division.

①
```
      0
  4 ) 4 3 6
  _____
      3
  _____
```

②
```
      0 7 R
  6 ) 6 4 7
  _____

  _____
```

③
```
      0   R
  5 ) 5 3 2
  _____
      2
  _____
```

④
```
        0 R
  7 ) 8 4 2
  _____
    1 4
  _____
```

⑤
```
        0 R
  8 ) 9 6 5
      8
  _____

  _____
```

⑥
```
        0 R
  3 ) 7 8 1
  _____
      1
  _____
```

⑦
```
    1 0
  5 ) 5 0 5
      5
  _____

  _____
```

⑧
```
    1 0   R
  7 ) 7 0 6
  _____

  _____
```

⑨
```
      0 5
  6 ) 6 3 0
  _____

  _____
```

ISBN: 978-1-77149-033-7

Do the division.

⑩

8) 8 5 2

⑪

3) 4 5 1

⑫

4) 8 3 4

⑬ 845 ÷ 7 = _____

⑭ 543 ÷ 5 = _____

⑮ 542 ÷ 3 = _____

⑯ 617 ÷ 6 = _____

⑰ 535 ÷ 5 = _____

⑱ 763 ÷ 7 = _____

⑲ 942 ÷ 9 = _____

⑳ 561 ÷ 4 = _____

㉑ 724 ÷ 6 = _____

㉒ 963 ÷ 8 = _____

Look at the picture. Solve the problems.

㉓　a.

If 4 boys share a box of stickers equally, how many stickers will each boy get? How many stickers will be left?

_____ = _____

Each boy will get _____ stickers.

_____ stickers will be left.

b.

If 6 girls share a box of stickers equally, how many stickers will each girl get? How many stickers will be left?

☺ Stickers
822

_____ = _____

Each girl will get _____ stickers. _____ stickers will be left.

 ISBN: 978-1-77149-033-7

Complete Canadian Curriculum • **Grade 5**

e.g.

$5 \overline{)302}$ ← 3 < 5; consider 1 more digit

$$
\begin{array}{r}
60\ \text{R}\ 2 \\
5\ \overline{)\ 3\ 0\ 2} \\
3\ 0 \\
\hline
2
\end{array}
$$

Remember to put a zero in the quotient.

302 ÷ 5 = **60R2**

Look at the picture. Solve the problems.

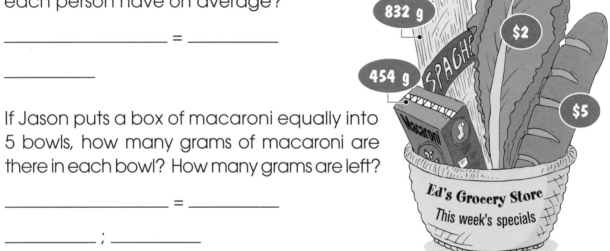

㉔ Mrs. Smith buys a pack of spaghetti for her family of 4 people. How many grams of spaghetti does each person have on average?

_____ = _____

_____

㉕ If Jason puts a box of macaroni equally into 5 bowls, how many grams of macaroni are there in each bowl? How many grams are left?

_____ = _____

_____ ; _____

832 g $2

454 g $5

Ed's Grocery Store
This week's specials

㉖ Mrs. Green spends $100 on buying lettuce for her restaurant. How many heads of lettuce does she buy in all?

_____ = _____   _____

㉗ The bakery has collected $350 from selling French loaves. How many French loaves have been sold in all?

_____ = _____   _____

㉘ A loaf is cut into 9 pieces. If Mr. Shaw needs 365 slices of bread, how many loaves of bread does he need to buy?

_____ = _____   _____

ISBN: 978-1-77149-033-7

Solve the problems. Do the long division in the spaces provided.

㉙ If Maria cuts the ribbon into 4 equal lengths, how long is each piece? How much ribbon is left?

Each piece is _____ cm. _____ cm of ribbon is left.

㉚ Each teaspoon can hold 9 g of sugar. How many teaspoons of sugar are there in one bag? How much sugar is left?

_____

㉛  Aunt Lucy uses 6 mL of dish detergent every day to do the dishes. How many days does a bottle of dish detergent last?

_____

㉜  Katie saves $8 each month for the dress. How many months does it take Katie to save enough money to buy the dress?

_____

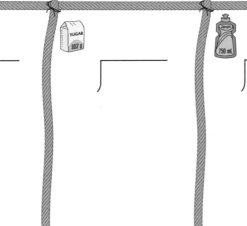

More about Multiplication and Division

- Do basic multiplication or division.
- Solve problems involving the multiplication or division of multi-digit whole numbers.
- Solve problems involving whole numbers up to 100 000 or 2-step problems.

The quilt will have:
12 columns and 14 rows

There will be 168 pictures on the quilt.

```
   12
x  14
   48
  120
  168
```

Find the answers.

①
```
    36
x   24
```

②
```
    79
x   15
```

③
```
    27
x   48
```

④ 9)523

⑤ 6)674

⑥ 4)815

⑦ 18 x 25 = _____

⑧ 64 x 19 = _____

⑨ 275 ÷ 3 = _____

⑩ 504 ÷ 5 = _____

⑪ 910 ÷ 6 = _____

⑫ 28 x 41 = _____

⑬ 67 x 33 = _____

⑭ 451 ÷ 4 = _____

ISBN: 978-1-77149-033-7

Look at the pictures. Solve the problems.

⑮   a.   A box has 945 pieces of gum. How many packs
          of gum are there in a box?

          _____ = _____   _____

      b.   How much do 15 packs of gum cost?

          _____ = _____   _____

      c.   If Leo and his family consume 2 packs of gum
          every day, how many packs of gum do Leo
          and his family consume in March?

          _____ = _____   _____

⑯

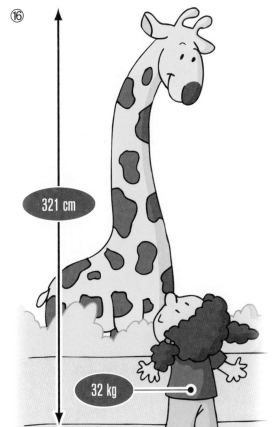

321 cm

32 kg

      a.   The giraffe is 3 times the height of Sue.
          How tall is Sue?

          _____ = _____

          _____

      b.   The giraffe is 18 times as heavy as Sue.
          How heavy is the giraffe?

          _____ = _____

          _____

      c.   Sue visited 7 zoo animals in
          112 minutes. How much time did she
          spend visiting each animal?

          _____ = _____

          _____

Read what the people say. Help them solve the problems.

⑰

> *How many boxes hold 100 000 sheets of paper?*

- 1 package: _____ sheets

- 8 packages: _____ sheets

- 1 box: _____ sheets

- 5 boxes: _____ sheets ←

- 20 boxes: _____ sheets ←

—make 100 000 sheets

_____ boxes hold 100 000 sheets of paper.

⑱

> *A sheet has 20 labels. How many packs do I need for 100 000 labels?*

- 1 sheet: _____ labels

She needs _____ packs for 100 000 labels.

⑲

> *How many boxes hold 200 000 markers?*

- 1 pack: _____ markers

_____ boxes hold 200 000 markers.

ISBN: 978-1-77149-033-7

Solving 2-step problems:

How much do 8 boxes of cookies cost?

1st $8 \div 2 = 4$ ← Find the number of 2's in 8.

2nd $\$5 \times 4 = \$20$ ← Find the cost.

8 boxes cost $20.

Solve the problems. Show your work.

⑳

How much do 81 boxes of juice cost?

81 boxes of juice cost $ _____ .

㉑

How much do 78 muffins cost?

78 muffins cost $ _____ .

㉒

How much do 52 CDs cost?

52 CDs cost $ _____ .

㉓

What is the total area of 96 small pieces of cloth?

Area: 5 dm²

The total area is _____ dm².

ISBN: 978-1-77149-033-7

Length, Distance, and Time

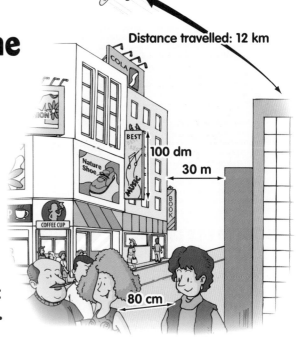

Distance travelled: 12 km

100 dm

30 m

80 cm

- Choose the most appropriate standard unit to measure length, height, width, and distance, using mm, cm, dm, m, or km.
- Do unit conversions.
- Find time intervals to the nearest second and elapsed time.

Choose the most appropriate standard unit to do each measurement. Write it on the line.

km   m   dm   cm   mm

①   the thickness of a dime   _____

②   the length of your arm   _____

③   the length of your thumb   _____

④   the distance between Toronto and New York   _____

⑤   the width of a swimming pool   _____

⑥   the length of a tunnel   _____

⑦   the thickness of a lunch box   _____

⑧   the height of Mount Everest   _____

⑨

a.   the distance between the girls

_____

b.   the distance between the girls and the whale

_____

ISBN: 978-1-77149-033-7

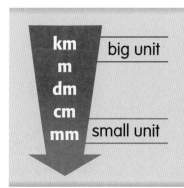

The relationships between the units:

1 km = 1000 m

1 m = 10 dm = 100 cm

1 dm = 10 cm

1 cm = 10 mm

e.g.

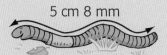

5 cm 8 mm

5 cm 8 mm = 50 mm + 8 mm
= 58 mm

The worm is 58 mm long.

Fill in the blanks.

⑩ 4 m = _____ cm

⑪ 8 km = _____ m

⑫ 6 dm = _____ cm

⑬ 9 cm = _____ mm

⑭ 8000 m = _____ km

⑮ 60 cm = _____ dm

⑯ 700 cm = _____ m

⑰ 50 mm = _____ cm

⑱ 7 km 8 m

= _____ m + 8 m

= _____ m

⑲ 9 cm 8 mm

= _____ mm + 8 mm

= _____ mm

⑳ 5 dm 6 cm

= _____ cm + 6 cm

= _____ cm

㉑ 4 m 9 cm

= _____ cm + 9 cm

= _____ cm

Do the conversion. Show your work. Then circle the greater measurement.

㉒

A to B : 4 km 20 m

C to D : 4150 m

㉓ Sam's height : 1 m 15 cm

Teddy's height : 9 dm 8 cm

You can find time intervals to the nearest second by using an analogue clock.

e.g. Start eating a cookie   Finish the cookie   Time taken

9:20:25   9:21:08

It took me 43 seconds to finish a cookie.

See how long it took each child to hop 50 times. Find the time taken. Then answer the questions.

㉔ Start   Finish

Sally: _____ S

Start   Finish

Frankie: _____ S

Start   Finish

Alexander: _____ S

Start   Finish

Tiffany: _____ S

㉕ Who took the longest time to hop 50 times?   _____

㉖ Who is the winner?   _____

㉗ *If I finished at* [clock] *, would I be the winner?*

Tiffany

_____

We can use subtraction to find time intervals. Sometimes we need to find the time interval in 2 steps.

e.g. 8:46 a.m. ⟶ 4:20 p.m.

1st 8:46 ⟶ noon

```
  12 : 0 0
–  8 : 4 6
  ─────────
   3 : 1 4
```
(3 h 14 min)

2nd noon ⟶ 4:20 p.m.
(4 h 20 min)

Time interval:
3 h 14 min + 4 h 20 min
= 7 h 34 min

The time interval is 7 h 34 min.

Find the travelling time of each train from Villa Village to Cook City. Then answer the question.

㉘

Train	Departure Time	Arrival Time	Travelling Time
A	8:25 a.m.	12:07 p.m.	
B	6:53 a.m.	11:51 a.m.	
C	10:12 a.m.	3:54 p.m.	
D	11:29 a.m.	4:16 p.m.	

㉙　　Which train is the fastest?　　_____

Ask your parent to give you a calendar. Then find the durations with the help of it.

㉚　From Sep 1 to Nov 30　•　_____ months or _____ weeks

㉛　From Apr 3 to May 7　•　_____ weeks or _____ days

㉜　From Apr 1 to Jun 30　•　_____ months or _____ weeks

㉝

If I start working on Project A on Mar 8, 2015 and the deadline is on Mar 7, 2017, how much time do I have to spend on this project?

_____ years or _____ months

ISBN: 978-1-77149-033-7

Perimeter and Area (1)

- Measure and record the perimeters and areas of regular and irregular polygons.
- Draw polygons with a given area or perimeter.
- Solve problems about perimeter or area.

Your face has an area of about 144 cm².

Find the perimeter of each polygon.

①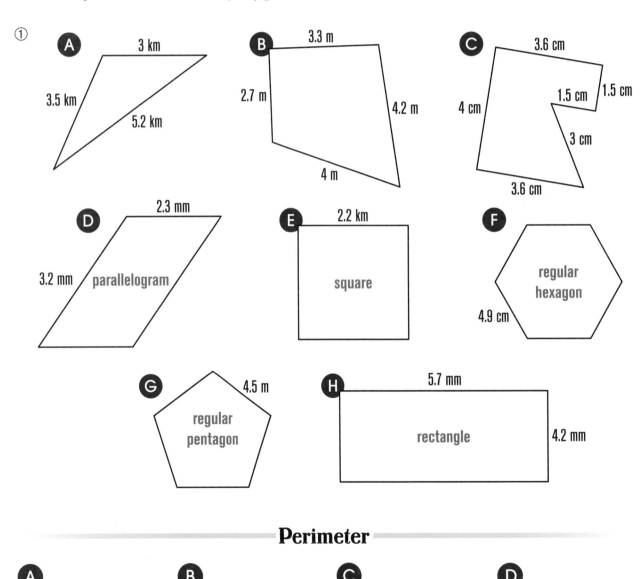

A
3 km
3.5 km
5.2 km

B
3.3 m
2.7 m
4.2 m
4 m

C
3.6 cm
1.5 cm
1.5 cm
4 cm
3 cm
3.6 cm

D
2.3 mm
3.2 mm
parallelogram

E
2.2 km
square

F
regular hexagon
4.9 cm

G
4.5 m
regular pentagon

H
5.7 mm
rectangle
4.2 mm

Perimeter

A _____   B _____   C _____   D _____

E _____   F _____   G _____   H _____

ISBN: 978-1-77149-033-7

Find the area of each shape.

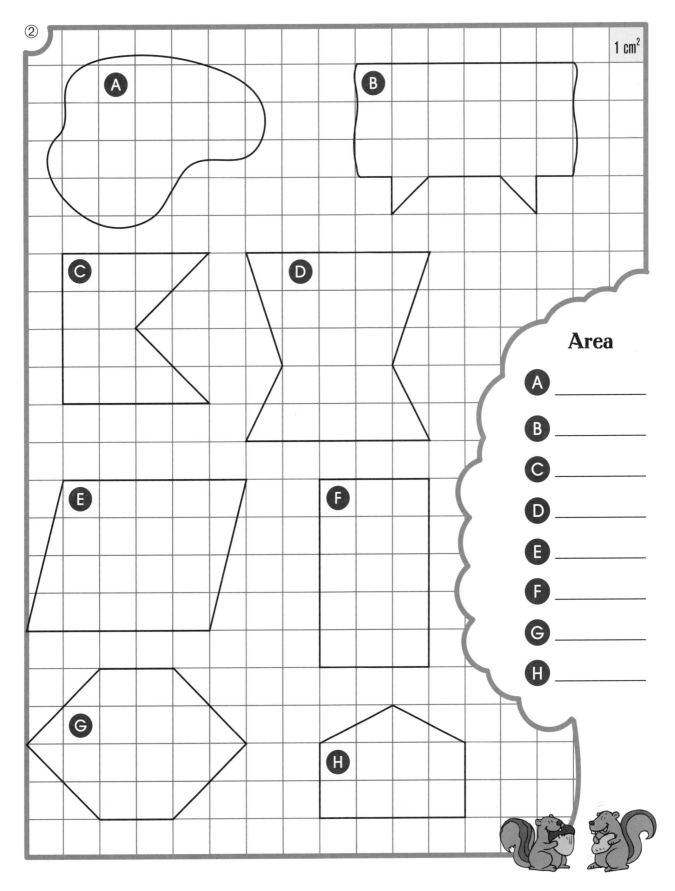

② 1 cm²

A

B

C

D

Area

A _____

B _____

C _____

D _____

E _____

F _____

G _____

H _____

E

F

G

H

Draw 4 different rectangles, each with a perimeter of 20 cm. Then find the area of each rectangle and write the answer in it.

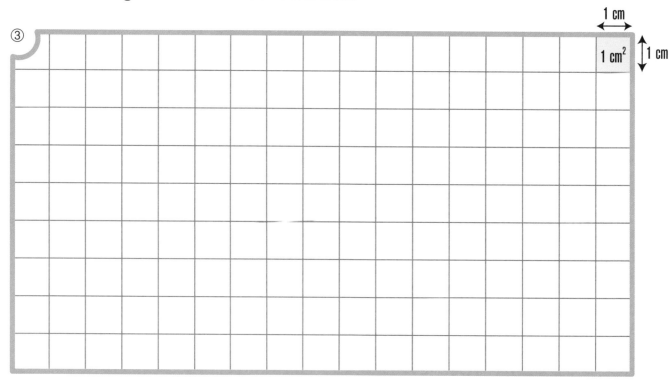

Draw 3 different rectangles, each with an area of 24 cm². Then find the perimeter of each rectangle and write the answer in it.

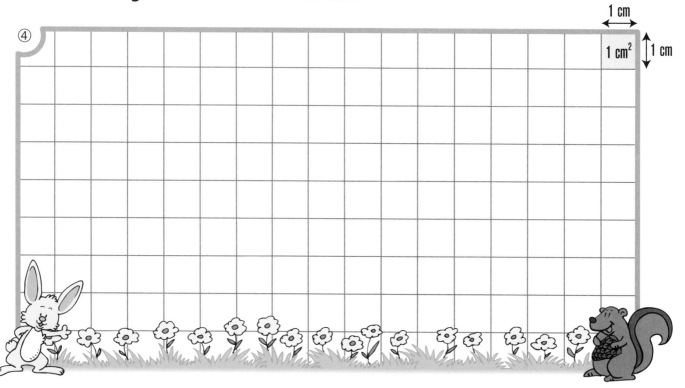

ISBN: 978-1-77149-033-7

Solve the problems.

⑤ 8 cm

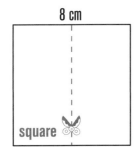

square

> If I cut along the dotted line to get two identical rectangles, what is the perimeter of each rectangle?

_____

⑥ 15 cm

13 cm

rectangle

> If I want to cut a square with the greatest area from this rectangle, what is the perimeter of that square?

_____

⑦

Area: 36 cm²

parallelogram

> If 42 parallelograms are needed to cover a carpet, what is the area of the carpet?

_____

⑧

Area: 126 cm²

trapezoid

> I've used 3 triangles of the same size to form this trapezoid. What is the area of each triangle?

_____

⑨ 20 cm

18 cm   18 cm

36 cm   36 cm

42 cm

> What is the "perimeter" of my dog?

_____

Perimeter and Area (2)

Area of the rectangle:
= 46 x 42
= 1932 (cm²)

46 cm

42 cm

- Use formulas to find the perimeters and areas of rectangles.
- Solve problems related to perimeters or areas.

The area of my picture is 1932 cm².

Read what Emily says. Then fill in the blanks and follow Emily's method to find the perimeters of the rectangles.

①

A rectangle has 2 lengths and 2 widths. The perimeter of a rectangle is the sum of 2 lengths and 2 widths.

8 cm

5 cm

- 2 lengths: _____   • 2 widths: _____

Perimeter = _____ + _____ = _____

My perimeter is _____ .

② 15 cm

10 cm

- 2 lengths: _____
- 2 widths: _____

Perimeter = _____ + _____

= _____ ( )

③ 8 m

25 m

- 2 lengths: _____
- 2 widths: _____

Perimeter = _____ + _____

= _____ ( )

ISBN: 978-1-77149-033-7

Formula for finding the perimeter of a rectangle:

Perimeter = 2 x length + 2 x width

width

length

Perimeter = 2 x 16 + 2 x 9
= 32 + 18
= 50

9 cm

16 cm

The perimeter of the rectangle is 50 cm.

Use the formula to find the perimeter of each rectangle.

④

A 16 cm

8 cm

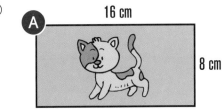

B 12 m

7 m

C 40 cm

72 cm

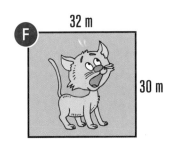

D 13 cm

18 cm

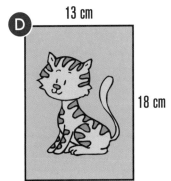

E 10 cm

16 cm

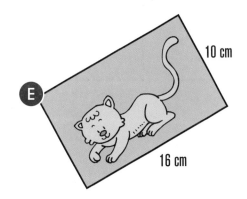

F 32 m

30 m

A Perimeter

= _____

= _____

= _____

B Perimeter

=

C Perimeter

=

D Perimeter

=

E Perimeter

=

F Perimeter

=

ISBN: 978-1-77149-033-7

Formula for finding the area of a rectangle:

Area = length x width

width

length

9 cm

16 cm

Area = 9 x 16

= 144

The area of the rectangle is 144 cm².

Find the lengths and widths of the rectangles. Then find the areas of the rectangles by counting and using the formula.

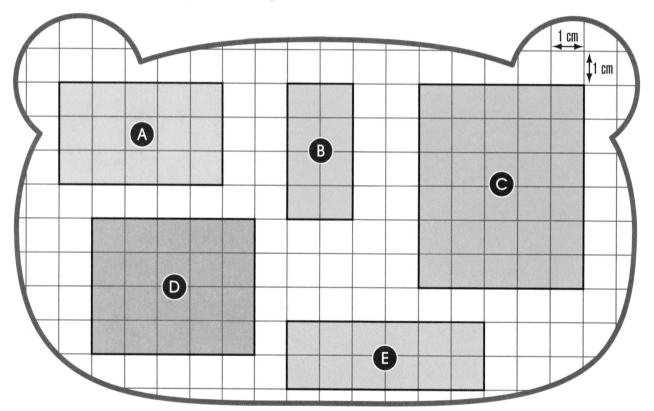

⑤

Area

	Length	Width	By counting	By using formula
A				
B				
C				
D				
E				

ISBN: 978-1-77149-033-7

Solve the problems.

⑥ What is the length of the rectangle?

Area = 153 cm^2 9 cm

The length is _____ .

⑦ If the length of the poster is 10 cm longer than the width,

a. what is the length?

The length is _____ .

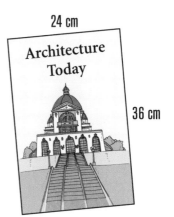

48 cm

b. what is the perimeter of the poster?

The perimeter of the poster is _____ .

⑧ a. What is the area of the picture?

24 cm

Architecture Today

36 cm

The area is _____ .

b. What is the perimeter of the picture?

The perimeter is _____ .

⑨

The width of my favourite picture is 32 cm. If its perimeter is 118 cm, what is its length?

Its length is _____ .

ISBN: 978-1-77149-033-7

Mass, Capacity, and Volume

It can hold 4 layers of 40 centimetre cubes.

Volume
= 40 x 4
= 160 (cm³)

- Choose the most appropriate standard unit to measure mass (e.g. mg, g, kg, or t).

- Understand the relationships between capacity and volume by comparing the volume of an object with the amount of liquid it can contain or displace.

- Use a formula to find the volume of a rectangular prism.

My volume is 160 cm³.

Complete the diagram and fill in the blanks with the short forms of the given units.

gram (g)	kilogram (kg)	milligram (mg)	tonne (t)

① **Big Unit**

Small Unit

② Relationships between the units:

a. 1 t = 1000 _____

1 kg = 1000 _____

1 g = 1000 _____

4 t = 4000 _____

6 kg = 6000 _____

7 g = 7000 _____

b. 5000 kg = 5 _____

6000 mg = 6 _____

4000 g = 4 _____

8000 g = 8 _____

9000 kg = 9 _____

3000 mg = 3 _____

Choose the appropriate unit for the mass of each object. Write "mg", "g", "kg", or "t".

③ a feather _____

④ an elephant _____

⑤ a man _____

⑥ a pencil _____

⑦ a pea _____

⑧ a whale _____

⑨ an apple _____

⑩ a watermelon _____

ISBN: 978-1-77149-033-7

A centimetre cube is a cube with length, width, and height of 1 cm.

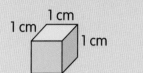

1 cm
1 cm
1 cm

Volume = 1 cm³

A cubic container with all edges 1 cm long can hold 1 millilitre of liquid.

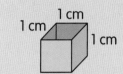

1 cm
1 cm
1 cm

Capacity = 1 mL

The relationship between volume and capacity: **1 cm³ = 1 mL**

The children use centimetre cubes to show the capacity and volume of each container. Help them record the measurements. Then fill in the blanks.

⑪

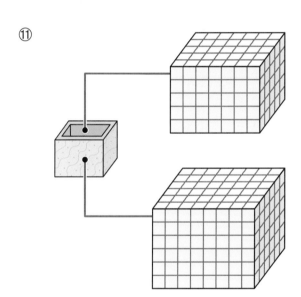

Capacity

- No. of cubes in each layer: _____
- No. of layers: _____
- Capacity: _____ mL

Volume

- No. of cubes in each layer: _____
- No. of layers: _____

  Volume: _____ cm³

⑫

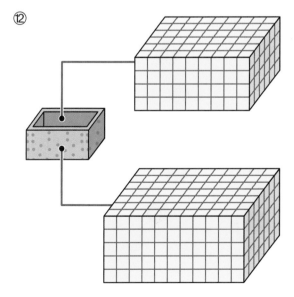

Capacity

- No. of cubes in each layer: _____
- No. of layers: _____
- Capacity: _____ mL

Volume

- No. of cubes in each layer: _____
- No. of layers: _____
- Volume: _____ cm³

ISBN: 978-1-77149-033-7

Formula for finding the volume of a rectangular prism:

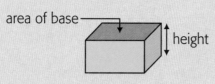

area of base ——— height

Volume = area of base x height

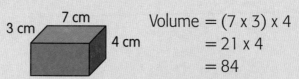

7 cm
3 cm
4 cm

Volume = (7 x 3) x 4
= 21 x 4
= 84

The volume of this prism is 84 cm³.

Look at each rectangular prism built with centimetre cubes. Fill in the blanks.

⑬

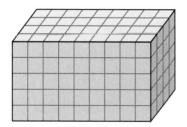

Area of Base = _____ cm²

Height = _____ cm

Volume = _____ x _____

= _____ (cm³)

⑭

Area of Base = _____ cm²

Height = _____ cm

Volume = _____ x _____

= _____ (cm³)

Find the volume of each rectangular prism.

⑮

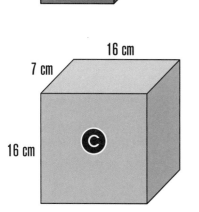

11 cm
2 cm
Ⓐ
9 cm

16 cm
7 cm
Ⓒ
16 cm

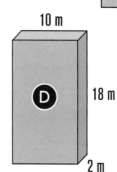

10 m
Ⓓ
18 m
2 m

8 cm
7 cm
Ⓑ
2 cm

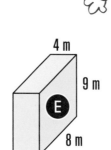

4 m
9 m
Ⓔ
8 m

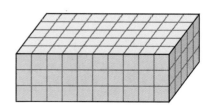

Volume

Ⓐ

Ⓑ

Ⓒ

Ⓓ

Ⓔ

ISBN: 978-1-77149-033-7

Draw a line on each solid to cut it into two rectangular prisms. Find the volume of each prism. Then find the volume of the solid.

⑯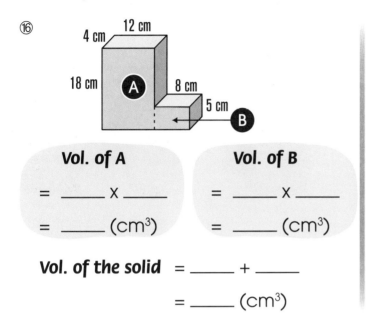

Vol. of A	Vol. of B
= ____ × ____	= ____ × ____
= ____ (cm³)	= ____ (cm³)

Vol. of the solid = ____ + ____

= ____ (cm³)

⑰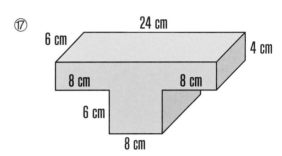

Vol. of the solid = ____ + ____

= ____ (cm³)

Help Elaine find the volume and the capacity of the aquarium with a thickness of 1 cm.

⑱ **Volume**

Length = 30 cm

Width = ____ cm

Area = ____ × ____ = _____ (cm²)

Height = ____ cm

Volume = ____ × ____ = _____ (cm³)

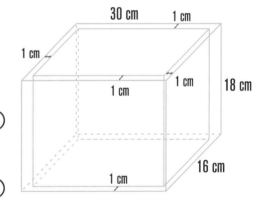

Capacity

Length = 30 − 2 = 28 (cm)

Width = _____ = _____ (cm)

Height = _____ = _____ (cm)

Area = ____ × ____ = _____ (cm²)

Volume = ____ × ____ = _____ (cm³)

Capacity = _____ mL

The thicker the glass for this aquarium is, the less water it can hold.

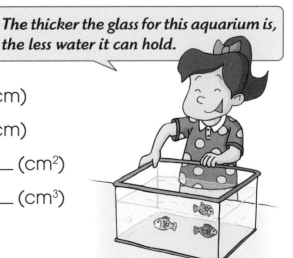

Fractions

There are $2\frac{3}{4}$ baskets of bones.

- Identify and write different types of fractions: proper and improper fractions and mixed numbers.
- Understand the meanings of equivalent fractions.
- Write fractions in simplest form.
- Compare and order fractions.

Fill in the blanks with the given words. Then sort the fractions.

Improper fraction	Mixed number	Proper fraction

$2\frac{3}{4}$

$\frac{3}{7}$

$1\frac{1}{5}$

$\frac{9}{5}$

$\frac{8}{7}$

$\frac{5}{6}$

$3\frac{4}{9}$

$\frac{2}{4}$

$1\frac{1}{3}$

$\frac{7}{5}$

$2\frac{7}{10}$

$\frac{8}{8}$

① **Types of Fraction**

_____ : a fraction with its numerator smaller than its denominator

e.g. _____

_____ : a fraction with its numerator equal to or greater than its denominator

e.g. _____

_____ : a number made up of a whole number and a proper fraction

e.g. _____

Write a fraction for the coloured part of each figure.

② 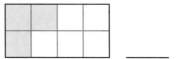 _____

③ 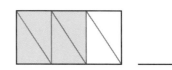 _____

ISBN: 978-1-77149-033-7

Write an improper fraction for the coloured parts of each group of diagrams.

④ 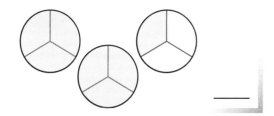 _____

⑤ 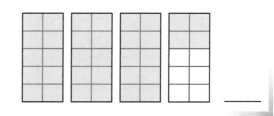 _____

⑥  _____

⑦ 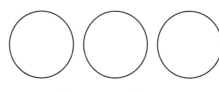 _____

Draw lines to cut one of the diagrams in each group and colour the correct number of figures and parts to show the mixed number given.

⑧ $3\dfrac{4}{5}$

⑨ $4\dfrac{3}{10}$

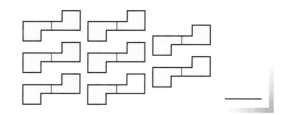

Write an improper fraction and a mixed number for the coloured parts of each group of diagrams.

⑩ **A**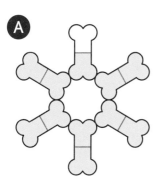

B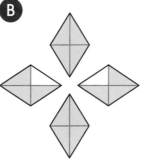

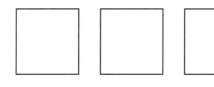

	Improper fraction	Mixed number
A		
B		

ISBN: 978-1-77149-033-7

Equivalent fractions: fractions that represent the same part of a whole

e.g.

$\frac{1}{2}$ is coloured.

$\frac{2}{4}$ is coloured.

$\frac{4}{8}$ is coloured.

$\frac{1}{2}$, $\frac{2}{4}$, and $\frac{4}{8}$ are equivalent fractions.

$\frac{1}{2}$ *is in simplest form since the numerator and the denominator have no more common factor except 1.*

Colour the parts and write a fraction to show the coloured parts in each figure. Then write the equivalent fractions in the space provided.

⑪ Colour 2 parts :

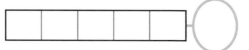

Colour 1 part :

Colour 4 parts :

Equivalent fractions

⑫ Colour 5 parts :

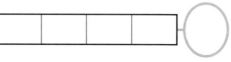

Colour 8 parts :

Colour 2 parts :

Equivalent fractions

Circle the fractions in simplest form.

⑬ $\frac{6}{10}$ $\frac{4}{7}$ $\frac{3}{5}$

⑭ $\frac{3}{4}$ $\frac{9}{12}$ $\frac{5}{8}$

⑮ $\frac{3}{9}$ $\frac{7}{10}$ $\frac{1}{3}$

ISBN: 978-1-77149-033-7

Steps to compare mixed numbers with the same denominator:

e.g. $4\frac{5}{8}$ $4\frac{6}{8}$

1st   Compare the whole number parts. The one with a greater number is greater. If they are the same, go to step 2.

2nd   Compare the fraction parts. The one with a greater numerator is greater.

1st $4\frac{5}{8}$ $4\frac{6}{8}$ the same; compare the fraction parts

$5 < 6$

2nd $4\frac{5}{8}$ $4\frac{6}{8}$

$4\frac{6}{8}$ is greater.

Circle the greater fraction.

⑯ $\frac{7}{9}$ $\frac{3}{9}$

⑰ $1\frac{4}{5}$ $3\frac{1}{5}$

⑱ $\frac{11}{8}$ $\frac{7}{8}$

⑲ $3\frac{1}{7}$ $2\frac{6}{7}$

⑳ $4\frac{3}{6}$ $3\frac{4}{6}$

㉑ $\frac{15}{9}$ $\frac{20}{9}$

Put the fractions in order. Then answer the question.

㉒ $1\frac{3}{5}$ $2\frac{1}{5}$ $\frac{4}{5}$

㉓ $\frac{6}{12}$ $\frac{3}{12}$ $\frac{18}{12}$

㉔ $1\frac{5}{10}$ $1\frac{3}{10}$ $2\frac{1}{10}$

   ____ > ____ > ____

   ____ > ____ > ____

   ____ < ____ < ____

㉕

Each bone is cut into 4 equal parts. If I have $3\frac{1}{4}$ bones, Tim has $\frac{15}{4}$, and Joe has $2\frac{2}{4}$, who has the most bones?

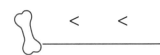

Gary

Number of bones in order from the most to the

fewest: _____ , _____ , _____

_____ has the most bones.

ISBN: 978-1-77149-033-7

Decimals (1)

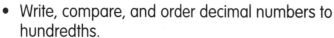

Can you see that 0.78 of the grid is coloured?

- Write, compare, and order decimal numbers to hundredths.

- Understand the place value in decimal numbers, the relationship between fractions and their equivalent decimal forms, and equivalent representations of a decimal number.

- Count forward or backward by hundredths.

Write a decimal for each diagram to show how much is coloured. Then write the decimal in words.

 ①

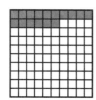 **A**

 **B**

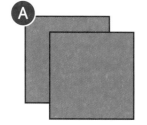

A _____ ; _____ and _____ hundredths

B _____ ; _____

C _____ ; _____

D _____ ; _____

E _____ ; _____

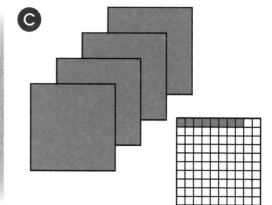 **C**

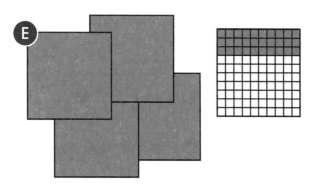 **E**

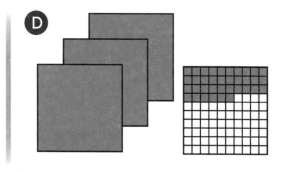 **D**

ISBN: 978-1-77149-033-7

Place value: the value of a digit that appears in a number

e.g. 3.68

- "3" is in the ones place; it means 3.
- "6" is in the tenths place; it means 0.6.
- "8" is in the hundredths place; it means 0.08.

ones	tenths	hundredths
3	6	8

Draw and colour the diagrams to match each decimal given.   Then write the decimal in words.

② **1.37**

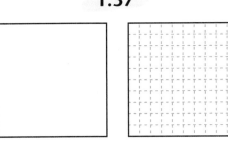

_____

③ **1.84**

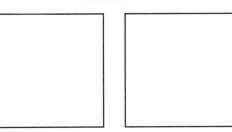

_____

Write the meaning of each highlighted digit.

④ 4.**28** _____

⑤ **3**.19 _____

⑥ 2.6**5** _____

⑦ 8.3**9** _____

⑧ 4.**5**3 _____

⑨ 7.5**8** _____

⑩ 2.7**1** _____

⑪ **8**.24 _____

⑫ 4.13 _____

Write as decimals. Then colour the greater one in each pair.

⑬ 4 and 27 hundredths

4 and 7 hundredths

⑭ 6 and 16 hundredths

1 and 66 hundredths

⑮ 3 and 11 hundredths

3 and 13 hundredths

⑯ 18 and 9 hundredths

9 and 18 hundredths

ISBN: 978-1-77149-033-7

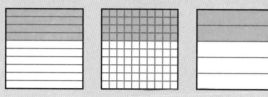

13

Fractions and Decimals

e.g.

Fraction: $\dfrac{4}{10}$ = $\dfrac{40}{100}$ = $\dfrac{2}{5}$

Decimal: 0.4 = 0.40 ← equivalent decimals

$\dfrac{2}{5}$ = 0.40; 0.40 is the equivalent decimal form of $\dfrac{2}{5}$.

Colour the diagrams to match the given ones. Then write a fraction and a decimal to tell how much of each diagram is coloured.

⑰

—— = 0.

⑱

=

⑲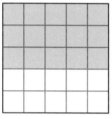

=

⑳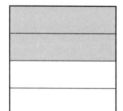

=

Circle the equivalent decimal form for each fraction.

㉑ 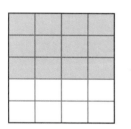 $\dfrac{10}{25}$ 0.40   0.04

㉒ $\dfrac{1}{2}$ 0.55   0.50

㉓ $\dfrac{12}{20}$ 0.60   0.80

㉔ $\dfrac{9}{10}$ 0.90   0.99

㉕ $\dfrac{5}{25}$ 0.40   0.20

㉖ $\dfrac{20}{50}$ 0.50   0.40

ISBN: 978-1-77149-033-7

Put the decimals in order.

㉗ 2.59 2.95 5.29 5.92 ＿＿＿ > ＿＿＿ > ＿＿＿ > ＿＿＿

㉘ 3.06 3.60 3.66 3.00 ＿＿＿ > ＿＿＿ > ＿＿＿ > ＿＿＿

㉙ 2.47 2.40 2.74 2.70 ＿＿＿ < ＿＿＿ < ＿＿＿ < ＿＿＿

㉚ 6.88 8.68 6.68 6.86 ＿＿＿ < ＿＿＿ < ＿＿＿ < ＿＿＿

Fill in the missing numbers.

㉛ 9.27 9.28 9.29 ＿＿＿ ＿＿＿ ＿＿＿ 9.34

㉜ 6.14 6.15 6.16 ＿＿＿ ＿＿＿ 6.19 ＿＿＿ ＿＿＿

㉝ 8.06 8.07 8.08 ＿＿＿ ＿＿＿ ＿＿＿ 8.12 ＿＿＿

㉞ 3.95 3.96 3.97 ＿＿＿ ＿＿＿ ＿＿＿ 4.02

㉟ 9.94 9.95 9.96 ＿＿＿ ＿＿＿ ＿＿＿ 10.01

Help Lucy use arrows to mark the locations of the bones on the number line. Then fill in the blanks.

㊱

The bones are at 5.96, 6.08, 5.99, 6.12, and 6.05.

a.

```
    5.90        6.00        6.10
```

b. Which bone is closest to the one at 5.99?

＿＿＿＿＿＿＿＿＿＿＿＿

c. Which bone is farthest from the one at 6.08?

＿＿＿＿＿＿＿＿＿＿＿＿

ISBN: 978-1-77149-033-7

14

Decimals (2)

I've never seen such a big bone in my life! It weighs 3.112 kg.

3 kg 112 g

kg	g		
3．	1	1	2

- Round decimal numbers to the nearest tenth.
- Multiply decimal numbers by 10, 100, 1000, or 10 000.
- Divide decimal numbers by 10 or 100.
- Do conversion between different units.

Use arrows to place the decimals on the number lines. Then round each decimal to the nearest tenth.

①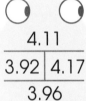

4.11
3.92 | 4.17
3.96

a.

3.90　　　　　4.00　　　　　4.10　　　　　4.20

b.　4.11 _____　　　　c.　3.92 _____

d.　4.17 _____　　　　e.　3.96 _____

②

8.95
9.14 | 9.08
9.03

a.

8.90　　　　　9.00　　　　　9.10　　　　　9.20

b.　8.95 _____　　　　c.　9.14 _____

d.　9.08 _____　　　　e.　9.03 _____

Round each decimal to the nearest tenth.

③　5.62 _____　　　④　4.71 _____　　　⑤　6.23 _____

⑥　10.54 _____　　⑦　15.82 _____　　⑧　20.27 _____

⑨　9.96 _____　　　⑩　9.07 _____　　　⑪　15.16 _____

⑫　8.08 _____　　　⑬　3.44 _____　　　⑭　2.93 _____

ISBN: 978-1-77149-033-7

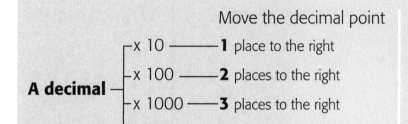

Move the decimal point

A decimal
- x 10 ——— **1** place to the right
- x 100 ——— **2** places to the right
- x 1000 ——— **3** places to the right
- x 10 000 —**4** places to the right

e.g. Multiply 3.25 by 10, 100, 1000, or 10 000.

3.25 x 10 = 32.5

3.25 x 100 = 325

3.250 x 1000 = 3250

3.2500 x 10 000 = 32500

Use arrows to show the movement of the decimal points. Then find the answers.

⑮ 6.25 x 10 = _____

⑯ 3.28 x 100 = _____

⑰ 4.06 x 1000 = _____

⑱ 5.13 x 10 000 = _____

⑲ 6.53 x 1000 = _____

⑳ 7.08 x 10 = _____

㉑ 8.67 x 10 000 = _____

㉒ 9.62 x 100 = _____

Look at the pictures. Fill in the blanks.

㉓ a. 10 bottles hold _____ L of detergent.

b. 10 000 bottles hold _____ L of detergent.

㉔ a. 100 bags hold _____ kg of candies.

b. 1000 bags hold _____ kg of candies.

㉕ a. The total length of 10 strings is _____ m.

b. The total length of 10 000 strings is _____ m.

ISBN: 978-1-77149-033-7

Move the decimal point

A decimal

÷ 10 — **1** place to the left

÷ 100 — **2** places to the left

e.g. Divide 4.6 by 10 or 100.

4.6 ÷ 10 = 0.46

04.6 ÷ 100 = 0.046

Use arrows to show the movement of the decimal points. Then find the answers.

㉖ 8.54 ÷ 10 = _____

㉗ 06.7 ÷ 100 = _____

㉘ 9.6 ÷ 100 = _____

㉙ 5.29 ÷ 10 = _____

㉚ 7.4 ÷ 10 = _____

㉛ 3.8 ÷ 100 = _____

㉜ 6.2 ÷ 100 = _____

㉝ 5.6 ÷ 10 = _____

Find the weight of each item. Then check the correct answer.

㉞

Each piece weighs _____ kg.

Each piece weighs _____ kg.

The heavier cookie

㉟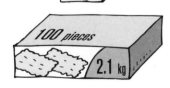

Each piece weighs _____ kg.

Each piece weighs _____ kg.

The heavier cracker

ISBN: 978-1-77149-033-7

Weight	Length/Distance	We can write measurements in an easier way with the help of the charts.

Weight

1 kg = 1000 g

1 g = 1000 mg

Length/Distance

1 km = 1000 m

1 m = 100 cm

1 cm = 10 mm

Capacity

1 L = 1000 mL

We can write measurements in an easier way with the help of the charts.

e.g. 4 kg 16 g = **4.016 kg**

kg	g		
4 .	0	1	6

← decimal point

3 m 42 cm = **3.42 m**

m	cm	
3 .	4	2

← decimal point

Write the measurements in decimals.

㊱ 3 kg 804 g

= _____ kg

kg	g		
.			

㊲ 4 L 78 mL

= _____ L

L	mL		
.			

㊳ 8 km 5 m

= _____ km

km	m		
.			

㊴ 6 m 17 cm

= _____ m

m	cm		
.			

㊵ 5 cm 8 mm

= _____ cm

cm	mm
.	

㊶ 9 kg 6 g

= _____ kg

kg	g		
.			

Write each measurement in decimals. Then answer the questions.

㊷

 A — 2 kg 16 g

_____ kg

 B — 2 kg 61 g

_____ kg

 C — 2 kg 6 g

_____ kg

Which pack is the heaviest?

_____

㊸

 A 8 cm 9 mm _____ cm

 B 8 cm 5 mm _____ cm

 C 8 cm 8 mm _____ cm

_____

Which bone is the longest?

 ISBN: 978-1-77149-033-7

1.2 5
+ 0.1 6
1.4 1

Addition and Subtraction of Decimals

- Add or subtract decimals to hundredths.
- Do estimates.
- Solve problems involving addition and subtraction of decimals.

1.25 m

0.16 m

Teddy, can you believe that I'm 1.41 m tall?

Write a vertical addition or subtraction to match each sentence.

①

A The sum of 2.68 and 3.44 is 6.12.

B The difference of 5.14 and 2.99 is 2.15.

C 4.67 and 6.28 makes 10.95.

D Subtracting 2.13 from 8.07 is 5.94.

A

B

+ _____

C

D

Find the answers.

②
```
  6.5 3
+ 2.4 9
```

③
```
  4.2 7
+ 3.9 4
```

④
```
  2.3 1
− 0.6 8
```

⑤
```
  7.4 6
− 5.3 9
```

⑥ 3.93 + 1.78 = _____

⑦ 15.26 − 9.44 = _____

⑧ 8.67 + 7.85 = _____

⑨ 4.62 − 2.88 = _____

⑩ 10.02 − 6.53 = _____

⑪ 3.87 + 12.64 = _____

⑫ 15.48 − 2.69 = _____

⑬ 7.06 + 5.89 = _____

 ISBN: 978-1-77149-033-7

Sometimes we need to find the equivalent decimals first before working out the vertical addition or subtraction.

e.g.

3.64 + 9.6 = **13.24**

$$3.64$$
$$+\ 9.60 \leftarrow 9.6 = 9.60; \text{the zero is a place holder.}$$
$$\overline{13.24}$$

8 − 4.73 = **3.27**

$$8.00 \leftarrow 8 = 8.00; \text{the zeros are place holders.}$$
$$-\ 4.73$$
$$\overline{3.27}$$

Find the sum and difference for each pair of numbers.

⑭   4.79   6.3

Sum	Difference

⑮   9.2   11.08

Sum	Difference

⑯   30.03   12.4

Sum	Difference

⑰   5.86   20.5

Sum	Difference

Look at the pictures. Fill in the blanks.

⑱   a.   These two watermelons weigh _____ kg in all.

 4.64 kg

 5.8 kg

    b.   The big watermelon weighs _____ kg more than the small one.

⑲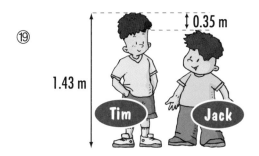

   ↕ 0.35 m

   1.43 m

   Tim   Jack

   a.   Jack is _____ m tall.

   b.   If Sue is 0.28 m taller than Jack, Sue is _____ m tall.

Look at the pictures. Round each decimal to the nearest tenth to do the estimate. Then answer the questions.

⑳

Estimate   Exact

a. The total capacity of these two pails is about _____ L.

b. The pails can hold _____ L of water.

㉑

Estimate   Exact

a. The total weight of these two pumpkins is about _____ kg.

b. These two pumpkins weigh _____ kg in all.

㉒

Estimate   Exact

7.18 m

50.76 m

36.25 m

a. There is a height difference of about _____ m between the buildings.

b. The tall building is _____ m taller than the short one.

c. The bird is about _____ m above the ground.

d. The bird is _____ m above the ground.

ISBN: 978-1-77149-033-7

Solve the problems.

㉓  If Aunt Elaine uses 1.27 kg of flour to make a cake, how much flour will be left?

_____ = _____   _____

㉔  If James pays $50 for a season pass, what is his change?

_____ = _____   _____

㉕ A chocolate bar weighs 1.08 kg. What is the total weight of two chocolate bars?

_____ = _____   _____

㉖ Aunt Sally has a ribbon that is 3.64 m long and she cuts it into 2 pieces. If one piece is 1.85 m long, how long is the other piece?

_____ = _____   _____

㉗ Each bag of dog treats costs $36.74. How much do two bags cost?

_____ = _____

_____

㉘ If Teddy gives 2.78 kg of treats to his friend, what will be the weight of the treats left?

_____ = _____

_____

ISBN: 978-1-77149-033-7

Money

- Read and write money amounts to $1000.
- Add and subtract money amounts to make purchases and changes.

It's so beautiful. It costs nine hundred sixty-five dollars and twenty-nine cents.

$965.29

Estimate and find the exact amount of money in each group.

①

Group	Estimate	Exact
A	dollars _____ cents	dollars _____ cents or $
B		
C		
D		

Draw the fewest bills and coins to show how much each child collected for the fundraising campaign. Then answer the questions.

Key

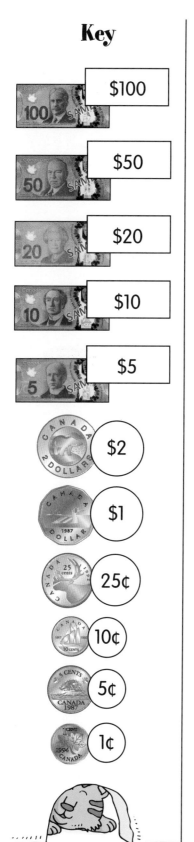

$100

$50

$20

$10

$5

$2

$1

25¢

10¢

5¢

1¢

②  Tim $326.91

 $297.08 Jack

 Katie $406.17

③ How much did the boys collect in all?

_____

④ How much more did Katie collect than Jack?

_____

Find the costs of the items. Then fill in the missing information on the receipts and answer the questions.

⑤

bookshelf **$127.49**

It costs $218.54 more than a bookshelf.

armchair

task chair

coffee table **$192.64**

It costs $76.85 less than a coffee table.

⑥

My Furniture Shop

ITEM	COST
Armchair	_____
_____	_____
Total	$538.67
Cash	_____
Change	$11.33

⑦

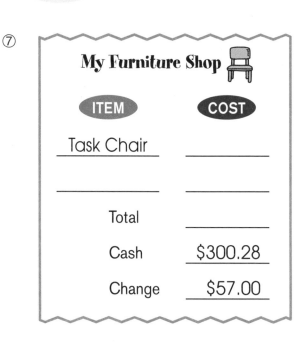

My Furniture Shop

ITEM	COST
Task Chair	_____
_____	_____
Total	_____
Cash	$300.28
Change	$57.00

⑧

If I want to buy two task chairs, how much do I need to pay?

_____ = _____ _____

⑨

If I want to buy one coffee table and one bookshelf, how much do I need to pay?

_____ = _____ _____

ISBN: 978-1-77149-033-7

Solve the problems.

⑩ a. Uncle James buys two jackets. How much does he need to pay?

_____

$129.76

b. Mr. Hunter pays $200 for a jacket. What is his change?

_____

⑪ a. Jason has $157.88 only. If he wants to buy a lawn mower, how much more does he need?

_____

$288.49

b. If a snow blower costs $624.35 more than a lawn mower, how much does a snow blower cost?

_____

⑫

I paid

for this necklace. Its original price was $965.29.

Do you know how much I saved?

_____ = _____

_____

2-D Shapes

I'm putting a fence around my beautiful rectangular flower bed.

- Identify polygons, regular polygons, and other two-dimensional shapes.
- Draw 2-D shapes with the given measurements.
- Sort 2-D shapes by their geometric properties such as parallel sides, symmetry, etc.

**Colour the regular polygons.
Then sort them. Write the letters.**

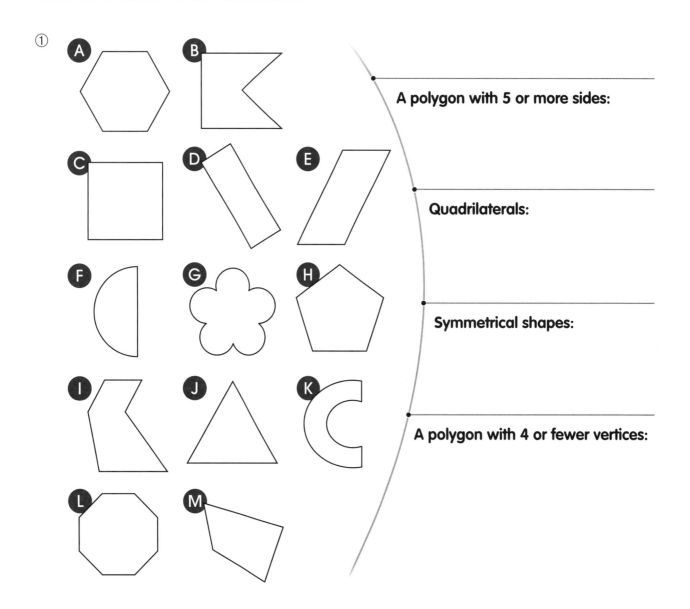

①

A polygon with 5 or more sides: _____

Quadrilaterals: _____

Symmetrical shapes: _____

A polygon with 4 or fewer vertices: _____

ISBN: 978-1-77149-033-7

Read what the dogs say. Then draw the shapes.

② a square with a side length 4 cm

a rectangle with length 5 cm and width 3 cm

a triangle with sides 5 cm and 3 cm

a quadrilateral with a right angle

a hexagon with a pair of parallel sides

a pentagon with two right angles

Draw lines on the shapes to match the sentences.

③ 🅐 The square is formed by nine congruent squares.

🅑 The hexagon is formed by six congruent triangles.

🅒 The trapezoid is formed by three congruent triangles.

🅓 The rectangle is formed by six congruent rectangles.

🅔 The triangle is formed by four small congruent triangles.

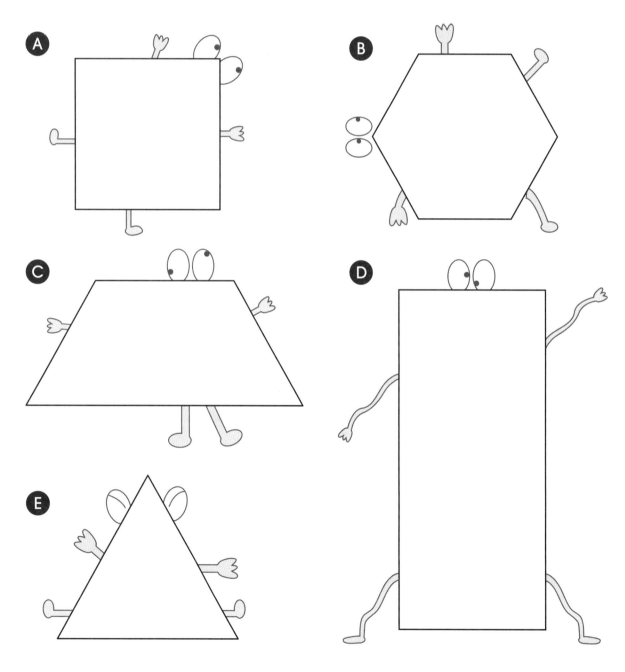

ISBN: 978-1-77149-033-7

Read what the children and the animals say. Help them draw the shapes and lines. Then answer the questions.

④ *Draw a big regular hexagon with sides of 4 cm. Then draw lines on it to show how it can be formed by six small congruent triangles.*

1 cm
1 cm 1 cm

What is the side length of each of the small triangles?

⑤ *Draw a big triangle with sides of 8 cm. Then draw lines on it to show how it can be formed by four small congruent triangles.*

1 cm
1 cm 1 cm

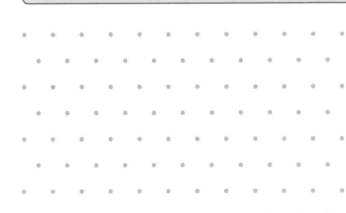

What is the side length of each of the small triangles?

ISBN: 978-1-77149-033-7

Complete Canadian Curriculum • Grade 5

Angles

- Describe angles related to right angles or straight angles and find the measures.
- Identify and classify acute, right, obtuse, and straight angles.
- Measure angles and construct angles up to 90°, using a protractor.

I've got a hat with an obtuse angle.

120°

Look at the angles. Complete the notes.

①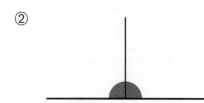

This is a _____ angle.

A right angle is _____ .

②

Two right angles form a _____ angle.

A straight angle is _____ .

③

This angle is _____ of a right angle.

It is _____ .

④

This angle is _____ of a right angle.

It is _____ .

⑤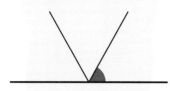

This angle is _____ of a straight angle.

It is _____ .

ISBN: 978-1-77149-033-7

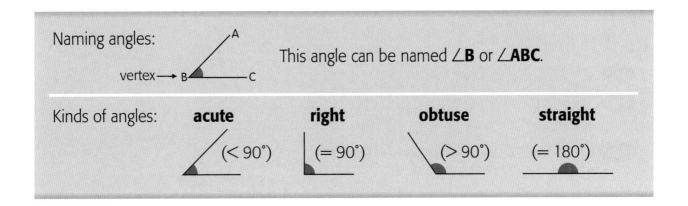

Naming angles:

This angle can be named ∠**B** or ∠**ABC**.

vertex → B

Kinds of angles:

acute	right	obtuse	straight
(< 90°)	(= 90°)	(> 90°)	(= 180°)

Name each angle. Then write what kind of angle it is.

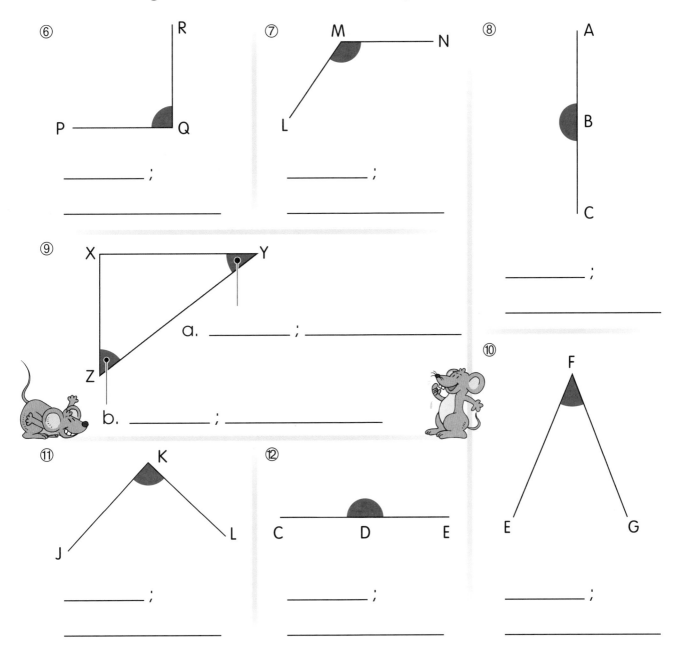

⑥ R

P ——— Q

_____ ;

_____

⑦ M   N

L

_____ ;

_____

⑧ A

B

C

_____ ;

_____

⑨ X   Y

Z

a. _____ ; _____

b. _____ ; _____

⑩ F

E   G

_____ ;

_____

⑪ K

J   L

_____ ;

_____

⑫

C   D   E

_____ ;

_____

Steps to measure an angle:

1st Put the 0° line on one arm of the angle.

2nd Place the centre of the protractor at the vertex.

3rd Mark the reading of the angle and record it.

e.g.

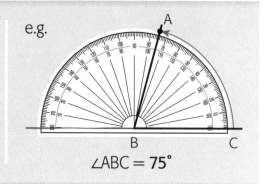

∠ABC = **75°**

Measure the size of each marked angle using a protractor.

⑬

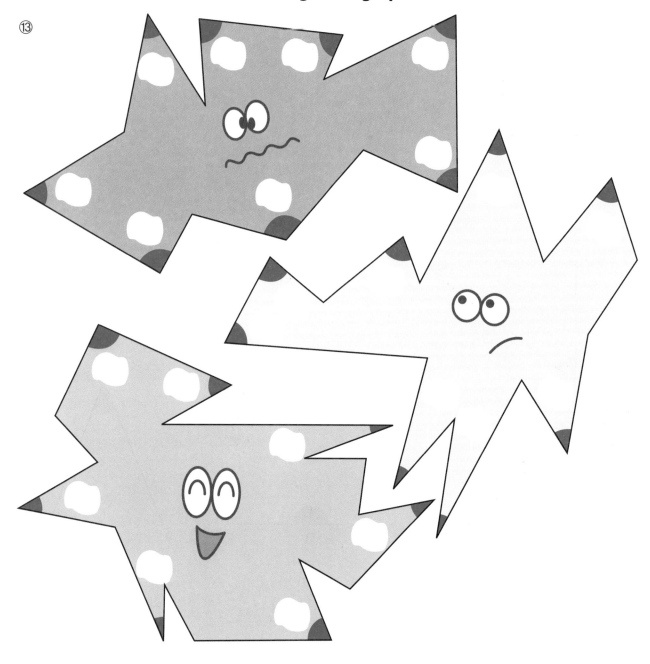

ISBN: 978-1-77149-033-7

Draw and mark the angles.

⑭

A ——————— B

H ——————— I

P

Q

L ——————— M

∠ABC = 70°

∠HIJ = 40°

∠PQR = 84°

∠LMN = 38°

∠XYZ = 55°

∠STU = 63°

∠EFG = 25°

X —— Y

S

E ——————— F

T

Help the girl measure and record the size of each marked angle. Then circle the smallest one.

⑮

Triangles

- Identify triangles and classify them according to angles and side properties.
- Construct triangles with the given acute or right angles and side measurements.

Can I have an equilateral triangle sandwich?

Measure and record the angles of the triangles. Then fill in the blanks with the given words.

acute   obtuse   right

① This triangle has 3 _____ angles. It is an _____ triangle.

② This triangle has 2 _____ angles and 1 _____ angle. It is a _____ triangle.

③ This triangle has 2 _____ angles and 1 _____ angle. It is an _____ triangle.

ISBN: 978-1-77149-033-7

Equilateral Triangle	Isosceles Triangle	Scalene Triangle
• 3 equal sides	• 2 equal sides	• no equal sides

Use a ruler to measure and record the sides of the triangles. Then name the triangles.

④

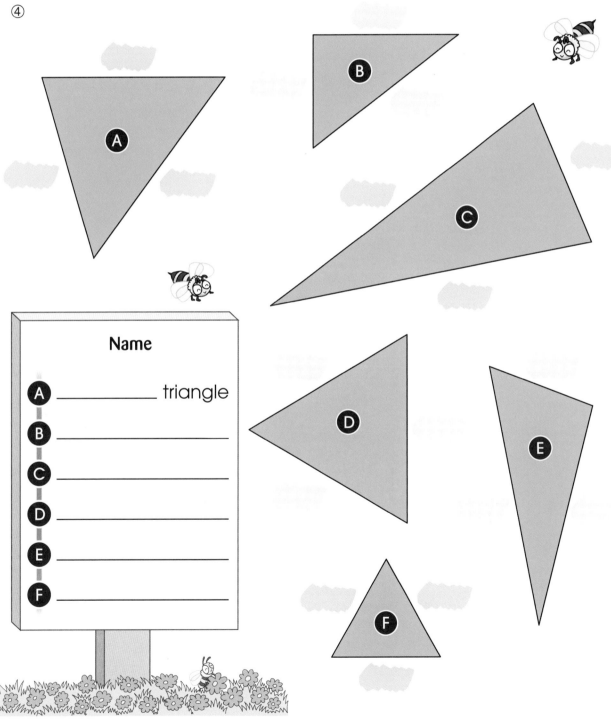

Name

A _____ triangle

B _____

C _____

D _____

E _____

F _____

Draw the triangles.

⑤   an acute triangle

⑥   a right triangle

⑦   an obtuse triangle

⑧   an equilateral triangle

⑨   an isosceles triangle

⑩   a scalene triangle

Sort the triangles. Write the letters.

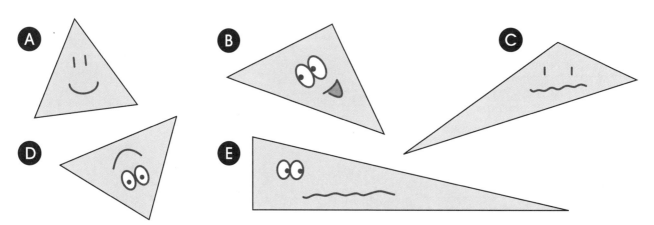

Ⓐ   Ⓑ   Ⓒ   Ⓓ   Ⓔ

⑪ **By Angles**

Acute triangle: _____

Right triangle: _____

Obtuse triangle: _____

⑫ **By Sides**

Equilateral triangle: _____

Isosceles triangle: _____

Scalene triangle: _____

ISBN: 978-1-77149-033-7

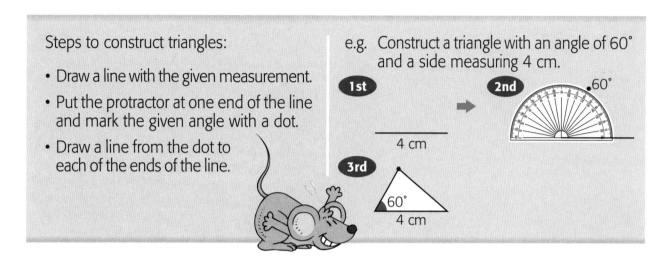

Steps to construct triangles:

- Draw a line with the given measurement.
- Put the protractor at one end of the line and mark the given angle with a dot.
- Draw a line from the dot to each of the ends of the line.

e.g. Construct a triangle with an angle of 60° and a side measuring 4 cm.

1st

4 cm

2nd   .60°

3rd

60°

4 cm

Draw the triangles. Then label them with the given letters.

⑬ A triangle with

A an angle of 75° and a side measuring 3 cm

B an angle of 28° and a side measuring 6 cm

C an angle of 42° and a side measuring 5 cm

Draw a triangle with an angle of 125° and a side measuring 4 cm. Label it **D** *.*

ISBN: 978-1-77149-033-7

3-D Figures

- Identify prisms and pyramids from their nets.
- Construct nets of prisms and pyramids.

Which nets make the coloured prisms? Put a check mark in the correct circles.

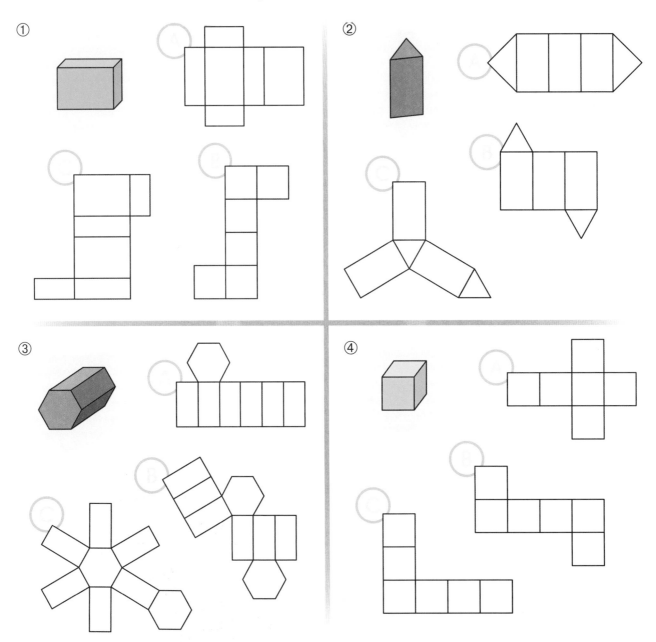

① ② ③ ④

ISBN: 978-1-77149-033-7

Colour the nets that make the coloured pyramids.

⑤  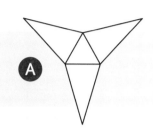 Ⓐ 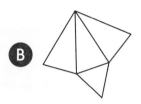 Ⓑ 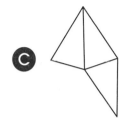 Ⓒ

⑥ 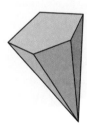 Ⓐ  Ⓑ 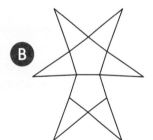 Ⓒ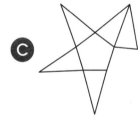

⑦ 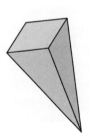 Ⓐ 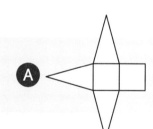 Ⓑ 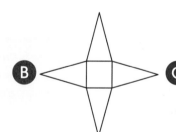 Ⓒ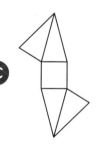

⑧ 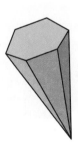 Ⓐ 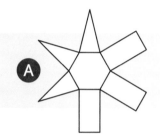 Ⓑ 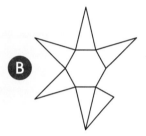 Ⓒ

⑨  Ⓐ 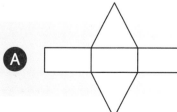 Ⓑ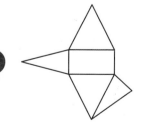

ISBN: 978-1-77149-033-7 Complete Canadian Curriculum • Grade 5 **83**

Draw the missing edges to complete the skeletons and the missing faces to complete the nets of the 3-D figures. Then match the skeletons with the nets that show the same figures.

⑩

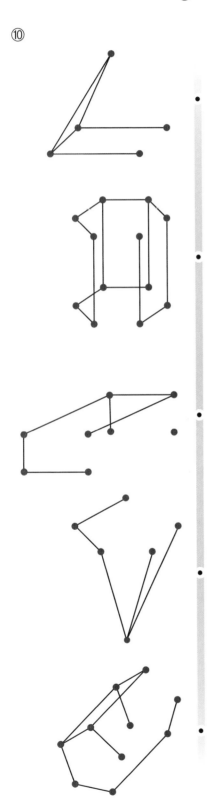

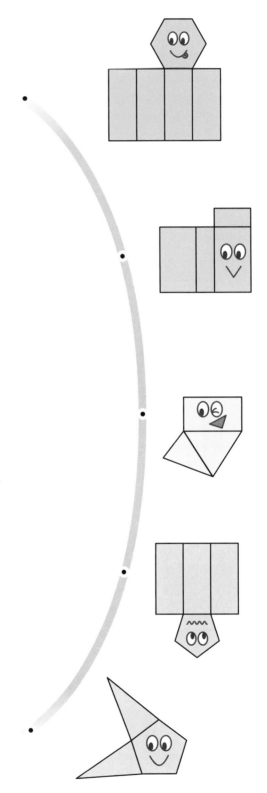

ISBN: 978-1-77149-033-7

Draw the missing faces to complete the net of each 3-D figure. Then name the figure. Write the numbers and describe the shapes of the faces that it has.

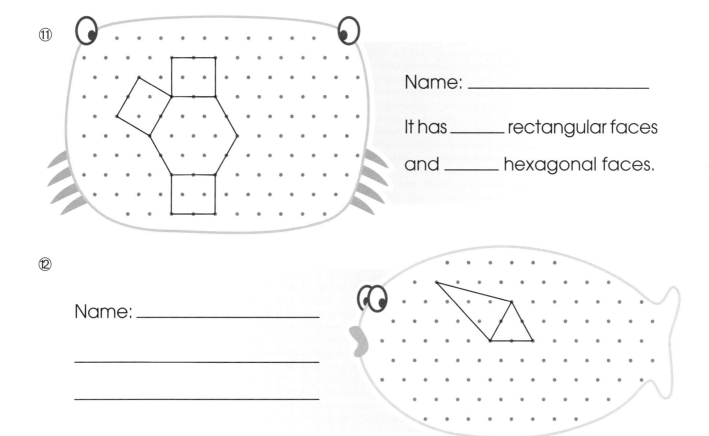

⑪

Name: _____

It has _____ rectangular faces

and _____ hexagonal faces.

⑫

Name: _____

_____

_____

Draw the net of the 3-D figure that the girl is describing.

⑬

I've built a 3–D figure which has 12 edges, and all the faces that it has are rectangular.

Transformations

This is translation!

- Identify and draw translation images.
- Create and analyze designs by translating and/or reflecting a shape or shapes.

Circle the correct words to complete what Emily says. Then check the pictures that show translations.

①

A translation is a transformation that moves a figure to a new position. The figure   changes / does not change   its size, shape, or orientation.

Translation

②

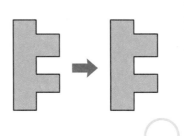

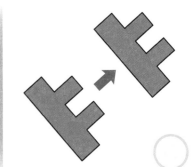

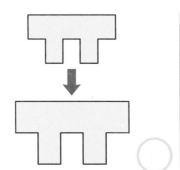

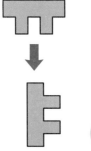

ISBN: 978-1-77149-033-7

Follow the directions to draw the translation images of the given shapes.

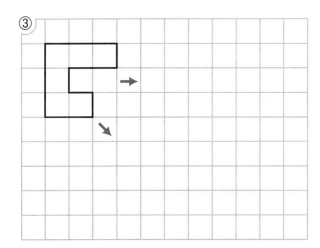

③

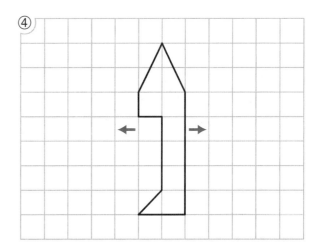

④

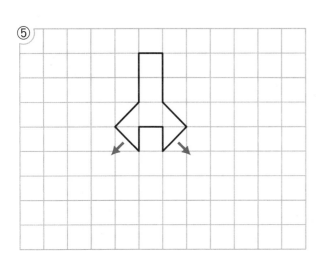

⑤

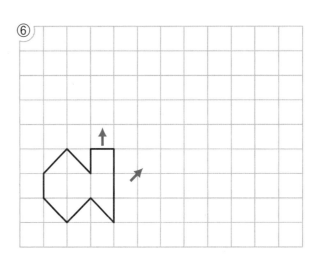

⑥

⑦

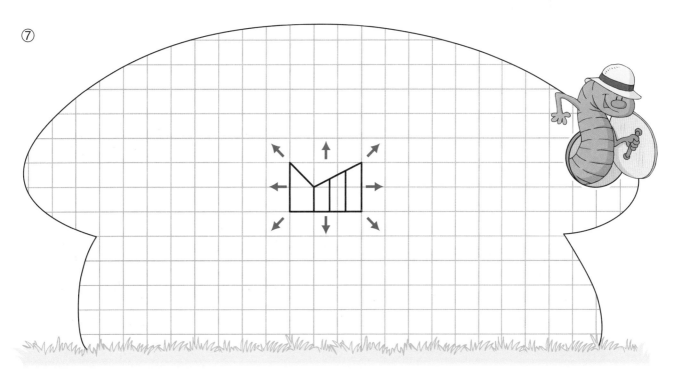

Create designs by

- translating | - reflecting | - translating and reflecting

Check the designs that are created by translating, reflecting, or translating and reflecting of a shape.

⑧

ISBN: 978-1-77149-033-7

Create designs by translating, reflecting, and translating and reflecting the shapes.

⑨

By **Translating**

By **Reflecting**

By translating and reflecting

Grids

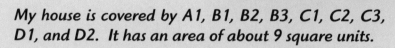

- Locate an object using the cardinal directions (i.e. north, east, south, and west) and grids.
- Describe movement from one location to another.
- Read and describe grids used on maps.
- Draw maps on grid systems.

My house is covered by A1, B1, B2, B3, C1, C2, C3, D1, and D2. It has an area of about 9 square units.

Draw the things on the grid. Then circle the correct answers and answer the questions.

①
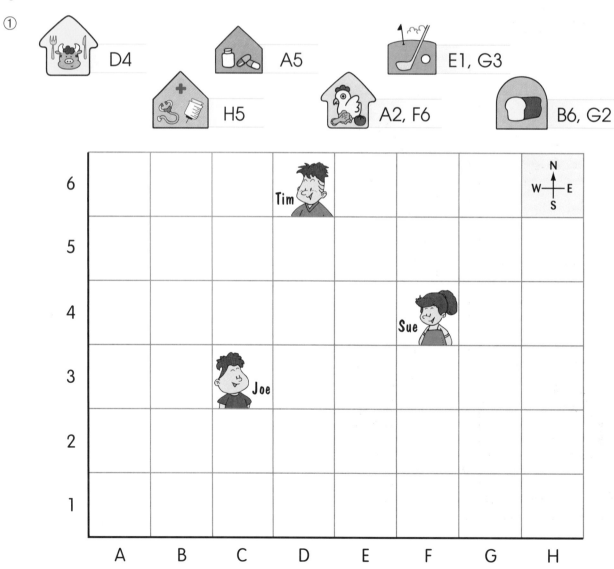

D4

A5

E1, G3

H5

A2, F6

B6, G2

ISBN: 978-1-77149-033-7

②

If I go 2 squares north and 2 squares west, do you know where I am going?

③

If I go 2 squares south and 1 square east, do you know where I am going?

④

We want to build a golf centre which has the same distance and is 2 squares away from the two golf courses. What are the possible locations?

_____

⑤ Joe is at the clinic and he wants to go home. Draw the shortest path that he should take on the map and describe it.

He should go _____ .

⑥ Sue is at the bakery at B6 and she wants to go to the other bakery. Draw the shortest path that she should take on the map and describe it.

_____

⑦ Tim wants to borrow some books from Joe and then give a present to Sue before going home. Describe the path that Tim should take to have the things done.

_____
_____
_____

Look at the zoo map.   Answer the questions.

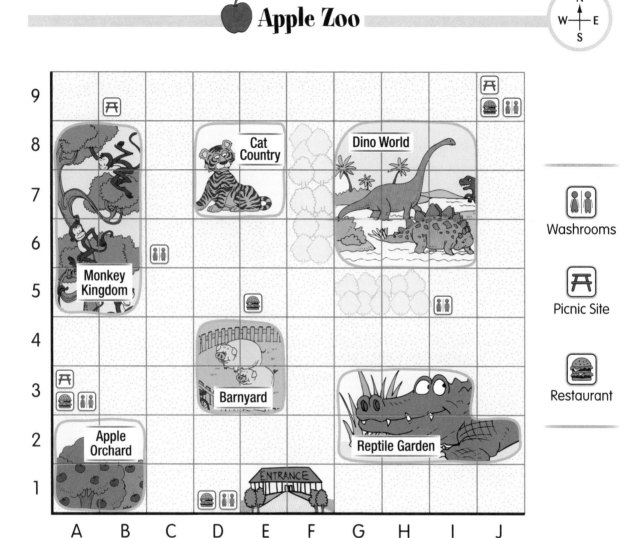

🍎 **Apple Zoo**

⑧   Locations of the washrooms: _____

⑨   Locations of the restaurants: _____

⑩   **I'm at Reptile Garden.   What's the shortest route to Monkey Kingdom?**

_____

_____

⑪ What is the area of each part in the zoo?

Area

Barnyard: _____ square units

Reptile Garden: _____ square units

Dino World: _____ square units

Monkey Kingdom: _____ square units

Cat Country: _____ square units

Apple Orchard: _____ square units

⑫ Which part of the zoo has the greatest area?

_____

⑬ There will be a big construction in the zoo.

Project 1 – Cutting down the trees from F6 to F8

• The entire Dino World will be extended 1 square west. What will be the new area of Dino World?

_____

Project 2 – Planting trees from G1 to J1

• What will be the area covered by the trees?

_____

Project 3 – Reptile Garden will be changed into a rectangle.

• How can that be done? What will be the new area?

_____

⑭

I'm going to make a donation to the zoo so that it can build an educational centre with an area of 2 square units beside Barnyard. What are the possible locations?

_____

ISBN: 978-1-77149-033-7

Patterning

- Create, identify, and extend numeric and geometric patterns.
- Make a table of values for a pattern or build a model to represent a number pattern presented in a table of values.
- Make predictions related to growing and shrinking geometric and numeric patterns.

I love patterning.

**Find out the pattern rule for each number pattern.
Then write the next two numbers.**

① 6   12   18   24   30   36   **Pattern rule:**

The next two numbers are _____ and _____ .

② 512   256   128   64   32   16   **Pattern rule:**

The next two numbers are _____ and _____ .

③ 575   550   525   500   475   450   **Pattern rule:**

The next two numbers are _____ and _____ .

④ 4   12   36   108   324   972   **Pattern rule:**

The next two numbers are _____ and _____ .

⑤ 172   167   162   157   152   147   **Pattern rule:**

The next two numbers are _____ and _____ .

ISBN: 978-1-77149-033-7

Make a table of values for each described number pattern. Then fill in the blanks.

⑥ *Start with 15 and add 4 to each term to get the next term.*

Term number	Term
1	
2	
3	
4	
5	
6	

The 8th term is _____ .

⑦ *Start with 20 and subtract 2 from each term to get the next term.*

Term number	Term

The _____ term is 0.

⑧ *Start with 6561 and divide each term by 3 to get the next term.*

Term number	Term

The _____ term is 1.

⑨ *Start with 5 and multiply each term by 2 to get the next term.*

Term number	Term

The 9th term is _____ .

Make a table of values for each number pattern. Then check the pictures that match the pattern.

⑩

Start with 4 and add 3 to each term to get the next term.

Term number	Term
1	
2	
3	
4	

Ⓐ

Ⓑ

⑪

Start with 21 and subtract 4 from each term to get the next term.

Term number	Term

Ⓐ

Ⓑ

⑫

Start with 13 and subtract 4 from each term to get the next term.

Term number	Term

Ⓐ

Ⓑ

ISBN: 978-1-77149-033-7

Follow the pattern to draw the next two pictures.   Make a table of values to match the pictures.   Then answer the questions.

⑬ a.

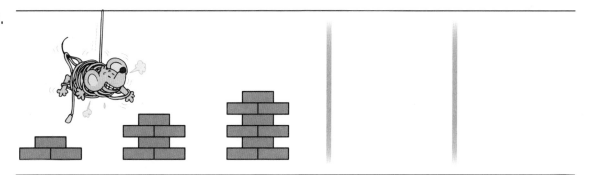

b.

Tower	No. of Blocks
1st	3

c.

How many blocks are there in the 8th tower?

_____

⑭ a.

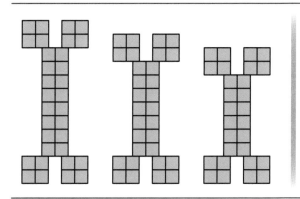

b.

Bone	No. of Squares
1st	

c.

How many squares are there in the 7th bone?

_____

Simple Equations

- Understand variables as changing quantities in an equation.
- Use symbols or letters to represent the unknown quantities to write equations that describe relationships involving simple rates.
- Find the missing numbers in equations.

I know you can go 10 km in 1 h. Did you know that I can use D = 10 x t to tell how far you will go in a given time?

$$D = 10 \times t$$

distance travelled   time

Look at the pictures. Then use equations to describe the relationships.

①  $3 each

Total cost = 3 x No. of hamburgers purchased

_____ = 3 x _____ ,

C = Total cost

n = No. of hamburgers purchased

②

Total no. of muffins = 6 x No. of boxes

_____ = 6 x _____ ,

_____ = Total no. of muffins

_____ = No. of boxes

③  Juice 2 L

Total amount of juice = 2 x No. of bottles

_____ = 2 x _____ ,

_____ = Total amount of juice

_____ = No. of bottles

④  A LUCKY Dog $9

Total cost = 9 x No. of books

_____ = 9 x _____ ,

_____ = Total cost

_____ = No. of books

ISBN: 978-1-77149-033-7

Circle the symbols or letters in the equations. Match the equations with the situations. Then write what the symbols or letters represent.

 ⑤

$c = 100 - n$

$c =$ _____

$n =$ _____

Mrs. Smith divides 100 children into equal groups. She wants to know the number of children in each group.

$w = 100 \times$

_____ = _____

_____ = _____

I take some candies from a bag of 100 candies. There are some candies left in the bag.

$y = 100 \div k$

_____ = _____

_____ = _____

A watch costs $100. Jason wants to know how much he needs to pay for a watch and a doll.

▲ $= 100 + x$

_____ = _____

_____ = _____

A box of raisins weighs 100 g. I want to know the total weight of some boxes of raisins.

Check the equations that can be used to represent each situation.

⑥

> *I have a bag of 40 cookies. If I eat some cookies, how many cookies will be left?*

(A) $n = 40 - k$

(B) $40 - k = n$

(C) $40 + k = n$

(D) $n \times k = 40$

⑦

> *I earn $100 a day. If I work for a few days, how much will I earn?*

(A) $c = 100 \times n$

(B) $c \times n = 100$

(C) $100 \div n = c$

(D) $100 \times n = c$

⑧

> *I have 12 stamps and 5 of them are from Canada. How many stamps are from other countries?*

(A) $12 + 5 = s$

(B) $12 = 5 + s$

(C) $12 = 5 + \square$

(D) $12 = \square - 5$

⑨

> *If I take away 3 gifts from under the tree, there will be 7 gifts left. How many gifts are there under the tree?*

(A) $n + 3 = 7$

(B) $7 + n = 3$

(C) $n - 3 = 7$

(D) $\square - 3 = 7$

(E) $\square = 7 - 3$

(F) $7 = s - 3$

 Complete Canadian Curriculum • **Grade 5**

ISBN: 978-1-77149-033-7

Simplify the equations first if needed.

e.g. $k - 4 = 6 + 9$ ← Simplify 6 + 9 first.

$k - 4 = 15$ ← Think: what number minus 4 is 15?

$k = \underline{\textbf{19}}$

Find the unknowns.

⑩ $11 = 88 \div$ ▢

▢ = _____

⑪ $9 \times \heartsuit = 144$

$\heartsuit$ = _____

⑫ ☺ $- 8 = 22$

☺ = _____

⑬ $50 - y = 34$

$y =$ _____

⑭ $18 + k = 20$

$k =$ _____

⑮ $h \times 7 = 126$

$h =$ _____

⑯ $45 = ❀ \times 3$

❀ = _____

⑰ 🌳 $\div 8 = 24$

🌳 = _____

⑱ $138 \div m = 23$

$m =$ _____

Simplify the equations. Then find the unknowns.

⑲ $m + 9 = 20 - 4$

⑳ $b \div 4 = 3 + 3$

㉑ $8 \times k = 144 \div 3$

㉒ $y - 16 = 15 + 15 + 15$

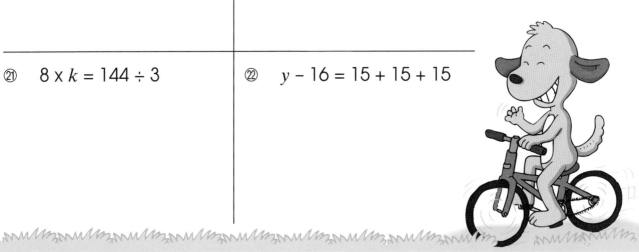

ISBN: 978-1-77149-033-7

Graphs (1)

- Read and describe the data presented in charts and graphs, including broken-line graphs.

He really likes fish.

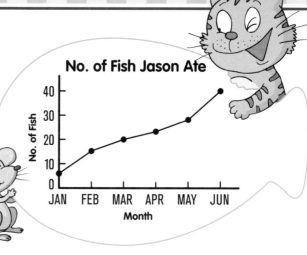

No. of Fish Jason Ate

Read the graph. Answer the questions.

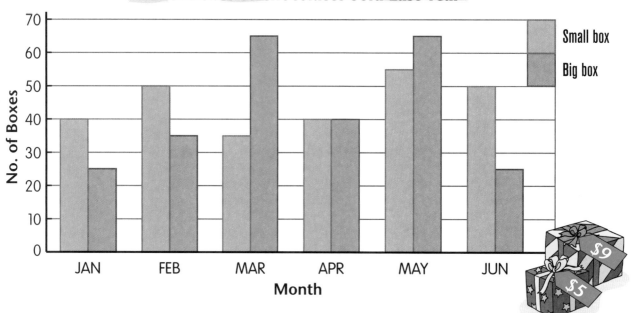

No. of Boxes of Chocolates Sold Last Year

① How many kinds of packaging are there? _____

② How many boxes of chocolates were sold in March? _____

③ How many more big boxes of chocolates were sold in May than in June? _____

④ In which month were the most chocolates sold? _____

⑤ How much was collected from selling the chocolates in

a. January?   b. April?   c. June?

_____   _____   _____

    ISBN: 978-1-77149-033-7

Broken-line Graph:

a graph formed by line segments that join points representing the data

I had lots of bones on Thursday.

No. of Bones the Dog Had

Uncle Jimmy has recorded the attendances at the local hockey matches. Look at the graph. Answer the questions.

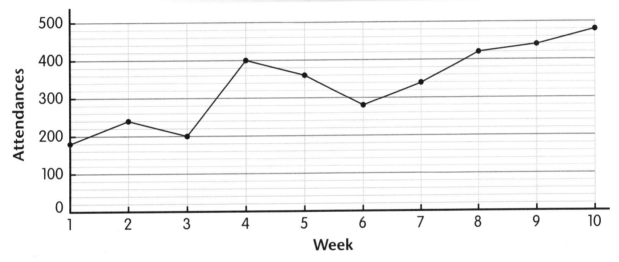

Attendances at the Local Hockey Matches

⑥ Which week had an attendance closest to 300? _____

⑦ Which week had the largest attendance? _____

⑧ How many more people were there

   a. in week 4 than in week 2? _____

   b. in week 8 than in week 5? _____

⑨

The matches I took part in all had attendances of 400 or more. In which weeks did I play?

_____

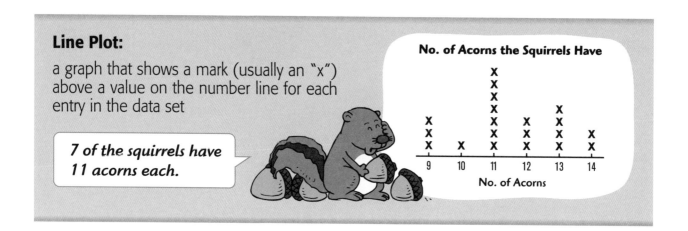

Line Plot:

a graph that shows a mark (usually an "x") above a value on the number line for each entry in the data set

7 of the squirrels have 11 acorns each.

No. of Acorns the Squirrels Have

No. of Acorns

Mrs. White has recorded the heights of the children. Read the line plot. Then answer the questions.

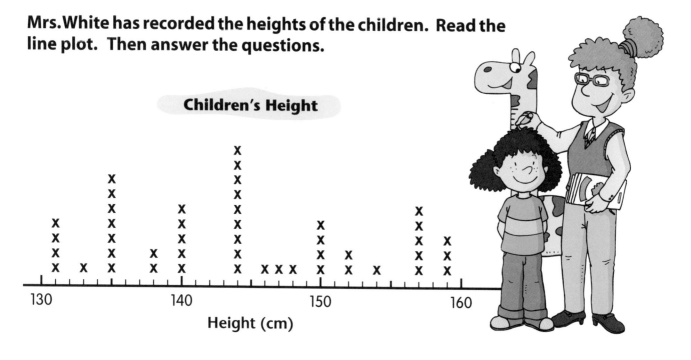

Children's Height

Height (cm)

⑩ What is the range of the data? _____

⑪ How many children are between 130 cm and 145 cm in height? _____

⑫ How many children are over 155 cm in height? _____

⑬ What is the most common height? _____

⑭ What is the greatest height in the record? _____

⑮ How many children were surveyed in all? _____

ISBN: 978-1-77149-033-7

Look at the graph showing the journey of Uncle Tim from his house to a campsite. Use the graph to answer the questions.

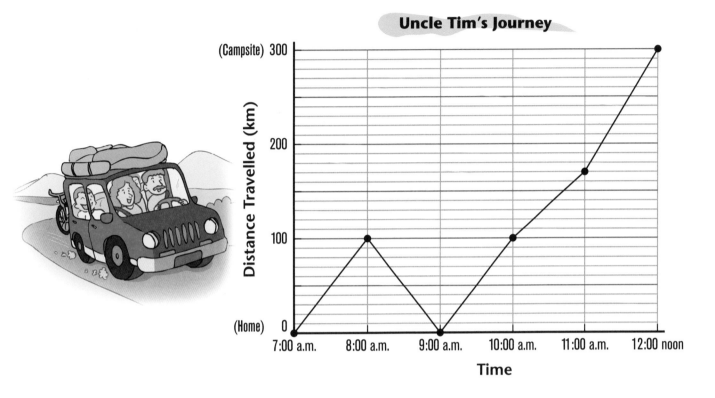

Uncle Tim's Journey

⑯ What time did Uncle Tim arrive at the campsite? _____

⑰ What was the distance between Uncle Tim's house and the campsite? _____

⑱ At 8:00 a.m., how far was Uncle Tim from his house? _____

⑲ From 10:00 a.m. to 12:00 noon, how far did Uncle Tim travel? _____

⑳

After setting off, we found that our cat Lulu was not in the car. So I drove back home and picked her up. Do you know what time I started driving back home and what time I arrived home?

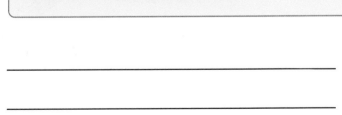

_____

_____

ISBN: 978-1-77149-033-7

Graphs (2)

- Complete graphs or make graphs to show data.
- Draw conclusions or describe the shape of a set of data presented in graphs.

No. of Treats in Each Box

Joe did a survey of the reading habits of his friends. Look at the results and complete the line plot. Then answer the questions.

Reading Time	5	3	4	8	9	3	11	10	14	7
(No. of hours in a week)	5	9	11	3	4	3	5	3	5	9
	7	5	3	5	9	5	3	4	5	4

①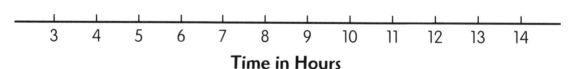

Children's Reading Time in a Week

```
3   4   5   6   7   8   9   10  11  12  13  14
```

Time in Hours

② How many children read more than 6 h a week?

_____

③ What conclusion can you draw from the line plot?

_____

ISBN: 978-1-77149-033-7

See how many combos were sold last week. Complete the table by rounding each figure to the nearest 10. Then make a double bar graph to show the data and answer the questions.

④

No. of Orders		Sun	Mon	Tue	Wed	Thu	Fri	Sat
Combo 1	Actual	98	46	42	55	38	94	101
	Rounded							
Combo 2	Actual	87	29	36	67	113	56	92
	Rounded							

⑤

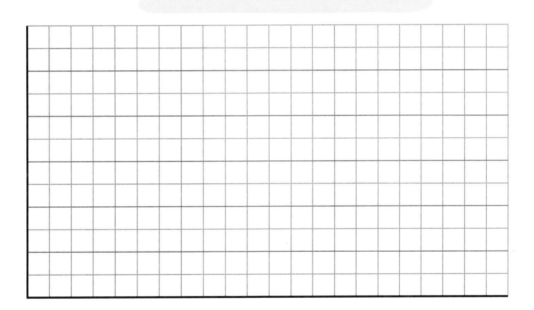

⑥

We had a promotion for Combo 2 last week. On which day do you think the promotion was held? Why?

_____

⑦ What conclusion can you draw from the double bar graph?

_____

The table shows the income of Douglas Bakery for each month last year. Round each figure to the nearest thousand and write the answer in the space provided. Then make a broken-line graph to show the data and answer the questions.

⑧

Income ($)

JAN	66 530
FEB	49 845
MAR	36 472
APR	33 617
MAY	28 825
JUN	30 334
JUL	31 149
AUG	30 816
SEP	37 113
OCT	38 605
NOV	47 018
DEC	68 076

⑨

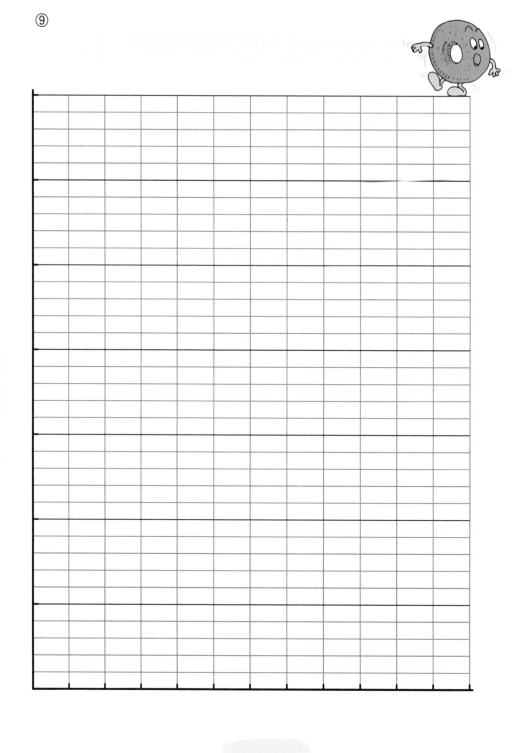

ISBN: 978-1-77149-033-7

⑩ In which month did the income reach $36 000? _____

⑪ In which months were the incomes over $60 000? _____

⑫ What was the difference in incomes between February and May? _____

⑬ What was the total income from October to December? _____

⑭ What was the average daily income in June? _____

⑮ In which month did Douglas Bakery have

    a.   the highest income? _____

    b.   the lowest income? _____

$25 $2 $9 $1

⑯ *If about half of the income in February was from selling strawberry cakes, about how many cakes were sold in February?*

about _____

⑰ *If 1000 pies were sold in October, about how much was collected from selling other items?*

about _____

⑱ *What conclusion can you draw from the broken-line graph?*

_____

_____

More about Graphs

The mean, the median, and the mode of the candies that I have are 8. Do you know how many candies are in each of my 3 boxes?

- Find the mean of a small set of data and use it to describe the shape of the data set across its range of values.

- Compare similarities and differences between two related sets of data by finding measures of central tendency, such as mean, median, and mode.

Help Judy find the mean number of the candies. Then find the mean of each group of data.

①

Find the total number of candies I have first. Then divide the sum by 4 to find the mean.

Total = 36 + _____

= _____

Mean = _____ ÷ 4 = _____

The mean number of the candies is _____ .

②

89 g   68 g   75 g

91 g   87 g   76 g

Total = _____

= _____

Mean = _____ ÷ _____ = _____

The mean weight is _____ .

③

750 mL   600 mL   850 mL   750 mL

750 mL   850 mL   680 mL   650 mL

Total = _____

= _____

Mean = _____ ÷ _____ = _____

The mean capacity is _____ .

ISBN: 978-1-77149-033-7

e.g. The weights of a group of children: 42 kg   39 kg   42 kg   50 kg   37 kg   36 kg

Mean = (42 + 39 + 42 + 50 + 37 + 36) ÷ 6

= 246 ÷ 6

= 41

Put the data in order:

Mode

36   37   39   42   42   50

Median = (39 + 42) ÷ 2

= 40.5

The mean weight of the children is 41 kg, the median weight is 40.5 kg, and the mode weight is 42 kg.

Find the mean, median, and mode of each group of data.

④

A

8 kg   4 kg   5 kg

9 kg   5 kg

7 kg   11 kg

B

80 muffins   29 muffins

29 muffins   42 muffins

28 muffins   50 muffins

	Mean	Median	Mode
A			
B			
C			
D			
E			

C

$56 $27 $13

$27 $25 $40

$27 $25

E

0°C   8°C   12°C

4°C   7°C   6°C

0°C   5°C   3°C

D

7 m   6 m   8 m   3 m

8 m   8 m   7 m   8 m

2 m   3 m

ISBN: 978-1-77149-033-7

Look at the bar graph. Find the mean number of the marbles that each group of children has and draw a line to show the mean on the graph. Then match the graphs with the correct descriptions.

⑤ **Set 1** **Marbles that Each Child Has**

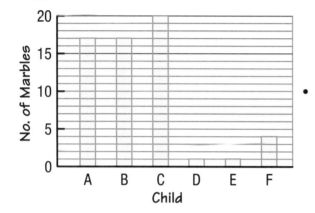

This set of data is spread out evenly around the mean.

Set 2 **Marbles that Each Child Has**

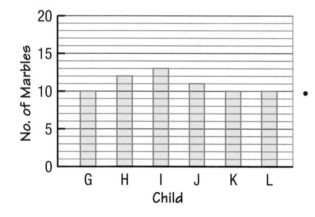

The data fall mainly into two groups on both sides of the mean.

Set 3 **Marbles that Each Child Has**

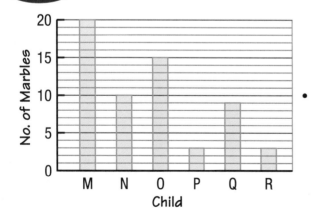

This set of data is not spread out evenly around the mean.

ISBN: 978-1-77149-033-7

Find the means, medians, and modes of the sets of data presented below. Then answer the questions.

⑥   a.   **Mary's Scores in 10 Games**

Stem	Leaves
5	3 3
8	6 7 7 7 7
9	0 1 9

Mean	Medium	Mode
_____	_____	_____

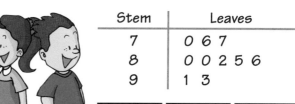

George's Scores in 10 Games

Stem	Leaves
7	0 6 7
8	0 0 2 5 6
9	1 3

Mean	Medium	Mode
_____	_____	_____

b.   The mean scores of Mary and George are _____ .

c.   The range of Mary's score is _____ . Her median and mode are both _____ , which is higher than the mean. Most of her data are above / below the mean.

d.   The range of George's score is _____ . As the mean, median, and mode have a difference of 1 or 2 points, his data set should / should not be around the mean.

⑦   **No. of Sausages Eaten Each Month**

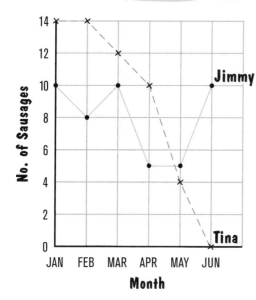

	Mean	Median	Mode
Jimmy			
Tina			

Write a sentence to describe the graph.

_____

_____

_____

_____

ISBN: 978-1-77149-033-7

Probability

- Determine all the possible outcomes in a simple probability experiment.
- Use fractions to represent the probability that an event will occur in probability experiments.

It's not fair! The probability of getting my favourite food is only $\frac{1}{4}$.

List out all the possible outcomes for each probability experiment.

① 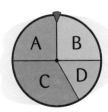 Toss a coin.

_____

②   Roll a cube numbered 1 to 6.

_____

③   Spin the spinner.

_____

④ 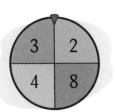 Roll a cube numbered 1 to 6 two times and find the sum.

_____

⑤  Spin the spinner two times and find the product.

_____

ISBN: 978-1-77149-033-7

Probability: a number showing how likely it is that an event will happen

e.g.

$$\boxed{2} \ \boxed{2} \ \boxed{2} \ \boxed{7} \ \boxed{8}$$

$$\text{Probability} = \frac{\text{No. of outcomes of a particular event}}{\text{Total no. of outcomes}}$$

Probability of picking a $\boxed{2}$

$$= \frac{3}{5} \quad \begin{array}{l} \leftarrow \text{There are 3 "2".} \\ \leftarrow \text{There are 5 cards.} \end{array}$$

Write a fraction to describe the probability of each event.

⑥

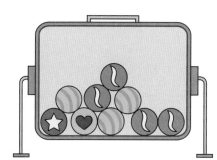

What is the probability of picking

a. a marble with a cat's eye? _____

b. a marble with stripes? _____

c. a marble with a star? _____

⑦

What is the probability of picking

a. a card with an animal? _____

b. a card with a vehicle? _____

c. a card with a plant? _____

⑧   What is the probability of landing on

a. a flower? _____

b. a pencil? _____

c. a car? _____

d. a ring? _____

e. a pail? _____

ISBN: 978-1-77149-033-7

Match the spinners with the correct tables. Then write fractions or draw pictures to complete the tables.

⑨

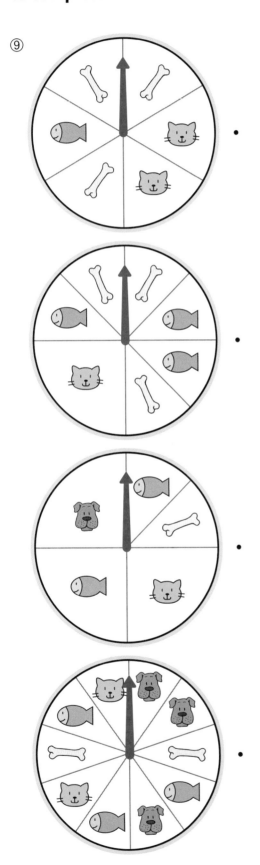

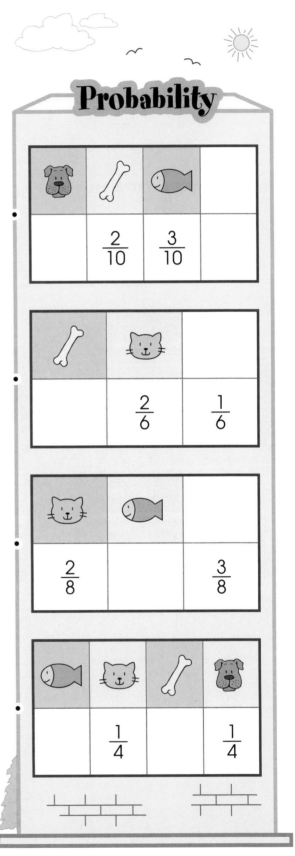

Probability

ISBN: 978-1-77149-033-7

Draw things on the spinners to match the descriptions. Then answer the questions.

Spinner **A** – 6 equal sections

- 3 sections – muffin
- 1 section – cookie
- the rest of the sections – cracker

Spinner **B** – 8 equal sections

- 3 sections – cracker
- 4 sections – cookie
- the rest of the sections – muffin

⑩

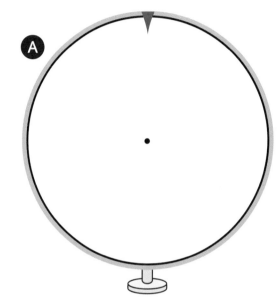
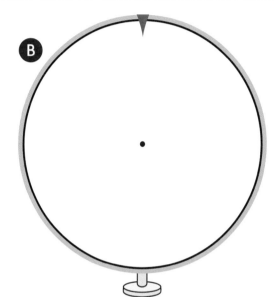

⑪ What is the probability that **A** will land on "cracker"? _____

⑫ What is the probability that **B** will land on "muffin"? _____

⑬
> *Which spinner should I choose to spin if I want to have a muffin? Why?*

_____

⑭
> *If the sections "cookie" and "cracker" on spinner A are replaced by "bone", what will be the probability of landing on "bone"?*

_____

ISBN: 978-1-77149-033-7

ENGLISH

ISBN: 978-1-77149-033-7   Complete Canadian Curriculum • **Grade 5**   **119**

European Microstates

Did you know that there are countries so small, many of us have never heard of them? Five of these smallest countries in the world are in Europe, commonly known as the five European microstates.

Andorra

This country is in the Pyrenees, the mountain range that separates France and Spain. It is a small principality, meaning it is ruled by a prince. It is about 470 square kilometres and has a population of about 78 000. Andorrans make up only about one-third of the population, almost half are Spanish, and the rest are Portuguese and French. The official language is Catalan.

Liechtenstein

Liechtenstein is also a principality. It is the fourth-smallest country in the world. Its area of 160 square kilometres is home to 36 000 people, most of whom speak German. There is great skiing to be found here.

San Marino

Founded in 301 CE, San Marino is one of the world's oldest republics. It is the third-smallest country in the world, with an area of 61 square kilometres and a population of about 32 000. Its people speak Italian and are in fact very much like Italians themselves. Tourism is the main industry, although banking, ceramics, clothing, wine, and cheese are also important to the country's economy.

Monaco

As the second-smallest country in the world, Monaco is located on the Mediterranean Sea along the coast of France, not far from the Italian border. It has a population of 35 000, which is not much until you learn that the country is only two square kilometres! It is the world's most densely populated country. Many wealthy people choose to live here, most of them being Monegasques, French, or Italians.

Vatican City

Known as the "headquarters" of the Roman Catholic Church, Vatican City is the world's smallest country, measuring only 0.44 square kilometres. It is located in Rome, the capital city of Italy. Although it is home to only about 800 citizens, 3000 people commute from Rome to work here every day. Millions of tourists visit each year to see its buildings and famous artwork.

ISBN: 978-1-77149-033-7

A. Match the names with the descriptions.

1. San Marino •   • one of the world's oldest republics

2. Vatican City •   • official language of Andorra

3. Catalan •   • capital city of Italy

4. the Pyrenees •   • world's smallest country

5. Rome •   • a mountain range

B. Answer these questions.

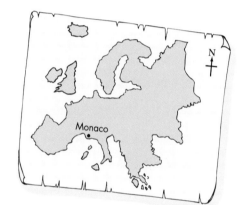

1. What is a principality?

    _____

    _____

2. Where is Monaco?

    _____

    _____

3. What can you say about Monaco in terms of its population density?

    _____

4. Why do you think Monaco is so popular among wealthy people?

    _____

5. The word "microstate" means "tiny state". Think of another word beginning with "micro" and tell what it means.

    _____

Nouns

Nouns can fall into three groups. A **common noun** names any person, place, thing, or animal. A **proper noun** names a specific person, place, thing, or animal. It always begins with a capital letter. A **compound proper noun** is a proper noun with more than one word.

Examples: country (common)
Andorra (proper)
the Roman Catholic Church (compound proper)

C. Write the underlined nouns in the correct groups.

Featured <u>Country</u>: **Monaco**

- second-smallest country in the world
- located on <u>the Mediterranean Sea</u>
- not far from the Italian <u>border</u>
- population: 35 000
- measures two square kilometres
- home to <u>Monegasques</u>, French, and Italians

1. Common:

_____

2. Proper:

_____

3. Compound Proper:

_____

D. Rewrite these sentences by correcting the common and proper nouns.

1. Many tourists visit Vatican City for its Famous Architecture.

_____

2. The Pyrenees is the Mountain Range between france and spain.

_____

3. Besides Tourism, things like Banking, Ceramics, Clothing, Wine, and Cheese are also important to San marino's Economy.

_____

_____

       ISBN: 978-1-77149-033-7

Verbs

Verbs can fall into two groups. A **transitive verb** must take an object. An **intransitive verb** does not need an object.

Examples: Most of the people in Liechtenstein <u>speak</u> German. (transitive)
Most of us <u>commute</u> every day. (intransitive)

E. **Write the transitive verb and the object of each sentence.**

	Verb	**Object**
1. Laurie measured the size of this box.	_____	_____
2. Bill chose Monaco to be his home.	_____	_____
3. Bob visits Rome every two years.	_____	_____
4. Kara sees the Pyrenees far away.	_____	_____
5. Cheryl learned German last year.	_____	_____

F. **Underline each intransitive verb. Then write a sentence.**

1. The more mistakes you make, the more you learn.

2. Marie paints every other weekend.

3. Walter always listens in class.

4. Thanks to the doctor, the blind man finally sees!

5. This parrot really talks.

6.
Some verbs can be both transitive and intransitive, like the word "see". Choose an intransitive verb from (F) and use it as a transitive verb in a sentence.

Have you ever wondered about the ship on the Canadian dime? It is a schooner called *Bluenose*, Canada's most celebrated sailing vessel.

Bluenose was launched in March 1921 at Lunenburg, Nova Scotia. It was both a racing and cod-fishing vessel. In fact, "Bluenose" is a nickname for Nova Scotians, and has been so since around 1760. No one really knows why, but some say it is because of the purplish-blue potatoes that were once widely grown in the province.

Bluenose had the largest mainsail in the world. It was 49 metres long and weighed 258 tonnes. Its mainmast was 38 metres high with a sail area of a whopping 1036 square metres! Its crew comprised five officers, 12 deckhands, and a cook. The schooner was built in response to the fact that the United States had won the trophy in the annual International Fishermen's Race in 1920. The following year, our Bluenose won the trophy back and remained undefeated for 17 years!

Bluenose was a hard-working vessel. Besides its racing and fishing duties, it also served as a showboat, representing Canada at the World's Fair in Chicago in

Bluenose

1933. But later, new boat designs made fishing schooners obsolete. Despite attempts to keep the ship in Canada and preserved as a national institution, our Bluenose was sold to a company in the West Indies in 1938. It became a "tramp schooner" – a cargo vessel sailing the waters of the Caribbean Sea.

Despite some misfortunes over the course of its career – it sank in 1946 when it struck a reef off the coast of Haiti – Bluenose was depicted on a Canadian postage stamp and put on our dime in 1937, becoming a little bit of history in our pocket. Then in 1955, the schooner and its captain Angus Walters were inducted into the Canadian Sports Hall of Fame. In 1963, the beloved schooner was back as *Bluenose II*, an exact copy of the original. It now belongs to the government of Nova Scotia and acts as a goodwill ambassador, to remind us of Canada's greatest sailing vessel.

A. Fill in the information about Bluenose.

Information about Bluenose

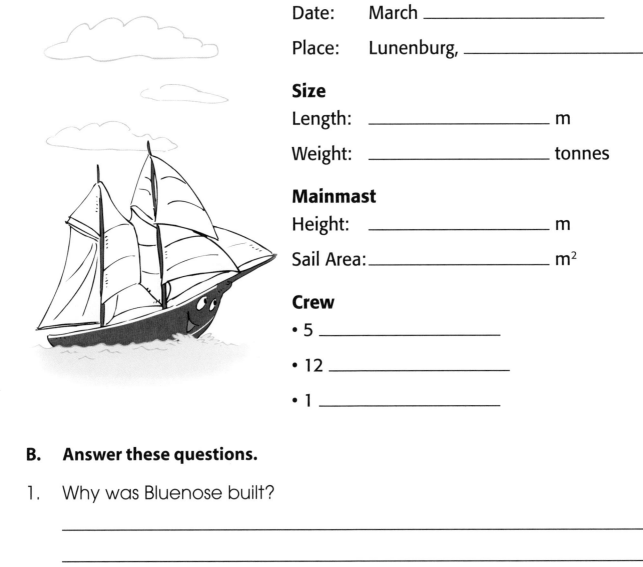

Launch

Date: March _____

Place: Lunenburg, _____

Size

Length: _____ m

Weight: _____ tonnes

Mainmast

Height: _____ m

Sail Area: _____ m^2

Crew

• 5 _____

• 12 _____

• 1 _____

B. Answer these questions.

1. Why was Bluenose built?

   _____

   _____

2. What happened to Bluenose in 1938?

   _____

   _____

3. How did Canadians preserve the memory of Bluenose before Bluenose II was built?

   _____

Adjectives

An **adjective** describes a noun. Sometimes, a noun can also function as an adjective.

Examples: Bluenose is a <u>Canadian</u> vessel that was <u>hand-built</u>.
Bluenose has been depicted on a <u>postage</u> stamp.

"Postage" is a noun, but it describes "stamp", so it functions as an adjective in this sentence.

C.   Underline each adjective and circle the noun that it describes.

1.   Bluenose had a large mainsail.

2.   Bluenose is Canada's national institution.

3.   The game room is just right across from where we are.

4.   Your timing was exact.

5.   There were many crew members on board.

D.   Complete this crossword puzzle with adjectives from the passage that describe Bluenose.

Adverbs

An **adverb** describes a verb. It often ends in "**ly**". Sometimes it is placed in front of the verb, and sometimes it is placed after.

Examples: Bluenose <u>easily</u> won the race.
Bluenose won the race <u>easily</u>.

E. Tell whether the underlined word is an adjective (ADJ) or adverb (ADV).

1. The province is full of <u>friendly</u> people. _____

2. Purplish-blue potatoes were once <u>widely</u> grown here. _____

3. Bluenose II is <u>exactly</u> the same as the original. _____

4. What a <u>lovely</u> name this is! _____

5. The schooner arrived <u>early</u>. _____

F. Rewrite each sentence by placing the adverb in a different spot.

1. We built the ships carefully.

   _____

2. The ship calmly sails the sea.

   _____

3. The cook chopped the onions skilfully.

   _____

4. The crew greeted the kids cheerfully.

   _____

Honeybees

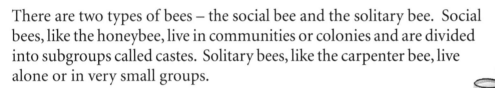

Honey has made many a food and meal tasty and enjoyable to eat. Yet the busy bees that fly about us when we have our outdoor meals are most annoying!

There are two types of bees – the social bee and the solitary bee. Social bees, like the honeybee, live in communities or colonies and are divided into subgroups called castes. Solitary bees, like the carpenter bee, live alone or in very small groups.

As their name suggests, honeybees make honey. They live in a beehive made up of honeycombs, a structure made of wax produced by the bees. Each honeycomb has many six-sided holes called cubbyholes or cells. It is in these cells that the bees put their nectar and honey or lay eggs.

As a community, honeybees are divided into three subgroups or castes: the queen bee, the worker bee, and the drone. Each caste has a very definite and rigid role or job. The queen bee only lays eggs into the waxy cells. The drones' only job is to mate with the queen bee, after which they die. It is the worker bees that are the really busy bees: they build the hive, collect the food, and care for the young. In each hive, there are about 50 000 to 80 000 worker bees. These bees produce the honey we eat.

The farming of honey is called apiculture or beekeeping. The farmer builds a small artificial hive, which is a box hung with many trays of wax in wooden frames. The worker bees fill these trays with honey, and when the trays are full, the farmer takes them out and collects the honey. When the hive is overpopulated, the bees fly away in search of a new hive, usually an empty hive that the farmer has built in advance nearby.

The worker bees collect flower nectar with their long tongues and deposit it into a special "honey stomach". The nectar reacts with chemicals in the stomach to start the honey-making process. The worker bees then fly to their hives and deposit the nectar-chemical mixture into the cells and later, honey is formed.

Next time when you spread honey on toast or use it in your tea, remember where it came from.

A. **Match the words with the meanings. Write the correct letters.**

1. colonies _____

2. cubbyholes _____

3. castes _____

4. rigid _____

5. apiculture _____

6. artificial _____

7. deposit _____

8. process _____

A six-sided holes in honeycombs

B not natural

C communities of bees

D not easily changed

E a series of actions

F farming of honey

G put

H subgroups

B. **Circle "T" for the true sentences and "F" for the false ones.**

1. Honeybees are social bees.   T   F

2. The carpenter bee lives in colonies.   T   F

3. Honeybees put nectar and honey in the cubbyholes.   T   F

4. The drones mate with the queen bee and help worker bees collect nectar.   T   F

5. An artificial hive consists of many trays of wax in wooden frames.   T   F

6. The bees die when a hive is overpopulated.   T   F

7. The worker bees collect flower nectars with their long antennae.   T   F

8. Chemicals in a bee's stomach are necessary in the honey-making process.   T   F

Easily Confused Adjectives and Adverbs (1)

Some adjectives and adverbs are often used incorrectly. We have to remember whether we are describing a noun or a verb when using them.

Examples: I'm doing <u>good</u>. (✗)   I'm doing <u>well</u>. (✔)
　　　　　Were you hurt <u>bad</u>? (✗)   Were you hurt <u>badly</u>? (✔)
　　　　　This candy is <u>real</u> good! (✗)   This candy is <u>really</u> good! (✔)
　　　　　Your house is <u>nearly</u> mine. (✗)   Your house is <u>near</u> mine. (✔)

C. Circle the correct adjectives or adverbs.

1. Kara needs to use the washroom really bad / badly .

2. The library is near / nearly the swimming pool.

3. This show turned out to be really good / well .

4. It is always good / well to think ahead.

5. Bob is near / nearly seven feet tall.

D. See if the words in bold are mistakes. Underline them if they are. Then write the correct words on the lines.

My brother can get **real** distracted by the TV and does his homework **really bad**. He knows perfectly **good** that the TV often airs **badly** shows. That is why he only watches documentaries, which are stories about **real** people. But he can be **real** consumed by them. Maybe my brother should become a documentary filmmaker, so that his work will also be his play! That would be a **real** good idea!

1. _____   2. _____   3. _____

4. _____   5. _____   6. _____

ISBN: 978-1-77149-033-7

Easily Confused Adjectives and Adverbs (2)

Some words like "late" and "high" can be used as adjectives or adverbs. But their "ly" form, "lately" and "highly", are used as adverbs with different meanings.

Examples: Sue is <u>late</u>. (adjective)
Sue came <u>late</u>. (adverb)
Has Sue been to the park <u>lately</u>? (adverb meaning "recently")

E. Fill in the blanks with the given words. Then identify each answer as an adjective (ADJ) or adverb (ADV).

hard   late   high   near

1. That flag is flying _____ above the rooftop.   (   )

2. This question on the test is very _____ for me!   (   )

3. My cousin arrived _____ for the party.   (   )

4. This is a very _____ phone call since it is midnight!   (   )

5. Jim got a very _____ score on the test.   (   )

6. Ben is standing _____ the pole.   (   )

7. You have to push the door _____ to open it.   (   )

8. Your birthday is _____ as it is already June.   (   )

F. Use each of these adverbs to write a sentence.

1. highly

_____

2. hardly

_____

Jess "n" Jacki
Party Planners

In May, my friend Jess and I started looking for summer jobs. After a couple of weeks of looking for work in the retail and fast food industries, Jess and I decided we wanted to try something different. We decided to go into business for ourselves! We got the idea from something we did last year.

Jess and I both love to dance. We have been taking dance lessons for years. One day last fall, my aunt asked us to organize a birthday party for her daughter. She thought we could organize a girls' dance party, so we gave it a try. First, we did a short dance show for the girls. Then we taught them a few steps. We taught them some ballet basics and cowboy line dancing too. Because it was a girls' party, we also brought along nail polish and sticker tattoos. The girls really loved it! Everyone had a great time.

Jess and I thought of ways to make our parties bigger and better. We went to the library and borrowed books on magic tricks and Japanese paper folding. Jess's uncle knows how to make balloon animals and taught us how. Then he gave us three beanbag balls and a book that teaches you how to juggle. Jess loves to practise. She is better at juggling than I am.

Later, we were asked to do a party for Canada Day. We got everybody to dress up in red and white. Before long, we were busy several times a week doing birthday parties, bar mitzvahs, and keeping children entertained during large family summer barbecues. The people loved us! We even came up with the idea of offering to supply cakes and snacks because my aunt is a pastry chef.

Now we have our own website, and have decided to work throughout the year doing one party a week. We call our business Jess "n" Jacki Party Planners. We love being our own boss, and we enjoy working together to make our business better and better. We love what we do and are proud to be able to share our passion with our customers!

ISBN: 978-1-77149-033-7

A. **Put these events in order for the website of Jess "n" Jacki Party Planners. Write 1 to 6.**

About Us: the Road to Our Sweet Success

☐   We were looking for summer work.

☐   We have our own website.

☐   We borrowed books from the library.

☐   We organized a Canada Day party.

☐   We organized a dance party.

☐   We learned how to juggle.

B. **Quote a sentence from the passage to support each of the following sentences.**

1.   Jess "n" Jacki Party Planners became more and more popular.

_____

_____

_____

2.   Jess and Jacki can potentially be contacted by anyone in the world looking for party planners.

_____

_____

3.   Even the relatives of Jess and Jacki became involved.

_____

_____

Comparatives and Superlatives (1)

We use "**more**" (**comparative**) and "**most**" (**superlative**) with adjectives that have two or more syllables. We should never use them with adjectives that are already in the comparative or superlative form.

Examples: Their parties are <u>the interestingest</u>. (✘)
Their parties are <u>the most interesting</u>. (✔)
Jess is <u>more better</u> at juggling than Jacki. (✘)
Jess is <u>better</u> at juggling than Jacki. (✔)

C. **Write "more" or "most" in each sentence.**

1. This is the _____ delicious cake I have ever had!

2. Jess and Jacki have a _____ organized party than Amy and Jill.

3. This barbecue is the _____ enjoyable one this summer.

4. The tricks this time are _____ elaborate than the ones before.

D. **Rewrite each sentence by correcting the underlined words.**

1. This kid is <u>more smarter</u> when he is outside the classroom.

   _____

2. Sally is <u>the most funniest</u> kid in class.

   _____

3. Lizzy is the <u>more beautiful</u> of all the daughters.

   _____

4. This story is <u>the most interesting</u> than the other one.

   _____

ISBN: 978-1-77149-033-7

Comparatives and Superlatives (2)

We should always use comparatives when comparing two things, and always use superlatives when comparing more than two things.

Examples: Of <u>all</u> the parties, this one is <u>better</u>. (✗)
Of <u>all</u> the parties, this one is <u>the best</u>. (✔)

E. Check the correct sentences. Put a cross for the wrong ones and rewrite them using the correct comparatives or superlatives.

1. ☐ In this year's list of movies, this one seems the least innovative.

_____

2. ☐ Of these two restaurants, this one is the best.

_____

3. ☐ Out of the whole class, Sarah got less juice.

_____

4. ☐ This is the best job ever!

_____

5. ☐ Is that the bigger one of this bunch?

_____

_____

6. ☐ The kids built the smallest snowman today than yesterday.

_____

_____

The Superfoods

Everyone knows it is important to watch what we eat. We know we must not eat too much fast food or sugary and fatty food, and must eat more raw fruits and vegetables. More and more doctors are telling us that there are foods that can really help us live longer, healthier lives because they have certain nutrients that help our body regenerate and fight disease.

Based on studies of diets in places where people live relatively long and healthy lives – like the Mediterranean region and Okinawa, Japan – doctors advise that if we want the same for our own families, we should make the following list of food a regular part of our diet:

- beans and lentils
- broccoli and spinach
- oranges and pumpkins
- soy
- tomatoes
- walnuts

- blueberries and raspberries
- oats
- salmon
- tea (green or black)
- turkey
- yogourt

When you cook, use olive oil rather than vegetable oil or lard, and spice up your meals with onion, garlic, and ginger. Not only will these items make your food more flavourful, they also have special properties that help you stay healthy.

Don't like spinach, you say? Try it in a salad, mixed with sections of juicy orange and sprinkled with a handful of walnuts, a drop of olive oil, and a dash of balsamic vinegar. You will surely like it then. And instead of boring, old breakfast cereal, make your own morning parfait by layering granola oats, plain yogourt, berries, and honey. Healthful eating *is* delicious!

ISBN: 978-1-77149-033-7

A. **Read the clues and complete the crossword puzzle with words from the passage.**

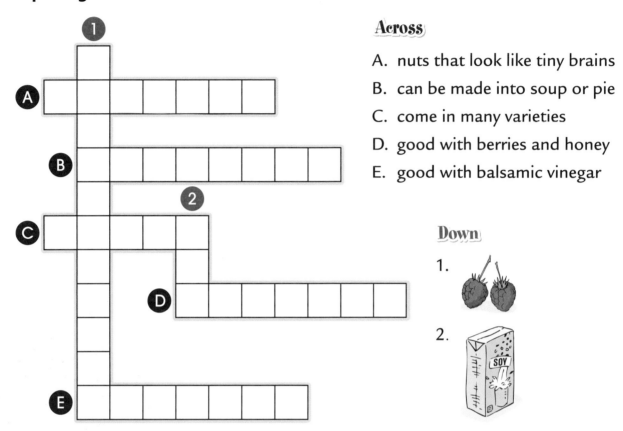

Across

A. nuts that look like tiny brains

B. can be made into soup or pie

C. come in many varieties

D. good with berries and honey

E. good with balsamic vinegar

Down

1.

2.

B. **Based on the information from the passage, plan a day of healthful meals.**

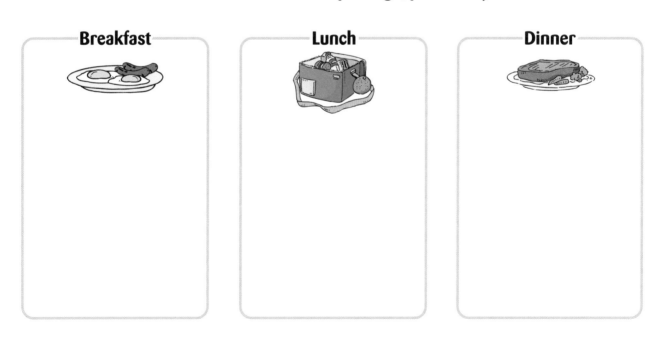

Breakfast

Lunch

Dinner

The Subject and the Predicate

The **subject** and the **predicate** are the two main parts of a sentence. The subject contains the noun or pronoun that performs an action. The predicate contains the verb and describes the action.

Example: The boy ate a salad with apples.
    subject – the boy (the noun is "boy")
    predicate – ate a salad with apples (the verb is "ate")

C.   Draw a line to separate the subject and the predicate in each sentence.

1.   Beth chews her food very carefully.

2.   Tom likes spinach.

3.   Kiwis contain a lot of vitamin C.

4.   The children ate a variety of vegetables.

5.   Sally added some walnuts to her tuna salad.

6.   Mom makes a very healthful breakfast for us every day.

D.   Unscramble the words of the predicate and write each sentence on the line.

1.   Sara (raw fruits vegetables every eats and day).

    _____

2.   My father (milk bought soy containing).

    _____

3.   Yogourt (with becomes a when treat berries mixed).

    _____

ISBN: 978-1-77149-033-7

Compound Subjects and Compound Verbs

Sometimes we have **compound subjects** and **compound verbs**, which means we have two or more subjects, and two or more verbs.

Examples: <u>Yogourt and berries</u> go well together. (compound subject)
The kids <u>ate and chatted</u> in the den. (compound verb)

E.   Check the sentences that contain compound subjects.

1.   Broccoli and spinach are both dark green vegetables. ☐

2.   Green tea and black tea are my favourite drinks. ☐

3.   Balsamic vinegar is very good with bread. ☐

4.   My picky mother needs to eat more fruits. ☐

5.   Mom and Sally are making dinner together. ☐

F.   Write a sentence with each compound verb. You may change the tense if necessary.

1.   sit and wait

_____

2.   cut and mash

_____

3.   shake and bake

_____

4.   sing and dance

_____

December 6, 1917 is a date that all schoolchildren in Nova Scotia most likely know about. On this day in Halifax, a 3121-ton French freighter called *Mont-Blanc* was entering the city's lovely harbour. It was part of a convoy of ships that had come from New York City, and was on its way back to France. It was filled with munitions – over 2600 tonnes of highly explosive chemicals such as nitrocellulose, TNT, wet and dry picric acid, and benzol. It was the time of World War I.

A Norwegian vessel, *Imo*, was also in the harbour. It had been delayed from leaving the day before. Because a third ship was blocking the right channel, the captain of *Imo* decided to leave the harbour through the left channel, where *Mont-Blanc* was coming through. Despite attempts of both captains to avoid a collision, the two ships collided in the centre channel. The result was the largest artificial explosion before the atomic bomb in 1945. *Mont-Blanc* became a fireball that rose over a mile into the air. The ship vaporized. The force of the explosion caused a tsunami 18 metres high, throwing *Imo* onto the land. A wave of air pressure snapped trees and demolished buildings for kilometres.

Over 1000 people died instantly, another thousand died later, and 6000 people were seriously injured. Because many of the residents in Halifax had been looking at the harbour through their windows, they were blinded by flying glass when *Mont-Blanc* exploded. The entire north end of the city was destroyed and 1500 people were left homeless by the destruction. Even in Truro, which is many kilometres away, windows were shattered. Property damage was estimated to be over $30 million, which was a huge amount in 1917.

Ironically, the large number of eye injuries led to medical advances in the treatment of such injuries.

Even today, nearly a century later, what happened in Halifax Harbour on that fateful day in December ranks as one of the largest human-made, non-nuclear explosions ever to occur.

The Halifax Explosion

ISBN: 978-1-77149-033-7

A. Match the five "W's" with the facts about the Halifax explosion.

- *Mont-Blanc* collided with *Imo*.

Who •

- Much of Halifax was destroyed.

- Halifax Harbour, Nova Scotia

What •

- A ship was blocking the right channel.

When •

- captain of *Imo*

- December 6, 1917

Where •

- captain of *Mont-Blanc*

- A very large explosion resulted.

Why •

- *Mont-Blanc* and *Imo* were going through the same channel.

- The explosion caused a tsunami.

B. Answer these questions.

1. What was going on in the world at the time of the tragedy?

    _____

    _____

2. What happened to *Mont-Blanc* after the collision?

    _____

3. What was the irony of the tragedy?

    _____

    _____

Subject-Verb Agreement

In a sentence, the subject and verb must **agree**. A single subject requires the singular form of the verb. A plural subject requires the plural form of the verb.

Examples: The ship <u>is</u> sailing ahead. (singular)
The two ships <u>are</u> sailing ahead. (plural)

C.   Circle the correct form of the verb.

1. The freighter has / have over 2600 tonnes of explosives.

2. Another ship is / are also in the harbour.

3. Some people is / are blocking Mr. Shaw's view.

4. The two cars collide / collides in the intersection.

5. The sun rise / rises over on the other side.

D.   Underline the verbs that do not agree with the subjects and correct them on the lines.

1. Everything vaporizes when the explosion occur.   _____

2. Sometimes, an explosion cause a tsunami that creates further damage.   _____

3. The ship becomes a fireball that rise into the air.   _____

4. Aunt Meg remain very quiet and avoids talking about the event.   _____

5. The students know about the tragedy and visits Halifax Harbour every year.   _____

E. **Change the singular subjects to plural ones and the plural subjects to singular ones. Make sure the subjects and verbs agree.**

1. The captain attempts a different course.

   _____

   _____

2. A load of munitions is on board.

   _____

   _____

3. Numerous trees snap and many houses are demolished.

   _____

4. The families are devastated and refuse to believe it.

   _____

F. **Write a sentence with each of these verbs. Make sure the verb agrees with the subject.**

1. happen

   _____

2. leave

   _____

3. find

   _____

4. rank

   _____

Cherry Blossom Time

Dear Sammy,

How are you? Is there still snow where you live? Where I live here in Japan, we get snow in the mountains in wintertime. But the snow is almost gone. Cherry trees are starting to flower now! I think there is nothing as pretty as a cherry tree in spring.

Each spring, we wait for the cherry blossoms to come out. There are four main islands of Japan: Kyushu, Shikoku, Honshu, and Hokkaido. Kyushu is in the farthest south, so cherry blossom time starts there and moves north. Announcers on the television news programs show us how the cherry blossom "front" is coming north, as if they are talking about some snowstorm. It is very exciting! When the cherry trees start to bloom, schoolchildren leave the classrooms and go to the parks. We sketch, paint, and have picnics under the cherry trees. Families and co-workers also take time to gather under the blossoms. We call this time *ohanami*. *O* means "honourable", *hana* means "flower", and *mi* means "to see".

When the cherry blossom front comes to the countryside around my town, it is like pale pink snow on the trees. After a while, the pink snow falls to the ground in the breeze. Cherry blossom time lasts such a short time – maybe that's why we love it so much.

I recently found out there are also many cherry trees in Vancouver and Washington, D.C. So they should have cherry blossom time, too. Do you have cherry blossom time where you live, Sammy? Why don't you come to Japan someday and see the beautiful blossoms with my family and me?

Your pen pal,

Kiyoka

ISBN: 978-1-77149-033-7

A. Fill in the blanks with words from the passage.

1. Cherry trees start to flower in _____ in Japan.

2. In Japan, there are four main _____ .

3. The cherry blossom "front" starts _____ and then moves _____ .

4. In *ohanami, hana* means " _____ ".

5. There are many cherry trees in _____ and Washington, D.C.

B. Fill in the blanks to complete these words from the passage. Then complete what Kiyoka says with the coloured letters.

b __ __ s s __ m s

H __ n s __ u

__ o __ __ __ i d o

__ o __ __ __ r a b l e

m __ __ __ t __ i __ s

b l __ __ __

p __ c __ __ __ s

We call cherry blossom time __ __ __ __ __ __ __ !

Direct and Indirect Objects

The **direct object** is the noun that receives the action of the verb. The **indirect object** is the noun that the action is directed to.

Examples: Kiyoka drew a <u>picture</u> of the blossoms. (direct)
Kiyoka gave <u>Sammy</u> the picture. (indirect)

In this sentence, "picture" is the direct object because it receives the action of the verb "gave".

C.   Tell whether the underlined object is "direct" or "indirect".

1.   The teacher and the children left the <u>classroom</u>.   _____

2.   A lady walked her <u>dog</u> in the beautiful park.   _____

3.   Sammy read her <u>dad</u> the letter before dinner.   _____

4.   A lot of children love <u>springtime</u> in Japan.   _____

5.   The breeze blows the <u>blossoms</u> to the ground.   _____

6.   Sammy sent <u>Kiyoka</u> a postcard.   _____

D.   Write the direct and indirect objects of each sentence.

Direct   Indirect

1.   Ann gave her sister a bracelet.   _____   _____

2.   Mom wrote Tom a little note.   _____   _____

3.   Though it is late already, I still told Bill a story.   _____   _____

4.   Jill sent her cousin a parcel by sea!   _____   _____

5.   I mailed you a letter when I was vacationing in Japan.   _____   _____

6.   Kelly showed Tom her project before heading home.   _____   _____

                ISBN: 978-1-77149-033-7

E. **Fill in the blanks with the correct objects to complete the sentences.**

1. her painting / the audience

   The artist showed _____

   _____ .

2. the customers / the menus

   The waiter handed _____ _____ .

3. the guests / a video

   My dad showed _____ _____ at our Christmas party.

4. Christmas cards / the children

   The teacher gave _____ _____ before sending them home for the holiday.

F. **Use each name as the direct object in one sentence, and as the indirect object in another sentence.**

1. **Sammy**

   Direct: _____

   Indirect: _____

2. **Kiyoka**

   Direct: _____

   Indirect: _____

3. **Uncle Peter**

   Direct: _____

   Indirect: _____

Winter Camp
at Lake Winnipeg

Dear Kiyoka,

Thank you for your letter. Springtime in Japan sounds fantastic. It is still winter here where I live. But I don't mind. I went to a winter camp last weekend. It was so much fun! The camp is on the shores of Lake Winnipeg. Lake Winnipeg is the world's tenth largest freshwater lake.

We went ice fishing at camp. We walked out onto the frozen lake to a small shack. It was nice and cozy inside, with chairs and a table, a small stove, and a toaster. The woman inside lifted a flap on the floor, and there was a hole in the thick ice! We put a fishing line down into the hole. We then had tea and toast and waited. We caught three nice fish right away. We were very lucky.

Then we went back to the lakeshore and cleared a space for building a campfire. Our camp leader taught us how to make a tasty meal. We chopped up some carrots and potatoes while she skinned the fish and cut it into fillets. We sprinkled on salt and pepper and some dried herbs, and then put everything inside pockets of aluminum foil. We let the campfire die down a bit; then we placed the pockets of foil inside the glowing sticks. We made hot chocolate while we waited for our meal to cook. Everything was delicious!

The next day, we learned how to do winter orienteering. It is like racing with snowshoes and a compass. It was very exciting! Maybe someday, you can come and spend the winter with my family.

Your pen pal,
Sammy

P.S. This is a picture of the ice fishing shack.

ISBN: 978-1-77149-033-7

A. **Look at the clues and complete the crossword puzzle with words from the passage.**

This is a sport in which we have to find our way across rough terrain using a map and compass.

This word is used as a verb in Kiyoka's letter.

Fish
8 pieces

B. **Write a short letter to a friend about an experience you had this season.**

_____

_____

_____

_____

_____

_____

Pronouns (1)

A **pronoun** is a word used to refer to a noun. We use **subject pronouns** like "we" and "they" when referring to the subjects of sentences. We use **object pronouns** like "us" and "them" when referring to the objects. We use **possessive pronouns** like "ours" and "theirs" when expressing ownership.

Examples: The <u>fish</u> was caught. <u>It</u> was caught. (subject)
Amy thanked <u>Joey and me</u>. Amy thanked <u>us</u>. (object)
This is <u>our house</u>. This house is <u>ours</u>. (possessive)

C. Write the stated pronoun in each case.

1. **Subject pronoun**
She went to winter camp with them. _____

2. **Object pronoun**
You are showing us such a good fishing trick! _____

3. **Possessive pronoun**
His fish is much bigger than ours. _____

4. **Possessive pronoun**
Their fish is more unusual than his. _____

D. Rewrite each sentence by replacing the underlined words with a pronoun.

1. We told <u>our camp leader Ben</u> that we wouldn't be long.

_____

2. Look! All of these are <u>Monica's fish</u>!

_____

3. Although it is still winter in Winnipeg, <u>Sammy and her friends</u> don't mind the cold at all.

_____

_____

     ISBN: 978-1-77149-033-7

E. Fill in the blanks with the correct pronouns.

Richard, Sam, and I are great friends. 1._____
have known one another since kindergarten.
Although I now go to a different school, my two
buddies still visit 2._____ every weekend. We
are inseparable! Because the three of us spend so
much time at my place, it feels like the house is 3._____ . Last month,
my mom bought 4._____ a video game called Roll-It-Up. When Richard
and Sam visited on Saturday, 5._____ showed 6._____ the game and
7._____ loved 8._____ ! It is too bad that Sam will be away for the
summer, so I won't be seeing 9._____ for two months. However, 10._____
promised Richard and me that he would tell 11._____ about his vacation
when he gets back.

F. Rewrite each sentence in different ways using a different pronoun each time.

1. Jenny wants my brother and me to go fishing with her.

    a. _____

    b. _____

2. Uncle Max has always been good at ice fishing.

    a. _____

    b. _____

3. "You should've asked if that marker belonged to me," said May.

    a. _____

    b. _____

    c. _____

Bethany Hamilton loves to surf. Growing up in Kauai, Hawaii, a place famous for its waves, Bethany had become a champion surfer by the time she was a teenager. Then on October 31, 2003, tragedy struck.

Bethany had gone surfing as usual with her friend Alana and Alana's father. It was a calm, clear day, and Bethany was relaxing on her board with her right arm on the board, and her left arm dangling in the water. Her friend was floating nearby. Suddenly, Bethany felt a clap of pressure and quick tugs at her arm. There was a flash of grey. The water around her was bright red. That was all the time it took.

Bethany says there was no pain at the time, and that she never panicked. She simply yelled to her friend that she had just been attacked by a shark, and started to make her way back to the shore. Alana's father used a surfboard leash to make a tourniquet for the stump of her upper arm, which saved her life. Her left arm was gone, bitten off by the three-metre tiger shark. The shark had also bitten off a chunk of Bethany's surfboard, 16 inches across and eight inches deep. The shark was later caught, though.

Bethany Hamilton
The Spirit of a Champion

Doctors say that Bethany's athletic training saved her life. Surprising everyone – except perhaps her parents – Bethany recovered and was back on her surfboard in less than a month! A few months later, Bethany competed at the 2004 National Scholastic Surfing Association Nationals Championships and took fifth place. Later that year, she secured a spot on the United States' National Surfing Team. The following year, Bethany came in first at the NSSA championships in the Explorer Women's Division. Bethany has won numerous awards, including the 2004 ESPY Award for "Comeback Athlete of the Year". She has written a book and often speaks about her experience, motivating others to overcome the obstacles in their lives.

Always with the spirit of a champion, Bethany says she is now interested in becoming a triathlete.

ISBN: 978-1-77149-033-7

A. **Use your dictionary to find the definitions of these words as they are used in the passage. Then use them in sentences of your own.**

1. surf: _____

_____

2. spirit: _____

_____

3. triathlete: _____

_____

4. tourniquet: _____

_____

B. **Imagine you are Bethany Hamilton being interviewed by a student newspaper reporter. Write your responses to these questions.**

1. What kept you from panicking after the shark attack?

_____

_____

2. How were you able to remain positive with one arm gone?

_____

_____

3. What do you say to those who have encountered similar obstacles?

_____

_____

Pronouns (2)

When we ask questions, we can use **interrogative pronouns**: "what", "which", "who", "whose", and "whom". We can use them indirectly too. When we want to refer to a noun occurring earlier in a sentence, we use **relative pronouns**: "which", "who", "whose", "whom", and "that".

Examples: <u>Which</u> is the one you told me about? (interrogative)
The mall, <u>which</u> is in the city core, is still open. (relative)

C. **Tell what type of pronoun is used in each sentence. Write "interrogative" or "relative".**

1. The champion, who is a hero to the kids, is getting a lot of attention.

    _____

2. I asked Alana what she was going to do for her Science project.

    _____

3. "Sam, do you know whose this is?" Amy asked.

    _____

4. Bethany, to whom the trophy was given, had a smile that stretched from ear to ear.

    _____

5. I asked Bethany what the secret to her success was.

    _____

6. My cousins love the guinea pig that I recently bought from the pet store.

    _____

ISBN: 978-1-77149-033-7

D.   Fill in the blanks with the correct pronouns.

1.   The student, _____ is new to the class, was shy at first but quickly warmed up to everyone.

2.   The fly ball, _____ Tony had wanted to give him a homerun, fell easily into my glove!

3.   "To _____ did you talk after school yesterday?" I asked.

4.   Tell me _____ you want from this rack and I will get you the right size.

5.   The little kid, _____ mother is away at work, mistakenly calls the babysitter "Mommy".

6.   Ask your little cousin _____ is making him so unhappy.

7.   I have no idea _____ Alice is going to do.

8.   I wonder _____ hid the little gift under my pillow.

E.   Use each of these as an interrogative pronoun in one sentence, and as a relative pronoun in another.

1.   what

_____

_____

2.   whom

_____

_____

ISBN: 978-1-77149-033-7

The Inca

Before the Spanish built their own empire in South America around the 16th century, there was the Inca, an ancient civilization that once lived in the mountains in what is now a country called Peru.

The Inca were good fighters. Over the years, they built a large empire of 12 million people. They worshipped the sun, and believed their leader descended from it. Though they were defeated in 1533 by the Spanish, the ruins of one of their high mountain settlements still exist today at Machu Pichu.

To the Inca people, the llama was an important animal. The llama is sure-footed on the steep and rocky crags of mountains, much like the big-horn sheep and mountain goats that we can see – if we are lucky – when driving through the mountains of British Columbia. The llama provided the Inca with food and clothing, and was the main method of transport. Because of the importance of this animal to the Inca, it is found in many of their legends.

The Llamas and the Flood
– based on an Inca legend

Two Inca shepherds were resting on a rock high in the mountains when they noticed that their llamas were acting strangely. These llamas seemed to be staring at the sky. The two shepherds approached the llamas and asked them what was wrong. The llamas replied that the stars said it was soon going to rain, and that an enormous flood would overtake the land below.

The two shepherds, who were good and honest mountain people, loved their animals very much and believed their story. They went to get their families and moved further up the mountain to live in caves. Concerned about the people living below, they sent a message down to the people on the flat land about the ensuing flood. The people down at the bottom, who were not too kind or sensible, scoffed at the message and ignored the mountain dwellers. Not long after, the rain came and continued for four months.

Those living below the mountains died. The shepherds and their families repopulated the Earth, and the llamas were happy to live up high, close to the stars.

   ISBN: 978-1-77149-033-7

A. Fill in the blanks with words from the passage.

The Inca:

* were good 1._____

* was an 2._____ civilization

* 3._____ the sun

* lived in what is now 4._____

The Llama:

* is 5._____ on steep mountains

* was the Inca's main method of 6._____

* provided the Inca with food and 7._____

* is found in many Inca 8._____

B. Answer these questions.

1. How big was the Inca empire?

_____

2. When did the Spanish build their empire in South America?

_____

3. In the legend, what disaster do the llamas say will overtake the land?

_____

4. If you were one of the shepherds in the legend, what would you have done after your message was ignored? Why?

_____

_____

Pronouns (3)

When the subjects of sentences do things that turn back upon the subjects, we use **reflexive pronouns**: "myself", "yourself", "himself", "herself", "itself", "ourselves", "yourselves", and "themselves". When they do the same things, we use **reciprocal pronouns**: "each other" and "one another".

Examples: I'm so bored that I'm starting to talk to <u>myself</u>! (reflexive)
These <u>two</u> sisters always look out for <u>each other</u>. (reciprocal)
These <u>three</u> sisters always look out for <u>one another</u>. (reciprocal)

C. Circle the correct reflexive pronouns.

1. The children enjoyed themselves / ourselves tremendously at Benny's birthday party.

2. Marie said to us, "Look! I made this pumpkin pie herself / myself !"

3. Sara looked at itself / herself in the mirror before heading out the door.

4. All the cousins on my father's side of the family are very good at making each other / one another laugh.

5. Tim tried to correct myself / himself by coming up with a kinder remark about the restaurant's design.

6. "Don't worry. Emily and I will look after each other / one another at the camp," said Jenny to her mother.

7. The cat is blocking our view because it is cleaning ourselves / itself in front of the TV.

8. Mother said to us, "Remember to behave yourself / yourselves at Grandma's."

ISBN: 978-1-77149-033-7

D.   Fill in the blanks with the correct pronouns.

Paul and Sam are brothers who work
as shepherds. They always keep
watch for 1._____ when
they are up in the mountains. They
also love their herds of llamas very
much. They do not always have to
keep the llamas close, though, since these wise animals can look after
2._____ .   One time, Sam said to the llamas as they were
grazing, "We're very grateful that you can look after 3._____
up here." Having heard this, one of the llamas responded, "In fact, we
can come up to the mountains 4._____ . We can also follow
other shepherds when you're busy on the farm." Still, Paul and Sam insist
on walking the beloved llamas 5._____ for fear the animals
might lose their way in the journey. Because these animals provide the
shepherds with food and clothing in return, the two groups – shepherds
and llamas – depend on 6._____ .

**E.   Write a short paragraph using two reflexive pronouns and two reciprocal
        pronouns.**

_____

_____

_____

_____

_____

_____

The Hummingbird – a Unique Flyer

Wing beats per second up to 200

Have you ever seen a tiny bird flitting from flower to flower? The wings move so fast that they appear to be just a blur. The bird appears not to be flying and seems to be hovering over the flowers. You hear a buzzing, humming noise. What kind of bird is it? You wonder. You have just seen a hummingbird!

Hummingbirds are the tiniest birds in the world. They are usually not more than 20 grams, though some can be as little as two grams! Their wings are quite long and pointy, which rotate rather than flap. This allows them to approach flowers in a way most other birds cannot. They move in this unique way to get very close to flowers for their food: besides feeding on insects like spiders, hummingbirds feed on nectar just like bees do.

This type of flying requires a lot of effort – the wings of a hummingbird beat up to 200 times per second! They can also fly up to 75 kilometres per hour. Because of this, hummingbirds need a lot of food each day to get their energy. They eat as much as half their body weight in nectar and insects every day! This is why the birds must spend most of their time flying around looking for food. Their feet are not well-developed as a result, since they are not for walking but for perching briefly on branches.

There are approximately 300 different types of hummingbirds, all inhabiting the western hemisphere from Canada down to Argentina. Canada and the United States are home to about 16 species, while the majority of hummingbirds live in the more tropical areas of Central and South America. Hummingbirds live for as long as five or six years in the wild, and many of them are migratory. For example, the ruby-throated hummingbird migrates across the Gulf of Mexico to take advantage of the warmer winter down south.

A. Find the words in the word search. Then write the correct words for the meanings.

rotate   hummingbird   tropical

hovering   western hemisphere perching

nectar   ruby-throated   migratory

a	e	g	e	h	u	m	m	i	n	g	b	i	r	d	e	p	m	s
e	d	b	n	t	x	p	q		p	n	m	s	z	p	y	e	o	c
h	c	y	o	r	o	k	e	s	a	t	u	r	r	e	z	r	j	h
r	e	r	p	o	k	j	u	e	p	r	p	o	t	r	h	t	m	o
p	n	l		p	j	d	r	t	e	y	p	t	y	c	f	r	i	v
i	e	o	c	i	l	x	s	a	c	a	o	a		h	i	t	g	e
m	c	p	z	c	b	c	t	i	a	e	k	t	i	i	a	r	r	r
e	t	w	r	a	u	h	r	y	l	s	a	e	o	n	w		a	i
h	a	s	a	l	q	a	u	p	a	w	j	A	w	g	q	k	t	n
r	r	u	r	u	b	y	–	t	h	r	o	a	t	e	d	g	o	g
n	w	e	s	t	e	r	n		h	e	m	i	s	p	h	e	r	e
s	e	w	n	e	w	z	d	h	k	r	a	c	d	n	a	s	y	w

1. _____ : move in circles

2. _____ : resting or settling

3. _____ : the world's smallest bird

4. _____ : hanging suspended in the air

5. _____ : changing one's area of habitation with the seasons

6. _____ : sweet substance produced by plants to attract pollinating insects

The Present Tense

When we want to talk about a habit or a simple truth, we use the **simple present tense**. When we want to talk about something that is going on or something that is planned for the future, we use the **present progressive tense**.

Examples: Hansel the Hummingbird <u>eats</u> a lot every day. (simple present)
Hansel <u>is perching</u> on a branch. (present progressive)
Hansel <u>is flying</u> south tomorrow. (present progressive)

B. Complete each sentence with the simple present tense or the present progressive tense of the given verb.

1. This hummingbird (weigh) _____ only two grams!

2. The hummingbird's unique way of flying (consume) _____ a lot of energy.

3. This ruby-throated hummingbird (leave)_____ very soon for the warmer winter in the south.

4. Most of the world's hummingbirds (live) _____ in Central and South America.

5. Just like bees, hummingbirds (feed) _____ on nectar. But unlike bees, they do not use it to make honey.

6. I can see that Hansel the Hummingbird (approach) _____ this beautiful flower with a lot of enthusiasm!

7. "Look! Hansel's wings (beat) _____ so fast they are a complete blur!" I say to Tom.

8. Considering how much hummingbirds have to eat, it is no surprise that they (spend) _____ most of their time looking for food.

ISBN: 978-1-77149-033-7

C. **Check the correct sentences. Put a cross for the wrong ones and rewrite them using the simple present tense or the present progressive tense.**

1. ☐ Ben and Jill are giving their dog a bath once every three weeks.

   _____

   _____

2. ☐ Gwen is dashing to the park after school every day.

   _____

3. ☐ Janice is pondering what to say this very moment.

   _____

4. ☐ Henry is travelling to the North Pole this winter.

   _____

D. **Use each of these verbs in the simple present tense in one sentence and in the present progressive tense in another.**

1. flit

   _____

   _____

2. flap

   _____

   _____

3. populate

   _____

   _____

A Letter from a New Pen Pal

Dear Samantha,

Hello! My name is Rakesh. I found your name and address from a Canadian magazine, which my aunt and uncle sent me from Toronto. They live there. In fact, they send me a magazine from Toronto every month. It's great, because I learn a lot about student life in Canada.

I speak Hindi — "Nah-mah-STAY" is how I say "hello" in my language — but I also speak and write English, as you can see. I'm an 11-year-old boy living in Mumbai, which used to be called Bombay. Can you guess what country I'm from? I'm from India! Perhaps you already knew that from the postmark on the envelope.

My family is not very big. I have a five-year-old sister named Kritika. My mom works for a magazine and my father is a computer programmer. We live in an apartment in the northern part of Mumbai. Mumbai is India's biggest city. Some say that there are 12 million people living here — but no one really knows for sure because many people here are homeless. Are there homeless people in your city? Sometimes when I take the train in Mumbai, I can see small shacks along the tracks. Families live in these shacks. It makes me sad.

I read in one magazine that the population of Canada is about 35 million. I think that's incredible! Your country is so big, and yet there are hardly any people compared to India. It's hard to imagine what it must be like to live in a place like that. My aunt and uncle said I can visit them in Toronto when I'm older. They said they would take me to Niagara Falls. My aunt sent me a postcard from there last year.

I hope you will write back to me, Samantha. I'm enclosing a photo of my sister and myself, and a bracelet made in Mumbai. I hope you like it. Write back soon and tell me more about your wonderful country!

Your friend in Mumbai,

Rakesh

ISBN: 978-1-77149-033-7

A. **Help Samantha write about her new pen pal in her scrapbook.**

Name: 1._____

Age: 2._____

Home

Country: 3._____

City: 4._____

- used to be called 5._____

- population is about 6._____

- the 7._____ in the country

Family

- mother works 8._____

- father works 9._____

- has a 10._____ who is 11._____ years old

- has 12._____ who live in 13._____

B. **Read what Samantha says and write a response.**

Why is it a good idea to have pen pals from other countries?
Where would you want to find your new pen pal, and why?

_____

_____

_____

_____

_____

ISBN: 978-1-77149-033-7 Complete Canadian Curriculum • **Grade 5** **165**

The Past Tense

When we want to talk about something that happened habitually or at a particular time in the past, we use the **simple past tense**. When we want to talk about something that continued to happen before and after a particular time in the past, we use the **past progressive tense**.

Examples: Sara <u>spent</u> her summers in Halifax for three years. (simple past)
Greta <u>called</u> Louisa at five o'clock today. (simple past)
We <u>were having</u> dinner when a mouse ran across the kitchen! (past progressive)

C.   Underline the mistake in each sentence and correct it on the line.

1.   Rakesh was attending English classes every Saturday last year.

_____

2.   When Leslie was spotting me in the crowd, she frantically waved.

_____

3.   Martin was practising his dance steps every day last month.

_____

4.   Rakesh's mom was admiring the lovely tableware when the guest musicians were arriving.

_____

5.   The kids planted flowers when their babysitter called them in for lunch.

_____

6.   We were playing with the ponies when Mrs. Fields was asking us to feed these chicks.

_____

7.   Samantha's mom was singing along with the radio while her cat purred.

_____

ISBN: 978-1-77149-033-7

D. **Choose the correct verbs for each sentence and use them in the simple past tense or past progressive tense.**

> watch bake pour stay catch begin
> leave go recognize enjoy walk ring

1. Clara _____ muffins for her party when the telephone

    _____ .

2. Robert and his brother _____ in Halifax two summers ago

    and _____ the seaside there.

3. Uncle Sam always _____ enough fish for a week when he

    _____ fishing every weekend last summer.

4. The spectators _____ the fireworks when it suddenly

    _____ to rain and everyone _____ .

5. Wendy _____ herself a cup of hot chocolate when

    a friend from kindergarten _____ her from afar and

    _____ over to say hello.

E. **Write about a memorable experience. Use two examples of simple past tense and two examples of past progressive tense.**

_____

_____

_____

_____

_____

Jeanne Mance
Angel of the Colony

Jeanne Mance was born in France in 1606. She came to North America in 1641 as a member of the mission of Paul Chomedey de Maisonneuve, who was sent to establish a settlement in New France. In addition to tending as a nurse to the soldiers who were in daily combat with the Iroquois of the area, Jeanne's role was to set up a hospital for the fledgling colony.

Jeanne provided basic medical care for both settlers and Aboriginal peoples. Later, in 1645, with funds that she had secured from French donors, she founded Hôtel-Dieu de Montréal, the oldest hospital in the city and one of the first in North America. Though Jeanne died in 1673, her hospital is still in operation today, with offshoots in other cities in Canada such as Québec City and Windsor.

Sometimes we use the term "founding father" to describe someone who establishes something, such as a town or an organization. Traditionally, women were not encouraged to do such things if they were not related to their church. But Jeanne Mance's dedication, courage, and skill certainly make her worthy of the term. Considered to be the first secular nurse of North America, Jeanne Mance is without doubt one of the "founding fathers" of New France.

Hymn to Jeanne Mance [1]

by Lady Amy Redpath Roddick

O brave Jeanne Mance whose fame is ours
As in a city's growth it flowers:
The seeds you humbly helped to sow
Give witness still and still they grow
Within tried hearts at mercy's call
In fanes and homes of Montreal,
In hospitals which hail you first
To soothe the sufferer, slack his thirst.

Heroic figure of the past
With Maisonneuve so staunchly classed,
Co-worker with ecstatic souls
Who showed the way to heavenly goals:
We have to-day a debt unpaid
Should we now fail where you have laid
Foundation on the rock of God
In turning thus our virgin sod.

[1] *From Library and Archives Canada*

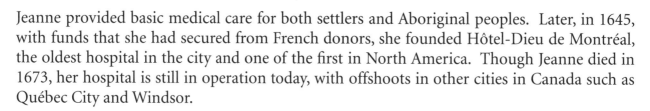

ISBN: 978-1-77149-033-7

A. Draw lines to match the descriptions with what is on the right.

1. those who establish something .

2. colony of the French people in North America .

3. natives of Canada •

4. one of the first hospitals in North America .

5. year that the oldest hospital in Montreal was founded .

• Hôtel-Dieu de Montréal

• New France

• founding fathers

• Aboriginal peoples

• 1645

B. Find the words or lines from "Hymn to Jeanne Mance" that mean the following.

1. a. heroic: _____   b. money owed: _____

   c. comfort: _____   d. one who suffers: _____

2. We will owe Jeanne Mance a lot if we don't do a good job at running the hospital that she set up.

   _____

   _____

   _____

3. Jeanne Mance's fame blossoms just like the growth of the city that she helped found.

   _____

   _____

   _____

   _____

The Future Tense

When we want to talk about something that will happen, we use the **simple future tense**. When we want to talk about something that will happen over a period of time, we use the **future progressive tense**.

Examples: Susan <u>will visit</u> us again next year. (simple future)
The music <u>will be playing</u> for the evening. (future progressive)

C. Circle the correct future tense in each sentence.

1. Our neighbours   will host / will be hosting
    the summer barbecue for the next two years.

2. When Jeanne returns, she   will show / will be showing   you the
    directions to the station.

3. The boat   will turn / will be turning   around once it gets close to the
    waterfalls.

4. "Oh dear," sighed Mr. Graham. "The skunk has made a home and
    will share / will be sharing   the backyard with us for the summer.

5. Since it   will snow / will be snowing   for the rest of the day, Marianne
    will read / will be reading   a book by the fireplace instead.

6. My cousin Kevin   will arrive / will be arriving   from Charlottetown
    tomorrow. I'm very excited since he   will stay / will be staying   with
    us for the entire Christmas holiday!

D. Help these people finish what they say. Write the correct letters.

Ⓐ they'll be begging me for hours to buy them candy

Ⓑ they'll beg me to buy them a tub of ice cream

Ⓒ we'll have to make sure we leave nothing behind

Ⓓ we'll watch a hockey game at the Air Canada Centre

1. *I'm at the grocery store with my kids, and I know that _____ .*

2. *I'll be spending the whole day at the fairground with my kids, where _____ .*

3. *We're leaving in a few minutes for Toronto, so _____ .*

4. *In two days, we're taking our kids to Toronto, where _____ .*

E. Write down some of your plans for the future. Use the simple future tense or the future progressive tense.

1. Tomorrow, _____

_____ .

2. This summer, _____

_____ .

3. When I grow up, _____

_____ .

Canadian Sports

Canadians love sports. Did you know that many of our most loved sports were invented by Canadians or developed in Canada?

Five-pin bowling was developed in Canada by Thomas Ryan in 1909. It is no surprise that the bowling pin resetter was invented in the same country in 1956.

Basketball, a major spectator sport in the United States, was actually invented in 1891 by a Canadian physical education instructor named James Naismith, who wanted to keep his students active indoors over the winter.

Ringette, invented as a sister game for hockey so that girls could also play, was the creation of Sam Jacks, the Director of Parks and Recreation for the City of North Bay. The first game was played – with sticks and rubber rings – in Ontario in 1963, and is now played around the world.

Wheelchair rugby was invented in Winnipeg in the 1970s. It was a demonstration event in 1996 at the Paralympic Games in Atlanta, and became a full medal sport at the Sydney Paralympic Games in 2000.

Canadian football is different than American football. The ball is bigger, the field is wider and longer, and the end zone is deeper. There are twelve players instead of eleven, and three downs instead of four.

Besides hockey, **lacrosse** is Canada's other national sport, invented by the Aboriginals of North America. It is like field hockey, but the ball is passed in the air to and from net-like rackets. It is becoming more and more popular around the world.

Synchronized swimming, a form of water ballet, was invented in Canada. It was once an Olympic sport. For that reason, some call it a Summer Games equivalent of figure skating.

Can you think of any other sports that were first developed in Canada?

   ISBN: 978-1-77149-033-7

A. **Read the clues and complete the crossword puzzle with words from the passage.**

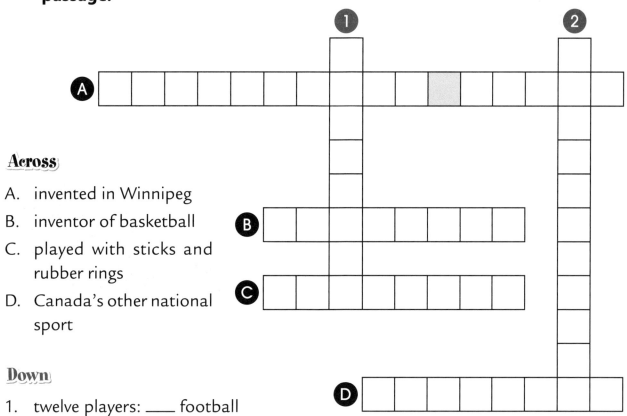

Across

A. invented in Winnipeg

B. inventor of basketball

C. played with sticks and rubber rings

D. Canada's other national sport

Down

1. twelve players: ____ football

2. inventors of lacrosse

B. **Circle "T" for the true sentences and "F" for the false ones.**

1. Basketball was invented to keep kids active indoors over winter. T F

2. Although five-pin bowling was invented by a Canadian, the bowling pin resetter was invented by an American. T F

3. Synchronized swimming can be considered the Summer Games equivalent of figure skating. T F

4. The end zone of Canadian football is deeper than the one in American football. T F

5. The first game of ringette was played in Quebec. T F

ISBN: 978-1-77149-033-7

Active Voice and Passive Voice

When we want to focus on the performer of the action in a sentence, we use the **active voice**. When we want to focus on the receiver of the action, we use the **passive voice**.

Examples: <u>Willie</u> spotted a hare in the backyard yesterday. (active)
A <u>hare</u> was spotted by Willie in the backyard yesterday. (passive)

C. **Complete each sentence using the active or passive voice. Focus on the part of the sentence that is in italics.**

1. performer: *Mrs. Maple* (verb: bake)
   receiver: a pumpkin pie

   Last Saturday morning, _____

   _____ .

2. performer: the nature-loving Aboriginal girl (verb: explore)
   receiver: *the ravine*

   Because of its beauty, _____

   _____ .

3. performers: the basketball players (verb: patron)
   receiver: *the diner around the corner*

   _____

   _____ after practice.

4. performers: *Vikki and her teammates* (verb: swim)
   receivers: many lengths of the pool

   _____

   _____ to build up stamina.

ISBN: 978-1-77149-033-7

D. **Classify the underlined sentences into the active voice or passive voice and answer the questions.**

Have you ever been amazed by something called *aurora borealis*? It is the northern lights. <u>They are seen more often by people who live near the Arctic.</u> These diffused lights can be pink and orange, or yellow and white. <u>The colours create a spectacular light show.</u> Sometimes, they even look like giant curtains! <u>The curtains appear to be shielding the Earth.</u> They may last for hours once they appear. <u>But the occurrence of northern lights cannot be predicted.</u> Maybe that is what makes these lights so special.

1. Sentences in the active voice:

    a. _____

    b. _____

2. Sentences in the passive voice:

    a. _____

    b. _____

3. Rewrite 1b and 2a in the other voice.

    _____

    _____

4. The sentences in 1b and 2a work better in their original voice for the paragraph. Why?

    _____

    _____

    _____

My Best Friend

Dear Diary,

I had a bad day at school. Tonetta was acting strangely with me – AGAIN! She was playing with Bernice, the new girl, during recess, and when I came over to join them, Tonetta grabbed Bernice and they went running away! I watched them go, and then they both turned around and made faces at me. I decided to go to the library after that. I don't know why Tonetta is doing this to me. She used to be my best friend. I'm really sad.

Dear Diary,

Mom asked me what was wrong today. I finally told her what Tonetta has been doing. As soon as I started telling her, I began to cry! Mom listened while I talked and cried. When I was finished, Mom said it was not good. I thought she was going to tell me to just put up with it, but she didn't. She said that Tonetta was acting like a kind of bully, and that I needed to stand up for myself. Mom and I practised what I'm going to say next time Tonetta is rude to me. I'm going to ask her if it makes her feel good to hurt her old friend.

Mom says the reason why Tonetta is doing this may have to do with how she feels about herself, not how she feels about me. We both hope that Tonetta will understand this someday. But for now, I think I'll just be friends with my other classmates.

Dear Diary,

Mom left this note under my pillow today:

Dear Evelyn,
When I was about your age, I also had a friend who suddenly became a problem for me at school. I told my granny about it, who said that I should think of myself as my own best friend. I have always remembered her advice, and I hope that you will remember it as well, my darling daughter.

Love,
Your other Best Friend,
Mom

ISBN: 978-1-77149-033-7

A. **Use your dictionary to find the definition of "bullying". Then make a web of examples.**

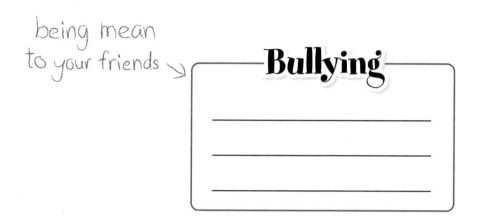

being mean to your friends

Bullying

_____

_____

_____

B. **Give your opinions.**

1. Do you think Evelyn is being bullied by Tonetta? Why or why not?

   _____

   _____

2. Why do you think Tonetta is being rude to Evelyn?

   _____

   _____

3. Do you like the advice that we should think of ourselves as our own best friend? Why or why not?

   _____

   _____

The Present Perfect Tense

When we want to talk about something that happened at a particular time in the past, we use the simple past tense. But when we want to talk about something from the past that is linked to the present (indicated by words like "finally", "yet", and "so far"), we use the **present perfect tense**.

Examples: I <u>saw</u> the rainbow yesterday. (simple past)
I <u>have seen</u> a rainbow before. (present perfect)

C. **Complete the sentences with the simple past tense or the present perfect tense of the given verbs.**

sing   ring   hear   think

1. The parents _____ never _____ this song from the choir.

2. "_____ you _____ the doorbell yet?" Ben asks Tom.

3. Our dog Sonic, ever so excitable, started wagging his tail as soon as he _____ the doorbell.

4. Janice _____ this song many times before.

5. During choir practice last Tuesday, we _____ a new song.

6. "When I didn't hear from you last week, I _____ you had lost my phone number," said Kate to Jill.

7. "Do you think Tonetta _____ ever _____ about the way she is behaving?" Evelyn asks Amy.

8. I forgot my key and _____ the doorbell many times before my brother opened the door for me.

D. Check the correct sentences. Put a cross for the wrong ones and rewrite them using the correct tense.

1. ☐ Evelyn has finally told her mother about Tonetta.

   _____

2. ☐ Little Tim has finished his homework at six o'clock today.

   _____

3. ☐ The teachers did not notice anything wrong so far.

   _____

4. ☐ My mother has not come home from dance class yet.

   _____

5. ☐ My brother has thrown one of his slippers out of the window a minute ago but luckily it didn't land on anyone's head!

   _____

   _____

6. ☐ Evelyn's mother slipped a note under her daughter's pillow when she was sound asleep.

   _____

   _____

   _____

E. Think of a verb. Use it in the simple past tense in one sentence and in the present perfect tense in another.

   _____

   _____

The Skeleton Coast

Have you ever heard of the Skeleton Coast? It sounds like a scary place, but it is really one of the most awesome landscapes on the planet.

The Skeleton Coast is a stretch of coastline in a country called Namibia, located in southwestern Africa. It is a place where barren dunes of desert sand rise up along the Atlantic Ocean in peaks as high as 500 metres. These dunes are a part of the Namib Desert, which takes up most of the area of Namibia. The place seems spooky and desolate, especially when the fog rolls, as it often does.

The coastline is often shrouded in fog, because a current of cold water – called the Benguela Current – passes through the waters of the coast, making the sea breezes cold too. These cold sea winds blow towards the land, which is hotter. The air mixes along the coast, producing a thick fog, which is unusual for desert areas.

The frequent fogs are the reason why this stretch of coastline is called the Skeleton Coast. There have been hundreds of shipwrecks in these waters over the years. Stories abound of shipwrecked sailors washing ashore into the desert, desperate with thirst, only to perish in the dunes. If you are there, you will see the remains of many ships that have been washed up on the shore, looking in many ways like the skeletons of old ships.

But the fog which has brought death to countless sailors over the centuries is what brings life to this unique desert land. Areas of low green desert bushes, fed by the moisture-laden winds, can be found in the canyons of the area. Animals like the desert elephant, springbok, brown hyena, and spiral-horned oryx antelope make this desert their home. And at Cape Cross, there are even seal colonies and an assortment of birds including the flamingo, pelican, and rare tern.

As much as it became a place of doomed sailors and ship remains, this seemingly scary coast is actually a land of fascinating wildlife, and a fine example of how even a harsh environment can be home to abundant life.

ISBN: 978-1-77149-033-7

A. Circle the correct answers.

1. In which continent is the Skeleton Coast located?

   A. Asia　　　　　　B. Africa　　　　　　C. Antarctica

2. Much of Namibia is _____ .

   A. wet soil　　　　B. mountains　　　　C. desert

3. An unusual characteristic of the Skeleton Coast is its _____ .

   A. skeletons　　　B. thick fog　　　　C. hot air on land

4. The winds of the Skeleton Coast are _____ .

   A. non-existent　　B. very dry　　　　C. full of moisture

5. In southwestern Africa, there are _____ and _____ .

   A. sheep; cows　　B. seals; penguins　C. pelicans; elephants

6. The Skeleton Coast got its name partly from _____ .

   A. being the site of shipwrecks and deaths of sailors in the past
   B. being a land of desolation and extinct wildlife
   C. being in the most remote region of Africa

B. Write about an imaginary place similar to the Skeleton Coast. Include these words in your paragraph.

   barren　　　**spooky**　　　**desolate**　　　**life**　　　**unique**

_____

_____

_____

_____

_____

Punctuation (1)

For a complete sentence, we use the **period** (**.**), the **question mark** (**?**), or the **exclamation mark** (**!**). If a sentence is borrowed (e.g. from a book) or in direct speech, we use **quotation marks** (**" "**). To show a pause in a sentence, we use the **comma** (**,**). We also use the comma instead of the period when ending a sentence in certain instances of direct speech.

Examples: The Skeleton Coast is in Namibia.
Have you ever heard of the Skeleton Coast?
"Look out for the rising sand, Camille!" Adrian exclaimed.
"This place is home to many animals," Kevin said.

C. **Write the missing punctuation mark(s) in each sentence.**

1. The sand dunes of the Skeleton Coast can rise as high as 500 metres

2. The frequent fogs are the reason why this stretch of coastline is called the Skeleton Coast, Samuel quoted from his reading.

3. Of the elephant, springbok, brown hyena, and spiral-horned oryx antelope which one would you want to see the most?

4. Where do you want to visit next? my father asked me.

5. Do you think the Skeleton Coast is really all that spooky

6. "Yes, seal colonies can be found in Africa" said Tom matter-of-factly.

7. "What a wonderful example of life in extreme environments" our teacher exclaimed in wonder.

8. Oh dear Look at all these ship remains!

9. "You won't believe what my friend has done" Amy said in anger.

10. "Sara look at those seals over there," her mother said.

ISBN: 978-1-77149-033-7

D. **Circle the wrong punctuation mark in each sentence. Then put the correct one above it where necessary.**

1.   When cold air mixes with hot air, moisture is produced? creating fog.

2.   "I seem to hear voices speaking to me as the fog rolls." Anna whispered to me.

3.   "The cold Benguela Current causes the sea breezes to be cold as well."

4.   "From the shores of northwest Africa, can I see the Atlantic Ocean," Bob asked.

5.   "Maybe there were not that many sailors who perished here!" Marie tried to make her sister feel better in her calm voice.

6.   "I can't take this anymore," Fran called out in exasperation.

E. **Put the missing punctuation marks in this paragraph.**

Lizzie and Paula go swimming every weekend Lizzie is training to be a competitive swimmer, while Paula swims for fun Someday Lizzie tells Paula, I'm going to be an Olympic silver medalist! A bit puzzled, Paula asks A silver medalist Why don't you want to be a gold medalist Sounding matter-of-factly Lizzie answers Silver is my favourite colour. Gold is a little too shiny for me When I'm up on the podium, I want to be wearing my favourite colour! Finding Lizzie's aspirations a little unusual Paula is quiet and thinks to herself Sounds like Lizzie Always making unpredictable choices

ISBN: 978-1-77149-033-7 Complete Canadian Curriculum • **Grade 5**

The Story of K'iid K'iyass

Canada is a country famous for its trees. Perhaps the most famous tree of all was the giant golden Sitka spruce. Its home was Port Clements, on Queen Charlotte Islands in British Columbia. What happened to it is a sad story, though.

This tree was at least 300 years old. It stood on the banks of the Yakoun River, in one of the last stands of virgin coastal forest of the Pacific Northwest. It was a popular site of ecotourism and moreover, was sacred to the Haida, the Aboriginal people of the area. They called the tree K'iid K'iyass – "Old Tree" – and it had been a part of their local oral history for generations.

Golden Sitka spruces are rare. This tree was not green – it was gold! It had a golden colour because of a lack of chlorophyll, which is the green substance needed for photosynthesis. Yet, K'iid K'iyass was able to thrive, because of the area's misty climate, or because the sunlight reached the tree by reflecting off the water of the river next to it. Even among rare trees, however, K'iid K'iyass was special: it was very tall, over 40 metres high and more than two metres in diameter at its base. Unlike most Sitka spruces, which branch out haphazardly, it was uniformly conical. K'iid K'iyass stood like a perfect, shining golden Christmas tree in a forest of green. It stood as a monument that united people who were loggers and people who were against lumber companies' methods, like clear-cutting. All agreed that K'iid K'iyass was never to be cut down.

Then on the night of January 20 in 1997, a man crept into the forest and cut deeply into K'iid K'iyass with a chainsaw. He had once been a logger and knew how to damage the tree. When he was done, he sent letters to newspapers and the logging company leasing the land, saying what he had done was a protest against the destruction of the forests taking place all around K'iid K'iyass. Despite attempts to save the tree, K'iid K'iyass fell a few days later. The misguided protester was charged with criminal mischief and illegal cutting of timber. Strangely, while on his way by kayak to a court hearing, he disappeared and has not been found since. Though the wreckage of his kayak was later washed up in Alaska, many in the community suspect that he faked his death to escape his trial.

Fortunately, a branch from the dying Old Tree was rescued, and a baby golden Sitka spruce is growing in Port Clements today in protective custody. With golden needles shining under the sun, this spruce will one day become a rare giant in the forest.

A. Fill in the blanks with words from the passage.

1. My teacher is a supporter of _____ . "Not only do tourists get to explore exotic places of the natural environment," he says, "they also get to support conservation efforts."

2. The _____ in the community are going on strike because the company they work for will not give up clear-cutting methods.

3. "This ancient statue was carved many years ago as a gift for god," our teacher explained to us the _____ nature of an artifact in the museum.

4. For the Aboriginal peoples of Canada, much of the knowledge from one generation to the next is not handed down in the form of books, but by means of _____ history.

5. From what her best friend told me, Bernice appeared to have made a hasty and _____ decision when she dropped out of school to travel around the country.

6. The tipi is the traditional dwelling of Canada's Plains Aboriginal peoples. It is _____ in shape, built with poles and cloth or animal hide.

7. "_____ we stand, divided we fall!" Little Timmy recites a line from a song written in 1768, to the surprise of his elder brother and sister.

Punctuation (2)

When we want to introduce a list, or give an explanation for something, we can use the **colon** (**:**). When we want to show possession, or indicate where the missing letters are in a contraction, we use the **apostrophe** (**'**).

Examples: We need three vegetables: lettuce, celery, and onions. (list)
It's easy to prepare: just toss everything together. (explanation)
This salad is Joey's creation. (possession)
I'd love to try this salad! (contraction of "I would")

B. Tell how the colon or apostrophe is used in each sentence. Write the correct letter.

Baby Golden Sitka Spruce

A to introduce a list

B to give an explanation

C to show possession

D to indicate missing letters

1. Here are some examples of trees in Canada: spruce, cedar, birch, and maple. _____

2. Despite a lack of chlorophyll, Old Tree thrived in the forest possibly because of the area's misty climate. _____

3. Old Tree stood as a monument that united people who were loggers and people who were against clear-cutting: it was a tree that everyone agreed not to cut. _____

4. "The man cared about the forests in the province and had good intentions," Dad explained, "but he didn't have to damage a rare tree to make his point." _____

5. Old Tree was special even among rare trees: it was very tall and uniformly conical. _____

6. A baby Sitka spruce is growing in British Columbia's Queen Charlotte Islands. _____

    ISBN: 978-1-77149-033-7

C. **Write the missing colons and apostrophes in the paragraph.**

Canada has produced some very talented people writer Alice Munro; scientist David Suzuki; dancer Rex Harrington, and retired hockey player Mario Lemieux. A prolific writer, Munros short stories always deal with the fascinating complexities of the human heart, winning international acclaim. Suzukis charm and knack for public speaking make him a scholar and a great communicator his show *The Nature of Things* draws the publics attention to the importance of protecting our environment. Harrington makes his ballet performances look so easy from his natural flare, you wouldnt have guessed how much hard work is required behind the scenes. Finally, Lemieux – whose name means "the best" in French – captained Team Canada into a gold medal at the 2002 Winter Olympic Games. Despite cancer and back pains, Lemieux never fails to play a good game, and is one of the NHLs greatest hockey players in history.

D. **Write your own paragraph containing the uses of the colon and the apostrophe.**

_____

_____

_____

_____

_____

_____

_____

18

As one of Canada's most memorable poems, "In Flanders Fields" was written as a tribute to soldiers everywhere. Its author John McCrae, who was a Canadian soldier and doctor in World War I, wrote the poem after his friend was killed on May 2, 1915 in Ypres, Belgium. (McCrae himself died of pneumonia in 1918 while on duty.) But when the poem was finished, McCrae tossed it away in the field. Were it not for a fellow soldier who picked up the poem and sent it to England, we would probably not be reading it today. The poem was first published in *Punch Magazine* in December of 1915.

In Flanders Fields
– a Poem of Remembrance

In Flanders Fields

In Flanders Fields the poppies blow
Between the crosses, row on row,
That mark our place; and in the sky
The larks, still bravely singing, fly
Scarce heard amid the guns below.

We are the Dead. Short days ago
We lived, felt dawn, saw sunset glow,
Loved, and were loved, and now we lie
In Flanders fields.

Take up our quarrel with the foe:
To you from failing hands we throw
The torch, be yours to hold it high.
If ye break faith with us who die
We shall not sleep, though poppies grow
In Flanders fields.

If you visit Flanders Fields in Belgium, you will still see the poppies waving among the crosses. Each year in November, we wear the bright red poppy over our hearts to remind ourselves of the soldiers that died in battle and the ones that have survived. We should try to imagine the lives that the fallen soldiers may have had, to think of the sacrifices that they made, and realize the futility of war.

A. **Use your dictionary to find the definitions of these words. Then use them in sentences of your own.**

1. lark: _____

    _____

2. tribute: _____

    _____

3. pneumonia: _____

    _____

4. futility: _____

    _____

B. **Explain the following in your own words.**

1. "Short days ago/We lived, felt dawn, saw sunset glow,"

    _____

    _____

2. "...and in the sky/The larks, still bravely singing, fly/Scarce heard amid the guns below."

    _____

    _____

3. "In Flanders Fields the poppies blow/Between the crosses, row on row,/That mark our place;"

    _____

    _____

    _____

Prefixes and Suffixes

A **prefix** is a group of letters placed at the beginning of a word – called the base word or root word – to change its meaning. A **suffix** is also a group of letters that changes the meaning of a word, but is placed at the end.

Examples: The prefix "re" in "rewrite" changes the meaning of "write" to "write again".
The suffix "able" in "memorable" changes the meaning of "memory" to "easily remembered".

C.   Form new words with the prefixes.

      un   re   im   in

1. place   _____

2. possible   _____

3. complete   _____

4. willing   _____

5. generate   _____

6. precise   _____

7. formal   _____

8. discrete   _____

D.   Circle the words that have a prefix, a suffix, or both. Then write their base words on the lines.

exaggerate   _____

present   _____

careful   _____

insecurity   _____

sincerity   _____

reunification _____

lampost   _____

bounty   _____

relate   _____

fulfill   _____

thoughtful   _____

perform   _____

ISBN: 978-1-77149-033-7

E. **Complete each sentence by rewriting the base word with the correct suffix.**

ial   able   ation   ance

1. "Be careful with that ornament. It's (break)

_____ ," my dad said.

2. The trillium is the (province) _____ flower of Ontario.

3. Many of us wear a poppy on (Remember) _____ Day.

4. The United Nations has put out another (public) _____ on world peace.

F. **Look at each base word and its changed meaning to write the correct prefix. Then make a sentence with the base word and a sentence with the new word.**

re   mis   de   in   dis

1. **view** ➔   view again: ___view

_____

_____

2. **cover** ➔   find out: ___cover

_____

_____

3. **place** ➔   put in the wrong spot: ___place

_____

_____

4. **organized** ➔ chaotic: ___organized

_____

_____

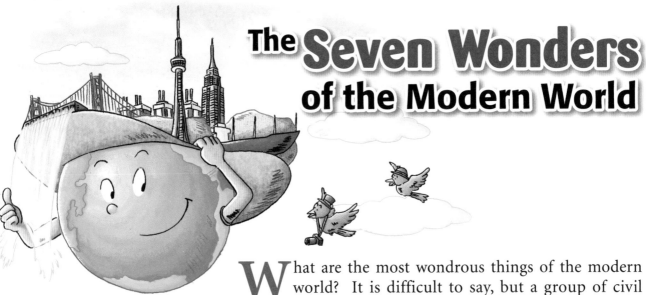

The Seven Wonders
of the Modern World

What are the most wondrous things of the modern world? It is difficult to say, but a group of civil engineers have tried to answer this question.

Civil engineers are people who build big things such as airports, hydroelectric dams, and impressive buildings. The American Society of Civil Engineers wanted to compile a list of engineering achievements to honour our ability to create things that seem almost impossible to build. So in 1994, the organization asked people around the world to tell them what they felt were the seven wonders of the modern world. Here is the resulting list of the greatest civil engineering feats of the 20th century:

Channel Tunnel
This underwater tunnel measures 50 kilometres and connects the United Kingdom with France in continental Europe.

CN Tower
As one of the world's tallest free-standing structures, this tower measures over 500 metres and weighs as much as 232 214 elephants!

Empire State Building
Built in 1930 in New York City, this building was the tallest in the world for 40 years.

Golden Gate Bridge
This is one of the world's most photographed bridges. Built in 1937, it was the world's longest and tallest suspension bridge for almost 30 years.

Itaipu Dam
At 8 km wide, this hydroelectric dam spans the Parana River between Brazil and Paraguay. It provides almost 75% of Paraguay's energy needs and 28% of southern Brazil's electric energy.

Netherlands North Sea Protection Works
Without this system of dams, floodgates, and storm surge barriers which make up the Netherlands' tidal defences, much of the country would be in the sea.

Panama Canal
Digging this canal through the Isthmus of Panama would have been the same as moving enough earth to open a five-metre-wide tunnel to the centre of the Earth!

          ISBN: 978-1-77149-033-7

A. Read the clues and complete this crossword puzzle with words from the passage.

Across

A. country below sea level: The ___

B. free-standing structure

C. built in 1937: ___ ___ Bridge

D. ___ Canal

E. in New York:

   ___ ___ Building

Down

1. Itaipu ___

2. connects France and the United Kingdom

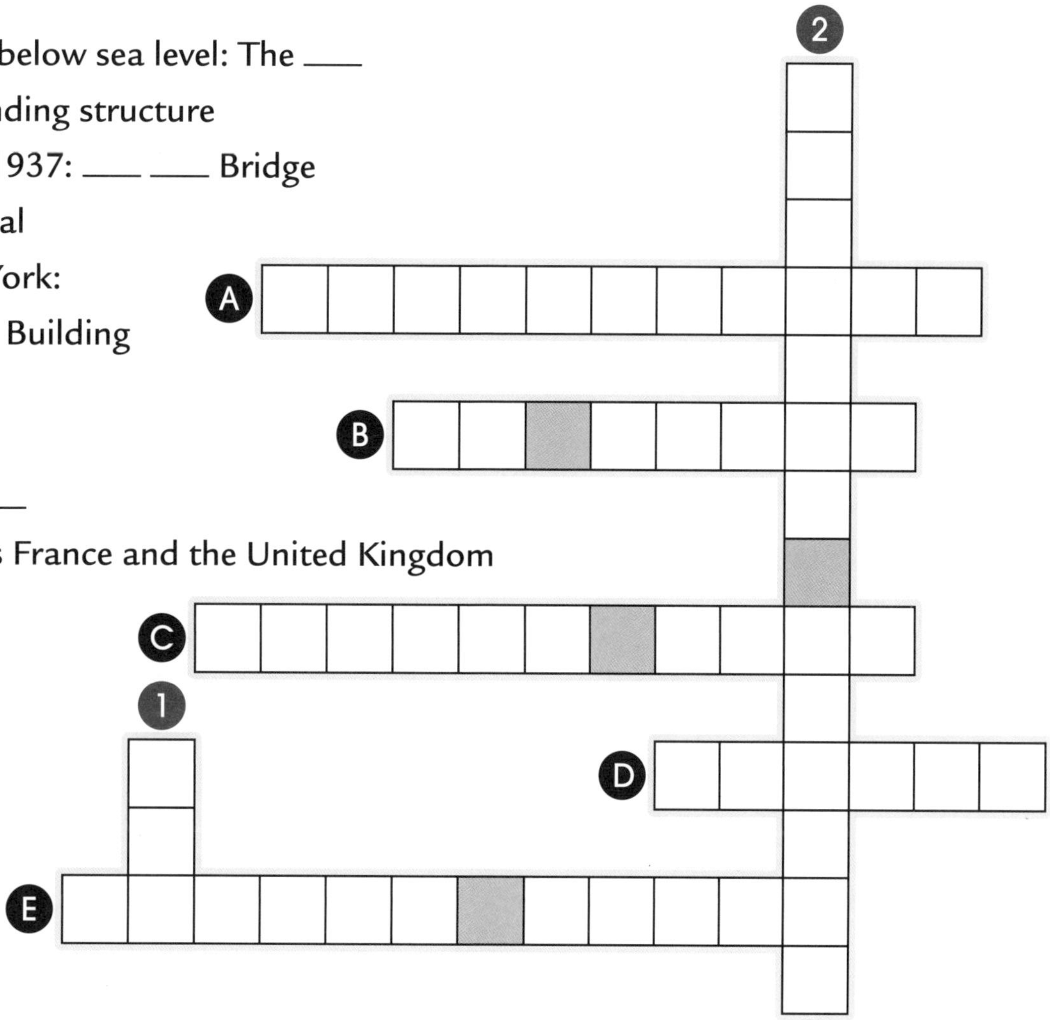

B. Imagine yourself to be a civil engineer. Which one of the seven wonders would you wish to have built? Why?

_____

_____

_____

_____

_____

19

Noun Phrases

A phrase is a group of words that can take the same spot in a sentence as a single word. A **noun phrase** contains a noun and other words such as articles and adjectives, and functions like a noun or pronoun. It may be the **subject**, **object**, or the **complement** in a sentence.

Examples: This city's buildings are very tall. (subject)
I can give you my own list of wonders. (object)
The CN Tower is one of the seven wonders. (complement)

C. Write "subject", "object", or "complement" for each underlined noun phrase.

1. A group of civil engineers compiled a list of seven engineering achievements. _____

2. The list of wonders honours our ability to build great things. _____

3. Most of Paraguay's energy is provided by the Itaipu Dam. _____

4. The CN Tower is one of the world's tallest free-standing structures. _____

5. France and the United Kingdom are connected by the Channel Tunnel. _____

6. The Netherlands' tidal defences are a system of dams, floodgates, and storm surge barriers. _____

D. Complete these sentences with noun phrases of your own.

1. _____ is my favourite wonder on the list.

2. I really want to photograph _____ .

3. The place I want to see most is _____ .

4. _____ opened my eyes to the world!

Verbals: Gerunds and Participles

A **verbal** is a verb form that does not function like a verb in a sentence, such as gerunds and participles. A **gerund** is a verbal that functions like a noun. A **present** or **past participle** is a verbal that functions like an adjective.

Examples: <u>Engineering</u> involves both math and design. (gerund)
The <u>painting</u> class takes place every Sunday. (present participle)
The <u>painted</u> door is a work of art. (past participle)

E. Fill in the blanks with the given words. Then circle the correct answers to tell their functions in the sentences.

> moving   free-standing   digging
> photographed   resulting

1. The Golden Gate Bridge is one of the world's most _____ bridges.

   verb
   adjective

2. As one of the world's tallest _____ structures, the CN Tower is also a landmark of Toronto.

   verb
   adjective

3. _____ the Panama Canal would have been the same as _____ enough earth to open a five-metre-wide tunnel to the centre of the Earth!

   noun
   verb

4. A squirrel was _____ a hole just now.

   noun
   verb

5. "Here is the _____ list of the greatest civil engineering feats of the 20th century," announced Michael.

   noun
   adjective

6. The plates on Earth are in fact constantly _____ , though at a very slow rate, which we cannot detect.

   noun
   verb

The **Seven Natural Wonders** of the World

In addition to a list of modern wonders, a list of natural wonders has also been made. They are places that have been sources of awe and wonder ever since people walked the Earth. As we are now much more familiar with the geography of our planet than before, these natural wonders have become places that we strive to protect.

Mount Everest in the Himalayan Mountain Range that borders Nepal and Tibet is the highest mountain on Earth.

The **Great Barrier Reef** in the Pacific Ocean off the northeast coast of Australia is the world's largest coral reef.

The **Grand Canyon** around the Colorado River in the state of Arizona in the United States is the largest canyon in the world.

Victoria Falls is a majestic 100-metre waterfall in Africa, where the Zambezi River falls into a two-kilometre-wide chasm to the Batoka Gorge.

The **Harbour of Rio de Janeiro** in Brazil is one of the most striking in the world, where tall mountains loom up from the water, and the city hugs the hillsides around the crowded beaches.

Paricutin is perhaps the world's youngest volcano. It erupted out of a cornfield west of Mexico in 1943! In the first year it grew 336 m high. Now it is 424 m high.

The **northern lights** are the natural phenomenon that appears in the night sky at high latitudes. At their best, they look like purple and green streaks dancing across the sky, a result of particles reacting with the Earth's magnetic field.

Some may think that these natural wonders are even more wonderful than our list of human-made wonders. What do you think?

ISBN: 978-1-77149-033-7

A. Draw lines to match the natural wonders with the locations.

1. Mount Everest •   • Australia

2. Paricutin •   • Brazil

3. The northern lights •   • Africa

4. The Grand Canyon •   • near Mexico

5. The Great Barrier Reef •   • Nepal and Tibet

6. Victoria Falls •   • The United States

7. The Harbour
   of Rio de Janeiro •   • high latitudes

B. Give your opinions.

1. What do you think are the criteria for something to be a natural wonder?

   _____

   _____

   _____

2. Why is it important to protect our natural wonders?

   _____

   _____

3. What other things or places do you think we should protect?

   _____

   _____

20

Adjective and Adverb Phrases

An **adjective phrase** contains an adjective and functions like an adjective in a sentence. An **adverb phrase** contains an adverb and functions like an adverb in a sentence.

Examples: Laura is <u>very happy</u> today. (adjective phrase)
Laura ran <u>very quickly</u> to the park. (adverb phrase)

C. **Write "adjective" or "adverb" for each underlined phrase.**

1. We are now <u>much more familiar</u> with our planet than before. _____

2. Laura finishes her lunch <u>quite fast</u>. _____

3. Laura's sister is <u>quietly excited</u> about the Christmas holiday. _____

4. Ted is doing his homework <u>unusually well</u>. _____

5. "Nobody sings this song <u>more wonderfully</u> than you do, Carol," says Bernice. _____

6. The northern lights dance <u>so beautifully</u> in the night sky. _____

7. "What can be <u>even more wonderful</u> than my list of seven wonders?" my little brother asks. _____

8. "Is there a list of <u>forgotten ancient</u> wonders?" asks my little cousin. _____

9. Bob is walking <u>very slowly</u> along the hillsides.

_____

10. "Can I help you?" someone asks Tommy. "You look <u>completely lost</u>."

_____

ISBN: 978-1-77149-033-7

D. **Underline the adjective phrases and circle the adverb phrases in this paragraph.**

For adventure seekers looking for mountains to climb, Mount Everest is a very popular choice. With its summit at 8850 metres, it is incredibly high. To reach the summit of Everest is to reach the top of the world because it is the highest mountain on Earth. To some climbers, it is like conquering the impossible. But failing to reach the top does not necessarily mean failure. There are really persistent climbers who so desperately want to keep going, but whose bodies simply cannot withstand the lack of oxygen at extremely high altitudes. Knowing only too well that there have been deaths on this mountain in the past, these people have no choice but to turn back. In their case, nothing is more sensible than walking back down, which can save their lives.

E. **Write a paragraph containing two adjective phrases and two adverb phrases using these words.**

more   most   very   quite

_____

_____

_____

_____

_____

_____

A Letter from Sammy

Dear Mom, Dad, Hugh, and Choco,

I'm so excited to be here in Japan that I don't even know what to start telling you about! First, the flight to Tokyo was a lot of fun. The flight attendants were all very kind to me. On the flight to Vancouver, Debra, the Chief Purser, introduced me to the lady sitting beside me. Her name was Mrs. Ward, and she was going to visit her son, who is teaching English in Japan.

At the stop in Vancouver, Debra took me to a special place to wait for my next flight. She called it a transit lounge. Then another flight attendant took me to my next plane, and Mrs. Ward was waiting for me there. When we arrived in Japan, an airline employee met me at the airplane door and took me through customs. I felt special. I had been scared to travel alone at first, but there was actually nothing to worry about.

Kiyoka and her parents were waiting for me in the arrivals hall. Kiyoka shouted out my name as I came through the doors. She grabbed my hand and I could feel it shaking. She was so excited – and so was I! Her parents said *Kon-ni-chi-wa* ("Hello") and *Ir-ra-sha-i* ("Welcome"). We got on a bus and travelled through Tokyo to a big station to take a train. Before long, I found myself in a Japanese home in the mountains, drinking green tea with Kiyoka and her grandparents. We can't talk much but we laugh a lot together. Kiyoka is good at translating what her grandparents say.

Already I have eaten sushi, I have slept on the floor on tatami mats, and I have learned to compliment Kiyoka's mother for her good cooking. I say *O-go-chi-so-sa-ma-desh-ta*, which means something like: you are a good cook. I helped Kiyoka pick some persimmons off their tree for dessert – it's called *kaki* in Japan. I know I've only been here for a day but I love Japan already! There is a small temple down the street, and Kiyoka will take me there tomorrow.

Love,

Sammy

ISBN: 978-1-77149-033-7

A. Put these entries in order for Kiyoka's vacation diary.

[   ] travelled through Tokyo on a bus

[   ] met a kind lady named Mrs. Ward

[   ] had green tea with Kiyoka and her grandparents

[   ] was greeted by Kiyoka and her parents at the airport

[   ] took a train to Kiyoka's house

[   ] picked persimmons for dessert

[   ] boarded another plane in Vancouver

B. Quote a sentence from Sammy's letter to support each of the following.

1. Sammy has only been in Japan for a very short time, but she has done many things already.

    _____

    _____

    _____

2. The train ride to Kiyoka's home did not feel long at all.

    _____

    _____

3. There are many languages in the world, but a smile speaks them all.

    _____

    _____

Conjunctions

When we want to join ideas together, we use **conjunctions**, which are also called **connecting words**.

Examples: I'm so excited <u>that</u> I don't know where to start.
We got on a bus <u>and</u> travelled through Tokyo.

C. Circle the conjunction in each sentence.

1. Kiyoka taught me some useful Japanese words, so I used them to compliment her mother for her cooking.

2. Someone met me at the airplane door when I arrived in Japan.

3. I had been scared to travel alone but there was in fact nothing to worry about.

4. Kiyoka shouted out my name as I came through the doors.

5. There is a small temple nearby and Kiyoka will take me there tomorrow.

6. I found myself in a Japanese home before I had time to take in the scenery along the train ride.

7. Debra took me to a place where I waited for my next flight.

8. Although I have only been in Japan for a day, I love this place already!

9. We stayed up until midnight!

10. If I had a longer summer holiday, I would stay longer in Japan.

D. **Fill in the blanks with the correct conjunctions.**

unless   since   whenever   where   while

1. Kiyoka acts as translator _____ her grandparents want to talk to Sammy.

2. "Canada is the country _____ I come from," said Sammy.

3. The girls picked persimmons outside _____ the others prepared dinner inside.

4. They can go to the temple any time _____ it is just down the street.

5. Kiyoka's grandparents do not eat fish _____ it is fresh.

E. **Choose five conjunctions from (C) to write your own sentences.**

1. _____

   _____

2. _____

   _____

3. _____

   _____

4. _____

   _____

5. _____

   _____

How Hurricanes Get Their Names

Have you ever wondered how hurricanes get their names? Many of the hurricanes we hear about in Canada are those that originate in the Atlantic Ocean. For some time since 1953, it was the U.S. National Hurricane Center that had been responsible for naming these hurricanes. But today, the lists of hurricanes around the world are maintained and updated by a specialized agency of the United Nations called the World Meteorological Organization.

The history of naming hurricanes is fascinating. Early on in the West Indies, for instance, names of saints were used. For example, if a hurricane occurred on February 3, it would be called Hurricane Blaise because, by the Christian calendar, February 3 is Saint Blaise's Day. (Every day is named after a saint in the Christian calendar. You probably know that March 17 is Saint Patrick's Day.)

Later, women's names started to be used to identify storms that resembled hurricanes. Some believe the practice began in Australia in the late 19th century. It became more common during World War II when the United States also adopted this method. Over time, however, people recognized that it was wrong to name hurricanes only after women. In 1978, both men's and women's names started to be used in alternate fashion – first on the Eastern North Pacific Storm lists and, a year later, on the lists for the Atlantic and the Gulf of Mexico.

There are over a dozen lists of names for the various regions around the world. For the Atlantic region, there is a list of 21 designated hurricane names for each year, which follows the alphabet, though there are no names beginning with the letters Q, U, X, Y, or Z. Each list is recycled every six years. If there are more than 21 hurricanes that year, later storms will be named after the letters of the Greek alphabet.

A name is retired if the hurricane is especially catastrophic. This is done as a mark of respect for the victims of that hurricane, who do not wish to be reminded of the event six years later. Since 2010, four names have been retired: Igor, Tomas, Irene, and Sandy.

ISBN: 978-1-77149-033-7

A. Answer these questions.

1. Who maintains the lists of hurricanes around the world?

   _____

2. How were hurricanes named in the West Indies in earlier days?

   _____

   _____

3. What is special about the Christian calendar?

   _____

4. What was changed in the practice of naming hurricanes in 1978?

   _____

   _____

5. What happens to the name of an especially catastrophic hurricane?

   _____

B. Read what John says. Then write a short response and make up some hurricane names.

Why do you think there are no hurricane names beginning with Q, U, X, Y, or Z? Can you think of any names beginning with these letters?

_____   Q _____

_____   U _____

_____   X _____

Y _____

Z _____

Clauses

A **clause** is a group of words that has the same structure as a sentence (containing a subject and a verb) but is part of a larger sentence. An **independent clause** can stand alone. A **dependent clause** cannot, and needs to be supported by an independent clause.

Examples: <u>The whole class laughed</u> when Mrs. Kemp told a joke.
(independent)

"We can go <u>wherever you like</u>," said Jan to Alice.
(dependent)

C. Underline the stated type of clause for each group of sentences.

Independent

1. A hurricane name is retired if the hurricane is especially catastrophic.

2. Names of saints had been used to name hurricanes before men's and women's names were used.

3. "I won't go out to the backyard unless that skunk leaves the deck," my sister says.

4. "I'm not coming out of my room until it's dinnertime!" my little sister pouts.

Dependent

5. We began using both men's and women's names for hurricanes after we recognized how wrong it was to use only women's names.

6. The practice of naming hurricanes with women's names became more common during World War II when the United States also adopted this method.

7. Whenever there is a squirrel in the backyard, my sister goes out to say hello.

8. "Why don't you help me wash the lettuce while I cut the carrots?" my mother asks.

D. Check the sentences that have a dependent clause. Then underline each dependent clause.

1. There were hurricanes whose names have been retired. ☐

2. The four names are Igor, Tomas, Irene, and Sandy. ☐

3. Did you see Teddy this morning? ☐

4. This is the place that Charlotte does not want to remember. ☐

5. The history of naming hurricanes is fascinating. ☐

6. It is fascinating only because you like storms. ☐

7. There are over a dozen lists of names for the various regions around the world. ☐

8. If there are more than 21 hurricanes in a given year, the additional storms will be named after the letters of the Greek alphabet. ☐

9. Ben thought of another way of naming hurricanes while he was doing his math homework. ☐

E. Complete each sentence by adding an independent clause.

1. As we were walking to the park,

   _____

   _____ .

2. Since we played well during our game, _____

   _____ .

3. Even though Ann did not win the race, _____

   _____ .

Strange Names
Strange Places?

If you ever thought that Moose Jaw in Saskatchewan and Medicine Hat in Alberta were strange Canadian place names, you haven't actually seen really strange place names yet. It's always fun to discover a new, weird place name to add to the list. Here's a sampling for you.

There are street names you would never expect to find. If you ever find yourself in Bandra, which is a neighbourhood in Mumbai, India, you might find yourself at Wit's End, a dead-end street. And if you are touring Hong Kong, don't be surprised if you come across Rednaxela Terrace. This strange name was created when the sign painter painted the letters backwards!

In the United States, you'll find a street in Massachusetts called Goah Way. And in Ohio, you'll find a road called Needmore Road. If you go to a place called Salt Lick in Kentucky – whose name is odd enough in itself – you'll probably find yourself driving down Mudlick Road. But that's not all. There is also Psycho Path in Michigan and Divorce Court in Pennsylvania.

The United States is full of quaint towns with strange names. You would probably have a great summer road trip just visiting the following places: Peculiar, Missouri; Embarrass, Wisconsin; Dull, Ohio; Unthanks, Virginia; Stinking Bay, Arkansas; Last Chance, Colorado, and Boring, Maryland (though you might want to avoid Accident in that same state). If you love to eat, then check out these towns: Goodfood and Hot Coffee, both in Mississippi; Buttermilk, Kansas; Tea, South Dakota; Oatmeal, Texas; Cheesequake, New Jersey, and Two Egg, Florida.

Have you ever wanted to visit a small town that has a big name? Head over to Wales in the United Kingdom, and ask someone to point you in the direction of – take a very deep breath – Llanfairpwllgwyngyllgogerychwyrndrobwllllantysiliogogogoch. The name translates into this: St. Mary's Church in the hollow of white hazel near a rapid whirlpool and the Church of St. Tysilio near the red cave. Most people call it "Llanfairpwllgwyngyll" or simply "Llanfair PG". But even this is not the longest place name in the world. There is in fact a town in Thailand with 163 letters in its name:

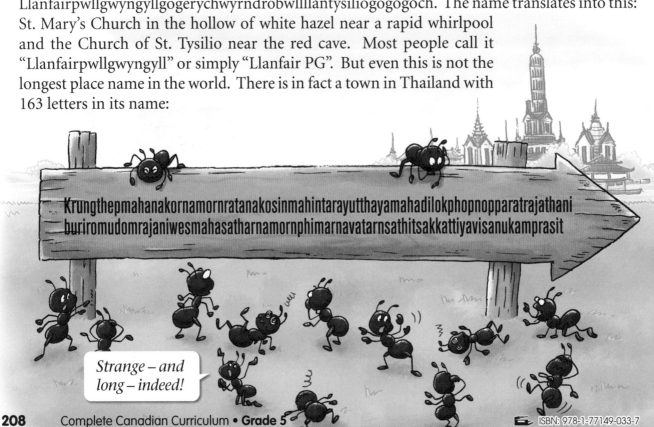

Krungthepmahanakornamornratanakosinmahintarayutthayamahadilokphopnopparatrajathani buriromudomrajaniwesmahasatharnamornphimarnavatarnsathitsakkattiyavisanukamprasit

Strange – and long – indeed!

ISBN: 978-1-77149-033-7

A. **Read the riddles and complete the crossword puzzle with the strange names from the passage.**

Across

A. "Mind if I pour myself another cup?"

B. "This place is certainly odd."

C. "This is part of a complete breakfast!"

D. "I've just about had it!"

E. "There's a missing 's'."

F. "Out of my way!"

Down

1. "We'd better get there fast!"

2. "There's nothing to do here."

3. "This place should go well with doughnuts."

4. "It's a little too short, this road."

Sentences

A **sentence** is a group of words that contains a subject and a verb. If the sentence has two or more independent clauses, it is a **compound sentence**. If it has one independent clause plus one or more dependent clauses, it is a **complex sentence**.

Examples: This is a quaint town and it has a strange name. (compound)
Don't be surprised if you come across Rednaxela Terrace. (complex)

B. **Read each sentence and write "compound" or "complex".**

If there is a dependent clause, then the sentence is complex. Every dependent clause begins with a conjunction.

1. There is Psycho Path in Michigan and there is Divorce Court in Pennsylvania. _____

2. Michelle wants to visit Goodfood but Richard wants to visit Hot Coffee. _____

3. I'll take you to Buttermilk if you take me to Tea. _____

4. "Rednaxela" was created when the sign painter painted the letters backwards! _____

5. Although you would want to avoid Accident, you might want to visit Boring since it's in the same state. _____

6. "We could visit Dull, or we could head down to Stinking Bay," I tell Gabriel. _____

7. My mom won't go to Cheesequake with my dad unless he takes her to Oatmeal. _____

ISBN: 978-1-77149-033-7

C. **Read this paragraph. Identify the underlined sentences as compound or complex.**

Has it ever occurred to you that the doughnut has multiple personalities? <u>It comes in many flavours and it comes in a variety of shapes.</u> <u>There is the Dutchie which looks like a pillow.</u> There is the cruller with its fun-loving twist. There is the fritter which is shapely and cute. And there is the classic "O", which is the shape that gave this dessert its name. <u>The shape looks like a ring but it also resembles a nut.</u> <u>Since this treat is made of dough, we decided to call it "doughnut".</u>

1. Compound Sentences:

a. _____

b. _____

2. Complex Sentences:

a. _____

b. _____

D. **Write a short paragraph containing one compound sentence and one complex sentence.**

_____

_____

_____

_____

_____

_____

ISBN: 978-1-77149-033-7

Farewell, Kiribati

Kiribati ("Ki-ri-bas") is a small country in the South Pacific. It is only 719 square kilometres in land area, comprised of one island and 32 atolls, which are ring-shaped coral reefs above the ocean surface, enclosing a body of water. Though individually small, these atolls spread across the Pacific Ocean in an area as large as the continental United States, looking like pale aqua gems dotting the deep blue sea. When viewed from atop, they are a lovely sight.

The population of Kiribati is 100 000. A third of its population lives in the capital city of Tarawa. Tourism, coconut-processing, and fishing are the main industries. On December 31, 1999, people around the world suddenly became familiar with this country: being the closest country to the International Date Line, Kiribati was the first to celebrate our entry into the new millennium. For those who were glued to their television sets that day, it was exciting to see the people of Kiribati dance and sing their welcome to the first sunrise of year 2000.

But Kiribati may not exist much longer. According to scientists worldwide, sea levels may rise up to 69 centimetres in the next 100 years, due to melting polar ice caps and glaciers from global warming. Soon, this low-lying country will be inundated by the sea. Salt water intrusion has already affected the drinking water supply in some parts of the country. Some habitats of marine life in Kiribati have begun to suffer as well. According to Greenpeace, two small atolls are already submerged. That is why New Zealand is accepting about 700 environmental refugees from Kiribati and the neighbouring country of Tuvalu every year.

But it is not just these South Pacific atoll nations that will be destroyed by rising sea levels. Equally at risk are the Maldives in the Indian Ocean and the millions of people who inhabit the coastal plains around the world. Over in the United States, the city New Orleans was damaged by Hurricane Katrina in 2005, and new buildings must be built on platforms that are close to one metre high. Rising sea levels will continue to affect many countries – long after we have bade farewell to Kiribati.

ISBN: 978-1-77149-033-7

A. Match the words with the meanings. Write the letters.

1. gems _____

2. atolls _____

3. glaciers _____

4. habitats _____

5. inundated _____

6. environmental refugees _____

7. millennium _____

A people who need to move due to natural disasters or other environmental causes

B coral reefs in the shape of rings surrounding a body of water in the ocean

C slow-moving masses of ice in very cold regions of the Earth

D precious stones

E 1000 years

F flooded

G homes

B. Complete these sentences.

1. The land of Kiribati is only 719 square kilometres, but the country covers an area as large as the United States because _____

_____ .

2. The main industries in Kiribati are _____

_____ .

3. The world suddenly became familiar with Kiribati in December of 1999 because _____

_____ .

4. Kiribati may not exist much longer because _____

_____ .

ISBN: 978-1-77149-033-7

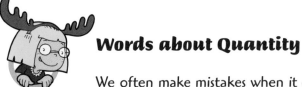

Words about Quantity

We often make mistakes when it comes to words that have to do with **quantity**. In order to use these words correctly, we need to know how many things we are talking about. We also need to know whether or not what we are talking about is countable.

C. **Read about each pair of words and fill in the blanks with the correct words.**

1. **Between vs. Among**

   When we are talking about only two things, we use "between". When we are talking about more than two things, we use "among".

   a. This is the biggest one _____ all the atolls.

   b. _____ Kiribati and Tuvalu, which country do you want to see?

   c. There are nine kilometres _____ these two atolls.

   d. There is worry _____ the people who live along coastal plains.

2. **Fewer vs. Less**

   We use "fewer" when referring to things that can be counted individually. We use "less" when referring to something that cannot be counted.

   a. In Canada, there is _____ daylight in winter than in summer.

   b. No _____ than four names of hurricanes have been retired since 2010.

   c. "I see _____ water in that tank now," says Anne.

   d. This year, there are _____ than 700 refugees from Kiribati and Tuvalu to New Zealand.

3. **Number vs. Amount**

"Number" is used when referring to things that can be counted individually. "Amount" is used when referring to something that cannot be counted, such as money and milk.

a. Can you tell me the _____ of atolls there are in Kiribati?

b. The _____ of places that will be inundated by the sea is rather alarming.

c. "You will never guess the _____ of wealth that some people have!" says Grace.

d. "50.5 kilograms is a bigger _____ than 5.05 kilograms," Bill tells his little sister as he helps her with decimal numbers.

D. Fill in the blanks with words from (C).

Tom and Alan have just been given their allowance. Off they go to the candy shop. 1._____ all the treats on the shelves, the one that catches their attention is a giant bag of marble candies! The two boys fish their pockets and look at the 2._____ of coins they have: they don't have enough to pay. A little disappointed, Tom says, "That's okay, we wouldn't be able to eat the whole bag 3._____ the two of us anyway." As they head out, the shopkeeper says, "I see you really want that bag of goodies. I can actually sell it to you for 4._____ ." Surprised and delighted, Tom and Alan put together their money to pay for it at the counter. Each of them eats no 5._____ than ten pieces before they even get home!

Going Camping with a Rock Star

My dad is a geologist. My mom calls him her "Rock Star". I like going with him on camping trips to the Canadian Shield, which is a huge landmass that stretches across half of Canada. It touches parts of the Northwest Territories, Saskatchewan, and Alberta; covers half of Manitoba, most of Ontario, Quebec, and Nunavut, and spans all of Labrador. It even reaches Greenland! The rock of the Canadian Shield goes back a very long time: anywhere between 350 million and 4.5 billion years old.

We always take our fishing rods – there are abundant lakes and rivers in the Canadian Shield – and a small pickaxe. I like looking for nice stones. Once, my dad took me to Ontario to look for amethyst, which is my mom's birthstone. Amethyst is a semi-precious stone that is violet in colour, but I like plain old rocks too. I love the way granite glints in the sun and comes in multiple colours. Sometimes I'm able to find granite stones that have other kinds of stones threaded through them. These ones are very colourful. There is a lot of granite in the Canadian Shield.

I also like finding mica. It is not very colourful, but I like the way it can break into tiny sheets. My dad explained that different rocks break – or cleave – in different ways. For example, mica cleaves into sheets and galena cleaves into cubes.

Sometimes it rains on our camping trips, so my dad and I would take out our cards or chess set to play, which we usually bring along. We also talk a lot. We talk about life, about how I'm doing in school, and about how he is doing at his job.

Sometimes we make lists of famous rocks. On our last camping trip, we tried to think of as many as we could. This is the list we came up with:

- Perce Rock, Canada
- Plymouth Rock, United States
- Stonehenge, United Kingdom
- Rock of Gibraltar, Gibraltar
- Blarney Stone, United Kingdom
- Devils Tower, United States
- Rosetta Stone (it's in a museum in England, but belongs to Egypt)
- Table Mountain, South Africa
- Mt. Rushmore, United States
- Ayers Rock, Australia (the rock is also called "Uluru")
- Hope Diamond (it's in a museum in the United States)
- Brighton Rock, United Kingdom
- Giant's Causeway, United Kingdom

And more will be made on future camping trips!

A. Use point form to complete this chart with information from the passage.

Stone	Colour	Other Information
Amethyst		

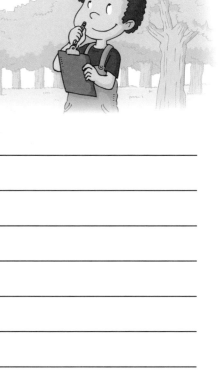

B. How does camping foster relationships? Write a response and support it with examples from the narrator's camping trips.

_____

_____

_____

_____

_____

_____

_____

Descriptive Writing

We use **descriptive writing** when we want to create a vivid picture of a person, thing, or an event in the reader's mind. One way of doing this is by using adjectives and adverbs to give detail. Another way is by replacing the existing words of a given sentence with more effective ones.

Examples: Naomi uses her pickaxe to find stones.
Naomi uses her pickaxe <u>delicately</u> to find stones.

There are many lakes and rivers in the Canadian Shield.
There are <u>abundant</u> lakes and rivers in the Canadian Shield.

C. **Fill in the blanks with the given adjectives and adverbs to make the sentences more descriptive.**

anxiously   easily   steadily   fun-loving   massive

slowly   carefully   always   hilarious   broad

1. Sara is very excited about her fishing trip.

   She is _____ getting her fishing gear.

2. Polly loves the woods. She _____ finds her way around.

3. David does not hurry when looking for stones. He _____

   searches _____ for nice ones.

4. Alan is very persistent. He _____ but _____ knits

   a scarf for his grandmother.

5. Shelley likes _____ paintings and has a habit of painting

   very _____ strokes.

6. My _____ little brother likes to make _____

   sounds to make all of us laugh.

D. **Underline the words that are different in each pair of sentences. Then explain why the second one is more descriptive than the first.**

1. The Canadian Shield makes up half of Canada.
   The Canadian Shield stretches across half of Canada.

   _____

2. Amethyst is a semi-precious stone.
   Amethyst is a semi-precious stone that is violet in colour.

   _____

3. I love the way granite looks in the sun.
   I love the way granite glints in the sun.

   _____

4. Different rocks break in different ways.
   Different rocks cleave in different ways.

   _____

E. **Write a descriptive paragraph on one of these topics.**

My Best Friend   My First Trip   My Room

   _____
   _____
   _____
   _____
   _____
   _____
   _____
   _____

Most people think that extreme sports are a relatively new invention in the sporting world, but a surprising number of extreme sports are not new at all; they are just adaptations of centuries-old, traditional games and rituals. Let's look at the examples of surfing and bungee-jumping.

The Long History of
Extreme Sports

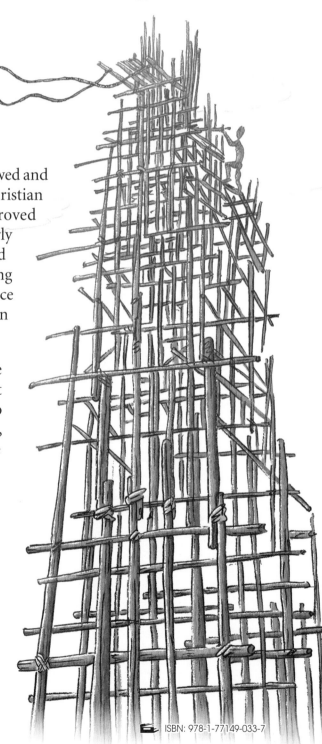

Surfing was invented in Hawaii centuries ago. It was called *he'e nalu* ("wave sliding"). Surfboards were first made from lumber and came in all shapes and sizes: from about one to four metres in length. Historically, all Hawaiian islanders could ride the waves, but it was mainly royalty who had the time to perfect the skills, which involved learning how to read the waves as much as knowing how to stay upright on the board.

The first western explorers who came to Hawaii were awed and impressed by the sight of wave sliding. However, Christian missionaries who came to the island later disapproved of the sport and banned it. It was not until the early 20th century that surfing was introduced to the world by Duke Kahanamoku, the Hawaiian-born swimming medalist at the 1912 and 1920 Olympic Games. Since then, the sport of surfing has developed into an important part of the beach culture.

Bungee-jumping was also invented by a group of people living in the Pacific Ocean, on the island of Pentecost in Vanuatu. Legend has it that the first person to ever jump was a woman named Tamalie. These days, however, the jump is performed only by men, who tie vines to their feet and jump from scaffolds. In addition to being a manhood ceremony, the jump is done to ensure a bountiful yam harvest. In 1979, a group of students from the Oxford University Dangerous Sport Club – who had seen a film about the vine jumpers of Pentecost – jumped from the Clifton Suspension Bridge in Bristol, England, and then later from the Golden Gate Bridge in San Francisco, *dressed in tuxedos and top hats!* Before long, bungee-jumping became the popular extreme sport that it is today.

ISBN: 978-1-77149-033-7

A. Circle "T" for the true sentences and "F" for the false ones.

1. Some extreme sports are adaptations of traditional games and rituals.   T F

2. Surfing was invented in Hawaii.   T F

3. Christian missionaries were impressed by the sight of wave sliding.   T F

4. Surfing was introduced to the world in the early 20th century.   T F

5. Bungee-jumping originated on an island in the Pacific Ocean.   T F

6. Bungee-jumping was introduced to the world by a group of British university students.   T F

7. Bungee-jumping was traditionally performed to ward off evil spirits.   T F

8. These days, only men would go bungee-jumping for fun on the island of Pentecost in Vanuatu.   T F

B. Between surfing and bungee-jumping, which extreme sport would you try? Why? Think of another extreme sport you might want to try and explain why.

_____

_____

_____

_____

_____

_____

Narrative Writing

We use **narrative writing** when we want to tell a story. This type of writing often involves telling about events in **chronological order**: the order that the events happen in time. A narrative may include vivid descriptions, and may be one or several paragraphs in length.

C. **Read the order of narration. Then use the given sentences to finish the narrative paragraph about surfing.**

Order of Narration:

1. *Tell when surfing made its comeback.*
2. *Tell why surfing made its comeback.*
3. *Tell who played an important role in its comeback and what they did.*
4. *Tell what happened as a result.*

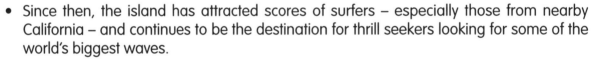

- Since then, the island has attracted scores of surfers – especially those from nearby California – and continues to be the destination for thrill seekers looking for some of the world's biggest waves.
- Along came a Hawaiian teenager named Duke Kahanamoku, who spent his days riding the waves.
- The missionaries' influence over the island had begun to decline by this time, which allowed the sport to regain its popularity.
- He and his buddies even created their own surfing club called "The Club of the Waves" and gave surfing a rebirth in Hawaii.

The comeback of surfing in Hawaii can be traced to the beginning of the 20th century. _____

_____

_____

_____

_____

_____

_____

ISBN: 978-1-77149-033-7

D. **Write a narrative paragraph on one of these topics.**

My Day at School   **My Baseball Practice**

My Club Meeting   **My Summer Vacation**

Topic: _____

Order of Narration:

1. _____

2. _____

3. _____

4. _____

5. _____

_____

_____

_____

_____

_____

_____

_____

_____

_____

Witch's Brew –
or, "EEEEeeeeeew!"

Ruth is the name of a witch I once knew,
Who loved to make soup she called "Witch's Brew".
(The soup was quite gooey – it was more like a stew.)
And let me tell you how she made it, too.

She took some soot from the roof
And some water from the pool.
She took some stuff from the chicken coop
And thought, "This will be lovely soup!"

She stirred it with a broom
(She'd forgotten her spoon.)
Adding roots, shoots, a boot,
And the juice of a prune.
She dug into her suitcase
And found two huge scoops of – *Gasp!* – food?
(No clue what it was, but it smelled really rude!)

Then she threw in some noodles
And a spoonful of glue.
Then a scoop of something gooey.
It was red, white, and bluey.
(I knew it was toothpaste! She put in some toothpaste!)
And – What do you know? – she threw in the tube too.

Her friend, the ghoul, took a spoonful,
A big scoop of her brew.
He sniffed it and snoofed it
And started to chew.

Next thing I knew, the dude flew from the room.
He tripped over the Hoover as he started to spew!
EEEEeeeeeew!
Wouldn't you?

 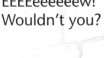

A. Find all the words in the poem that rhyme with "stew".

_____ _____

_____ _____

_____ _____

_____ _____

_____ _____

_____ _____

B. Answer these questions.

1. What do you think is the nastiest ingredient? Why?

_____

_____

2. Write your favourite rhyming lines from the poem. Why do you like them?

_____

_____

_____

_____

3. Lines within parentheses are used in several places throughout the poem. What is their use?

_____

_____

4. Writers and poets are allowed to use made-up words in their work because they have "poetic licence". What are the made-up words in this poem?

_____

_____

Writing Poetry

It is fun to write poems with rhyming words. When a pair of lines contains rhyming words in the end, they are called **rhyming couplets**.

Example: Ruth is the name of a witch I once knew,
Who loved to make soup she called "Witch's Brew".

C.   Write a word that rhymes with each of these.

1.   spell   _____

2.   vision   _____

3.   hour   _____

4.   jumpy   _____

5.   gold   _____

6.   tricks   _____

7.   conceal   _____

8.   treasure   _____

D.   Brainstorm some rhyming words related to the topic of "Elf".   Then use them to write the rhyming couplets in this short poem.

tricks – sticks

Elf

Ralph is the name of an elf who _____

Who _____ .

He took some yarn and _____

And some _____ .

He turned on his spinning wheel _____

Then _____ .

ISBN: 978-1-77149-033-7

E. **Think of a topic to write a poem about. Brainstorm some rhyming words related to the topic. Then write a poem about it using rhyming couplets.**

Folk Music
Brings the World Together

As we visit other countries and become more familiar with them, we also become more interested in the traditional folk music of cultures around the world. Though the music is different from culture to culture, the meaning and reason behind the music are the same.

Work songs and chants are a major type of traditional folk music. Whether the work was fishing, planting rice, harvesting grain, picking fruit, coal mining, logging, weaving, railway building, or even sponge diving, people sang songs to cheer themselves up and to get them through their long, hard day. Below are three well-known examples.

The Shanty-man's Life
(an American lumberjack song)
A shanty-man's life is a wearisome life, although some think it void of care.
Swinging an axe from morning till night in the midst of the forests so drear.
Lying in the shanty bleak and cold while the cold stormy wintry winds blow.
And as soon as the daylight doth appear, to the wild woods we must go.

Railway Song
(an American railroad song)
I've been working on the railroad all the livelong day
I've been working on the railroad just to pass the time away
Can't you hear the whistle blowing, rise up so early in the morn
Can't you hear the captain shouting: Dinah, blow your horn

The Banana Boat Song
(a Jamaican work chant)
Day-o, day-ay-ay-o! Daylight come and me wanna go home.
Day! Me say day, me say day, me say day-o.
Daylight come and me wanna go home.
Come, Mr. Tally Mon, tally my bananas.
Daylight come and me wanna go home.
Come, Mr. Tally Mon, tally my bananas.
Daylight come and me wanna go home.

A shanty-man's life...

ISBN: 978-1-77149-033-7

A. **Use your dictionary to find the meaning of each word. Think of a synonym for it. Then write a sentence with each word and a sentence with its synonym.**

1.  *wearisome*   synonym: _____

   _____

   _____

2.  *drear*   synonym: _____

   _____

   _____

3.  *bleak*   synonym: _____

   _____

   _____

B. **Pretend you are having a "long, hard day". Make up your own work song to help you get through the day.**

_____

_____

_____

_____

_____

_____

_____

_____

_____

Writing Letters (1)

Letters can be **formal** or **informal**. An informal letter may or may not have a purpose, and may use casual sentence structure. We often write informal letters when writing notes, e-mails, or greeting cards, where space is limited.

Example: Hey Kiyoka!

Back in Canada now. Will be starting school tomorrow and so I have some butterflies in my stomach...but I'm also excited because I'll be seeing my old friends and meeting new ones!

Hope you're doing well.

Sammy

C. Write a postcard using informal writing.

You are on a trip and have just bought a postcard for a friend.

Writing Letters (2)

A formal letter – or business letter – has a specific purpose. It begins with a formal salutation and ends with a closing and your name.

It usually contains three paragraphs:

Paragraph 1 states the purpose of your letter.
Paragraph 2 gives details about the subject of your letter.
Paragraph 3 suggests a course of action and/or solution and asks for follow-up.

D. Write a formal letter.

The city wants to build a high-rise condominium in your neighbourhood, which involves tearing down old but historically important buildings. You want to voice your concern to the mayor of the city.

Dear _____ :

_____

_____

_____

_____

_____

_____

_____

_____

_____

Sincerely,

_____

ISBN: 978-1-77149-033-7

SOCIAL STUDIES

ISBN: 978-1-77149-033-7

Complete Canadian Curriculum • **Grade 5**　　**233**

First Nations: Algonquin and Haudenosaunee (1)

The First Nations were people living in Canada before the Europeans arrived. There are more than 600 First Nations who identify themselves based on the geographic areas they live in.

A.   Circle the correct words.

Algonquin

The Algonquins migrated to places with good air / **food** supply. They lived in a type of hut called a wigwam. They were excellent hunters. Some of the animals they hunted were deer, moose, and **beavers** / penguins . They also fished and planted. Wild rice, seed, and berries were supplements to their diet. They travelled by birchbark canoes in water. In winter, they travelled in toboggans and **snowshoes** / skates . The women planted and the men hunted. Men were leaders of the family. The Algonquins believed the spiritual world interacts with the physical world.

Haudenosaunee

The Haudenosaunees settled more permanently than the Algonquins. They lived in **longhouses** / igloos . They were excellent farmers. Their main source of food came from farming crops, including the Three Sisters which were corn, beans, and coconuts / **squash** . They also fished and hunted deer, moose, and caribou. The men hunted while the women planted. Each longhouse was headed by a   man / **woman** , called clan mother, who looked after her extended family or clan. They had ceremonies and festivals to honour the spirits who were believed to change the seasons and provide good crops and **animals** / minerals .

ISBN: 978-1-77149-033-7

B. **Using the information from (A), compare the two First Nations.**

	Algonquin	Haudenosaunee
Dwelling	wigwam	long house
Food	deer moose, beavers, wild rice, seeds, berrys	coarn, beans, squash, fish deer, moose, caribou
Roles of Men and Women	Man: hunters Woman: farmers	Man: hunters Woman: housewifes
Religion		

C. **Use the information in (A) to answer the questions.**

1. What specific skills did the Algonquins develop because of their frequent migration?

   good food

2. How did agriculture affect the daily activities of the Haudenosaunees?

   good food

First Nations: Algonquin and Haudenosaunee (2)

The daily lives of different First Nations peoples were very different due to the available resources in the regions they occupied.

A. Label the Algonquin tribes on the map and list the Haudenosaunee tribes in the box. Then answer the questions.

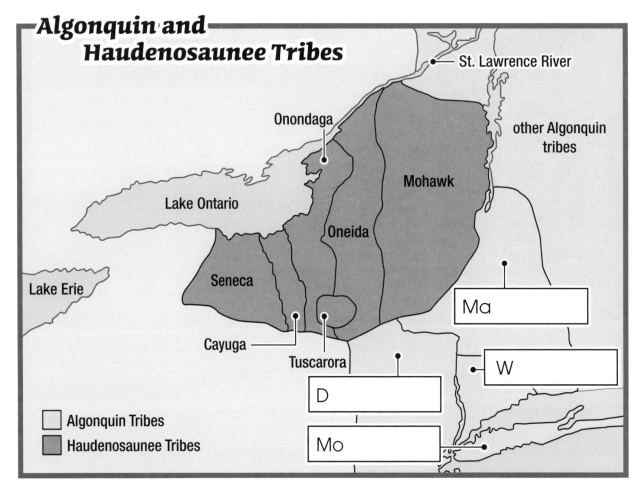

1. **Algonquin Tribes**

    Montauk

    Delaware

    Mahican

    Wappinger

2. **Handenosaunee Tribes**

ISBN: 978-1-77149-033-7

3. Check the region that the Algonquins occupied.

   (A) the north of Lake Ontario

   (B) the east of Lake Ontario

   (C) the north of St. Lawrence River

4. Check the region that the Haudenosaunees occupied.

   (A) by Lake Huron in Western Ontario

   (B) by Lake Ontario in Eastern Ontario

   (C) in Newfoundland and Eastern Quebec

5. Name the bodies of water that the Haudenosaunees had access to for their water source.

   _____

6. How did the locations of the Haudenosaunees benefit them in agricultural activities?

   _____

7. What caused the Algonquins to move from place to place?

   _____

8.

   We had a less structured government system than the Haudenosaunees. How did our frequent migration contribute to this?

   _____

   _____

   an Algonquian

3

Haudenosaunee Confederacy

The Haudenosaunee Confederacy was founded with the intention of uniting the nations and allowing them to live in harmony. It had a structured government system led by chiefs from all nations.

A. Fill in the blanks. Then answer the questions.

peaceful   Haudenosaunee   Longhouse   Tuscarora

The **Haudenosaunee Confederacy**, meaning "the People of the 1._____", is also known as the Iroquois Confederacy. It was formed to unite various 2._____ tribes and nations. Its purpose was to allow the nations to make 3._____ decisions. The nations that first joined the confederacy were the Mohawk, Oneida, Onondaga, Cayuga, and Seneca. In the early 1720s, the 4._____ , a nation located between the Oneida and Onondaga, also joined the Confederacy.

5.

Haudenosaunee Confederacy

Nations:

6.

The Wendat, also known as the Huron, was a group that was a distant relative of the Haudenosaunee who spoke a similar language.

St. Lawrence River

Wendat

Lake Ontario

Haudenosaunee

Why didn't the Wendat join the confederacy? (You may have to do some research*.)

_____

_____

*http://www.thecanadianencyclopedia.ca/en/article/huron/

ISBN: 978-1-77149-033-7

B. **Trading among the nations became easier after the formation of the confederacy. Match the pictures of the traded goods with the descriptions.**

Traded Goods

1. used for travelling in water
2. a kind of preserved food
3. shell beads that were used as money
4. used for fishing
5. the main source of their diet

A wampum strings

B corn

C fishing net

D smoked fish

E birchbark canoe

C. **Study the diagram about the confederacy's government system. Then fill in the blanks.**

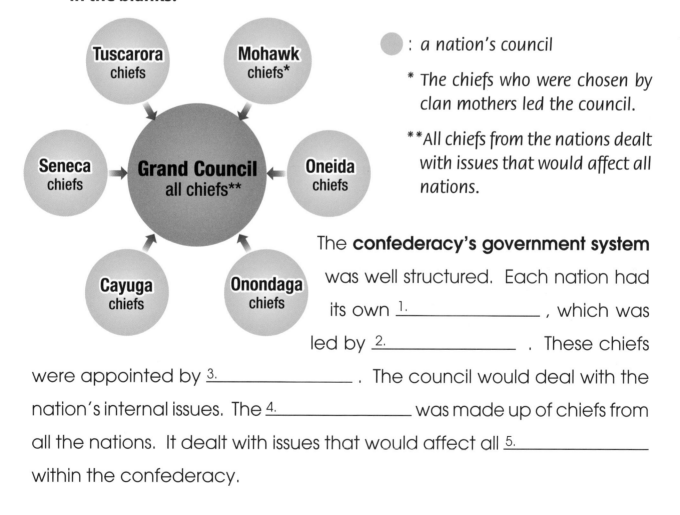

Tuscarora chiefs

Mohawk chiefs*

Seneca chiefs

Grand Council all chiefs**

Oneida chiefs

Cayuga chiefs

Onondaga chiefs

● : a nation's council

* The chiefs who were chosen by clan mothers led the council.

**All chiefs from the nations dealt with issues that would affect all nations.

The **confederacy's government system** was well structured. Each nation had its own 1._____ , which was led by 2._____ . These chiefs were appointed by 3._____ . The council would deal with the nation's internal issues. The 4._____ was made up of chiefs from all the nations. It dealt with issues that would affect all 5._____ within the confederacy.

European Explorers in Early Canada

European explorers began arriving in Canada as early as 800 CE. Since then, more Europeans have arrived and explored this new land for its riches and resources.

A. Trace the routes with the correct colours. Then answer the question.

European Exploration Routes

Of all regions in Canada, why was Newfoundland the first place the Europeans found and explored?

_____

_____

ISBN: 978-1-77149-033-7

B. **Look at the timeline of the European explorations in Early Canada. Fill in the blanks.**

European Exploration Timeline

Quebec City   overcrowding   Vikings   Newfoundland
King Francis I   Jacques Cartier   King Henry VII
North America   Asia   Atlantic   St. Lawrence River

800 ← European explorers began to arrive in Canada.

1000 ← The Norse, who are known as the 1._____ , were Scandinavians who travelled by sea regularly to explore and trade in waters and lands outside Scandinavia. They left Scandinavia because of 2._____ and political unrest. Leif Erikson led his crew to 3._____ and discovered Newfoundland.

1497 John Cabot, a famous English explorer, was hired by 4._____ of England to discover new lands and a route

1499 to Asia. In one of his voyages, he discovered 5._____ .

1524 Giovanni de Verrazano was sent by 6._____ of France to explore the east coast of North America and find a route to 7._____ . Verrazano did not find a route to Asia but explored the 8._____ coast of North America and Newfoundland.

1528

1534 9._____ , another French explorer, was sent by King Francis I to continue finding a route to Asia and claim the Newfoundland area for France. He travelled inland in North America and sailed up to the 10._____ and visited Stadacona and Hochelaga, which are now 11._____ and Montreal respectively.

1542

First Contact

When the Europeans arrived in Canada and met the First Nations peoples, challenges arose for both groups. They struggled to make sense of each other's way of life.

A. **Identify the challenges faced by the First Nations, European explorers, or both. Write the letters in the correct spaces.**

Challenges Faced by the First Nations and European Explorers

First Nations   Both   European Explorers

Ⓐ worrying about explorers taking over their land

Ⓑ adjusting to the new lifestyle

Ⓒ getting used to the cold climate and settling in

Ⓓ starting a different way of life away from their families and friends

Ⓔ worrying about the explorers imposing their ways and religion onto their people

Ⓕ dealing with diseases they had never encountered

Ⓖ interacting and communicating with people who spoke a different language and had a completely different culture

ISBN: 978-1-77149-033-7

B.   Read the passage. Then answer the questions.

How First Nations Helped the Europeans

Regardless of the potential threats the European explorers posed, the First Nations considered it wrong to leave the explorers suffering when they had means to ease their problems. They helped the Europeans with their basic necessities. They showed them new lands to settle as the explorers had no place to stay when they arrived. To help the explorers get adjusted to the harsh climate, the First Nations provided them with warm clothing and traditional nutritious foods like pemmican (a mixture of fat and protein). The First Nations also helped the explorers treat a disease called scurvy, which was caused by the lack of vitamin C. To supplement the diet of the patients, the First Nations gave the explorers fish and venison. They also taught them to make a herbal drink to treat the disease.

1.   Describe how the First Nations helped the explorers...

   a. settle: _____

   b. adjust to the harsh climate: _____

   c. treat a disease: _____

2.   Why were the First Nations being kind to the Europeans even though they presented the First Nations with challenges?

   _____

   _____

3.   Do you think the First Nations' response to the arrival of the Europeans encouraged more Europeans to come? Why?

   _____

   _____

Benefits of Contact

The first contact between the Europeans and the First Nations was peaceful. Soon, they started to learn about each other's traditions and culture.

A. Write the letters in the arrows to show the trade between the First Nations and the Europeans.

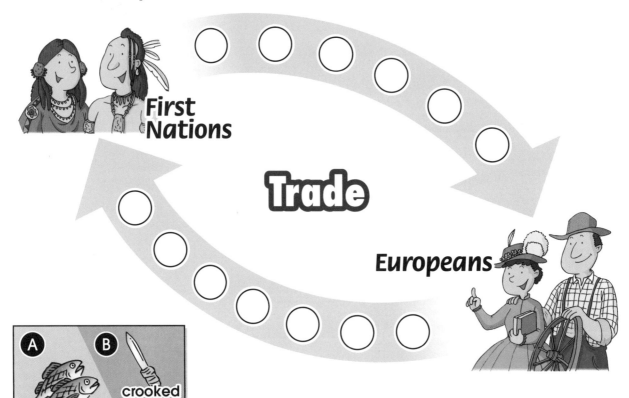

First Nations

Trade

Europeans

A fish

B crooked knife

C warm clothing

D brass pot

E metal axe

F canoe

G fresh meat

H herbal medicine

I wool blankets

J beaver pelts

K alcohol and tobacco

L European-style pipes

M powder horns (containers for gunpowder)

ISBN: 978-1-77149-033-7

B. Fill in the blanks. Then answer the question.

Things That Were Introduced to the...

First Nations:

> farm   metal   travel
> grains   hunt

- 1._____ tools:
  making their lives easier

- lightweight firearms:
  able to 2._____ more
  successfully

- horses:
  able to 3._____ faster
  and greater distances

- 4._____ animals:
  (e.g. chickens, cows, pigs)
  providing stable food sources

- 5._____ :
  (e.g. wheat and barley)
  an alternative food source

Europeans:

> survival   plants
> warm   lands

- new ways of life:
  including methods of travel
  and 6._____

- medicinal 7._____ :
  enhancing their survival skills

- new 8._____ :
  able to search for more furs

- sewing 9._____ clothing:
  keeping themselves warm
  throughout harsh winters

10. Some Europeans married into the
    First Nations community. How did this
    benefit both parties?

    _____

    _____

    _____

Negative Impacts on First Nations

The presence of the Europeans influenced the First Nations' culture and traditions. Some of the influences resulted in negative impacts on the First Nations.

A. Fill in the blanks.

Although the interactions between the First Nations and the Europeans benefited both groups, the Europeans' presence also posed negative impacts on the First Nations in different aspects including **overhunting**, **land exploitation**, **warfare**, **disease**, *and* **culture**.

decrease pelts	waterways cleared	British Wendats conflicts	decreased alcohol influenza	parenting Catholic culture

Overhunting

The First Nations hunted for beaver 1._____ to trade for goods and the introduction to guns made fur hunting a lot easier. The demand for fur and hunting with guns led to a drastic 2._____ in the beavers' population.

Land Exploitation

Forests were 3._____ for the Europeans, who took over lands near 4._____ , which were the First Nations' prime locations for food sources.

Warfare

The French fought alongside the 5._____ against the Haudenosaunee nations who sided with the 6._____ . Use of guns made 7._____ more deadly. Many people from the First Nations died from wars.

ISBN: 978-1-77149-033-7

Disease

The First Nations were exposed to diseases from which they had no immunity, such as 8._____ , tuberculosis, smallpox, scarlet fever, and measles. Their population drastically 9._____ after several outbreaks. The First Nations were also exposed to 10._____ which they had no tolerance for.

Culture

Trades were tied to religion. The French appointed 11._____ missionaries to influence the First Nations' way of life. Before trading took place, conversations around Christian practices of 12._____ , marriage, and burial of the dead were imposed. This led to the diminishing of the First Nations' traditional 13._____ and identity.

B. Read the quotes. Match to show whether each quote is from a First Nations person or a European.

"They are sharing valuable beaver pelts with us for cheap axes."

"We like the metal tools they are sharing with us."

• First Nations

• European

"The king will be happy with what we've established here."

"They are taking the best lands where we fish and hunt."

New Home

New France

During the 1600s, the king of France encouraged his people to migrate to his new colony called New France in Canada.

A. Circle the correct words.

Seigneurial System

The French colonists wanted to make New France like their homeland. King Louis XIII introduced a method of land ownership known as the seigneurial system for the French emigrants.

king

seigneur

habitant

King

- **borrower / owner** of all lands
- allocated large areas to different **noblemen / soldiers** called seigneurs

Seigneurs (noblemen)

- kept a **small / large** portion of land for themselves and their families
- divided up the rest of the land among **farmers / kings** called habitants
- built a small **church / temple** for worship
- built a **silo / mill** for the habitants to grind wheat

Habitants (farmers)

- paid rent to the **seigneur / king**
- gave the seigneur a portion of their **harvest / land**
- worked for the seigneur for a certain number of days each year, usually building **roads / parks** and bridges

B. Read the paragraph. Check the correct diagram and answer the question.

The lands given to seigneurs were usually beside a waterway, which was used for transportation and irrigation. Seigneurs would divide the land into strips for the habitants so that they could all have access to water.

1. Check the diagram that shows how the land was divided.
   (S – seigneur, H – habitants)

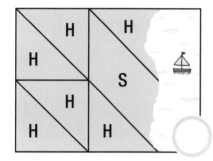 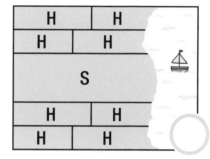 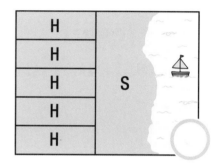

2. If you were a seigneur, would you divide the land the same way? Explain.

   _____

   _____

C. Look at the map. Then answer the questions.

1. The Europeans settled in the _____ part of Canada.
   eastern/western

2. Circle the three European settlements that were close to the St. Lawrence River.

3. How did the location of the European settlements benefit them in trades?

European Settlements and Major Trade Routes

   _____

   _____

Jesuit Missionaries

One of the first groups to emigrate from Europe to Canada were Jesuit missionaries. Their presence had significant impacts on the First Nations' culture and religion.

A. Read the paragraph. Colour and answer the questions.

Jesuit Missionaries

The king of France encouraged Roman Catholics to emigrate to New France. He sent Jesuits, a group of Catholic missionaries, with the intention of converting the First Nations peoples to Christianity so that New France would be like Europe. The Jesuits saw it as their obligation to save the "lost souls". They wore black robes from collar to toes and travelled to the interior lands to live with the First Nations peoples. They learned their languages and kept close contact with them. Some of them even married First Nations women, and their children born from this union were called Métis.

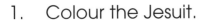

a Jesuit

1. Colour the Jesuit.

2. Why did the king send the Jesuits to New France?

_____

_____

_____

3. Who were the Métis?

_____

_____

_____

ISBN: 978-1-77149-033-7

B. Fill in the blanks to describe the missions and roles of the Jesuit missionaries. Then answer the questions.

Missions and Roles of Jesuit Missionaries

maps   king
priests   traditions
Sainte Marie

Mission

- build a community called 1._____ with the purpose of allowing the French and the First Nations to live in harmony

- set up parishes where people can train to become 2._____

- write about the 3._____ of the First Nations and draw 4._____ of the tribes

- submit reports to the 5._____ who sends money and people to support the Jesuits

Role

- manage all the 6._____ between the Europeans and the First Nations

convert
trades
Christianity

- 7._____ the First Nations to 8._____ through the frequent contact in trades

9. Why did the Jesuits who arrived in New France start learning the native languages?

_____

_____

10. Why did the king of France assign the Jesuits to trade with the First Nations?

_____

_____

ISBN: 978-1-77149-033-7 Complete Canadian Curriculum • Grade 5

New Home

Filles du roi

Filles du roi, also known as the King's Daughters, refers to a group of young European ladies who emigrated to New France with the sponsorship from the king.

A. Read the paragraph. Then circle the correct words and answer the question.

Filles du roi

In the 17th century, the number of single men far outnumbered single women in New France. They wanted to return to France because they could not find women to marry. To increase the French population and dominate the colony, the king selected approximately 800 single women who were called filles du roi, or King's Daughters, and sponsored their passage to New France. Once a couple married and had children, the family would be paid a good pension.

1. I will **gain / lose** control of my colony with the increasing French population. It means that the Haudenosaunee will have **less / more** control over this land.

king

2. I am selected to be a **fille du roi / slave**, so I can start a new life in the new country. The expense of the journey is covered by **the king / myself**.

fille du roi

3. Why would a French couple in New France be paid a good pension if they had children?

_____

_____

B. Read the passage. Then answer the questions.

Filles du roi were from different parts of France including Paris and Normandy. Some of them were from other countries including Germany, England, and Portugal. They were mostly between the ages of 16 and 25. They were all very poor and most of them were orphans while some were "spares" from very large families. They had very low levels of literacy skills. To be selected, the girls had to be physically fit enough to survive the hard work and have the potential to support their future husbands in New France. The time it took them to find their husbands varied but it was between a few months and three years. Marriage ceremonies were held at church parishes and administered by priests.

1. **Filles du roi**

    a. where they came from: _____

    _____

    b. ages: _____

    c. background: _____

    _____

    d. requirements: _____

    _____

2. Describe the marriage ceremony.

    _____

    _____

3. Why was it important to choose girls who were physically fit as filles du roi?

    _____

    _____

New Home

People in the Fur Trade

The Europeans were very interested in the First Nations' animal pelts, and the First Nations were interested in the Europeans' metal tools. Soon, the fur trade began.

A. Write the words in bold in the correct boxes. Then answer the questions.

The Europeans and the First Nations started trading and, very soon, the **fur trade** expanded and covered large areas of Canada. **Trading posts** were set up at various locations, usually near waterways. The **coureurs des bois** were French people who could navigate the interior lands of Canada very well. They helped the First Nations in hunting beavers, even in deep forested areas. Another group of French people, called **voyageurs**, were hired to navigate canoes briskly along some dangerous sections of waterways.

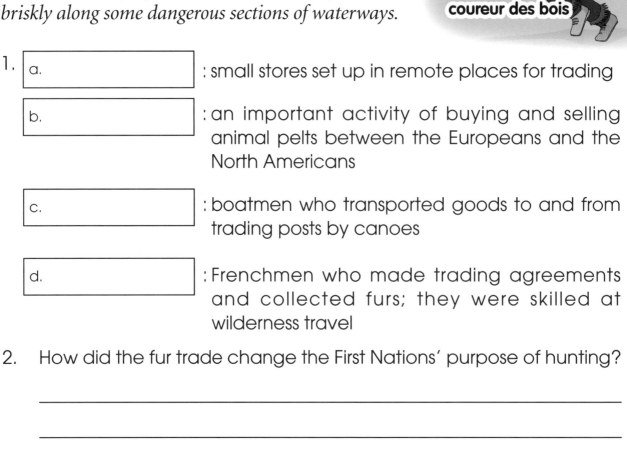

coureur des bois

1. a. [ ] : small stores set up in remote places for trading

   b. [ ] : an important activity of buying and selling animal pelts between the Europeans and the North Americans

   c. [ ] : boatmen who transported goods to and from trading posts by canoes

   d. [ ] : Frenchmen who made trading agreements and collected furs; they were skilled at wilderness travel

2. How did the fur trade change the First Nations' purpose of hunting?

   _____

   _____

   _____

ISBN: 978-1-77149-033-7

B. Fill in the blanks and do the matching.

First Nations Women in the Fur Trade

The voyageurs travelled to Canada every 1._____ to trade
spring/winter

2._____ . Some returned home after the trading was over,
herbs/furs

while others felt more at home in the First Nations community and

3._____ . Very often, these voyageurs took First Nations women
left/stayed

as 4._____ . These marriages were often 5._____
wives/employees   encouraged/discouraged

because they strengthened their relationship with the First Nations

and the voyageurs would 6._____ benefits in trading.
gain/lose

First Nations women brought tangible benefits to 7._____
survival/entertainment

along the journeys between trading posts, which were unfamiliar to

European women.

8.

my tasks

sew clothing   •

carry heavy cargo   •

stitch moccasins for   •
the team

set up tents and   •
campfires

cook stew and   •
prepare pemmican

12

Treaties and Land Claims

More and more Europeans arrived and occupied lands that were originally possessed by the First Nations. The First Nations then began advocating for their rights, which led to the writing of treaties and land claims.

A. Read the paragraph. Then complete the timeline.

Treaty

A treaty is a negotiated agreement between two or more nations that gives valid rights to the respective parties.

In 1764, the Niagara Treaty was signed. It was the first treaty signed between the British and the First Nations. It ensured that there would be fair and voluntary land dealings between the two parties. In 1787, they signed another treaty called the Gunshot Treaty. It stated the British had the right to the land and its resources within a large area stretching from Lake Ontario to north of the Great Lakes. It was a blank contract that was to be filled later. In return, the First Nations were offered some money, reserve lands, and annual gifts. Between 1871 and 1921, 11 treaties called the Numbered Treaties took place. They were signed between the federal government and various First Nations communities. In these treaties, the First Nations received reserve lands and various forms of government assistance by giving up their rights to large tracts of land and the resources within them.

Treaty Timeline   *1764*   *1787*   *1871 to 1921*

The _____ **Treaty**

Parties: _____ and _____

Purpose:

_____

_____

_____

The _____ **Treaty**

Parties: _____ and _____

Benefits to the First Nations:

_____

_____

_____

The _____ **Treaties**
(11 treaties)

Parties: _____ and _____

Benefits to the First Nations:

_____

_____

_____

ISBN: 978-1-77149-033-7

B. Fill in the years in which the land claims took place.

Land claim is a grievance filed by a nation in response to what they consider a violation of their rights, from which the issue may be settled with land or financial compensation. Below are some of the land claims in Canada.

1978 in Quebec
> James Bay and Northern Quebec Agreement

1992 in Eastern Yukon
> Gwich'in Comprehensive Land Claim Agreement

1993 in Nunavut
> Nunavut Land Claims Agreement

1994 in Northern Northwest Territories
> Sahtu Dene and Métis Comprehensive Land Claim Agreement

2000 in Northwestern British Columbia
> Nisga'a Final Agreement

2005 in Eastern Northwest Territories
> Tlicho Agreement

2005 in Newfoundland and Labrador
> Labrador Inuit Land Claims Agreement

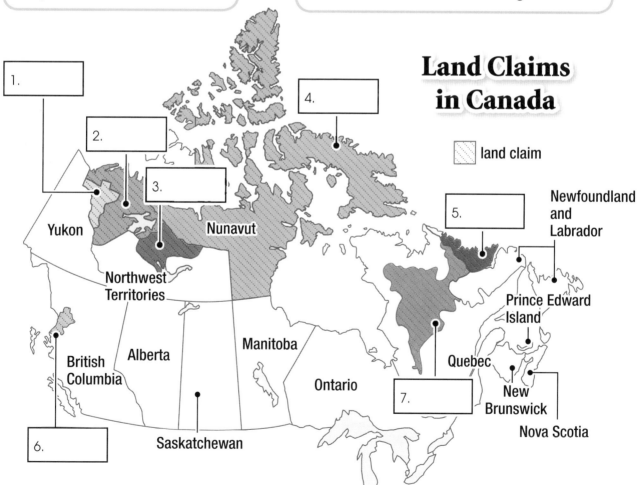

Land Claims in Canada

1.

2.

3.

4.

5.

6.

7.

land claim

Yukon

Nunavut

Northwest Territories

British Columbia

Alberta

Saskatchewan

Manitoba

Ontario

Quebec

Newfoundland and Labrador

Prince Edward Island

New Brunswick

Nova Scotia

13

Aboriginal Self-Government

In addition to the three levels of government, Canada also has a form of government called the Aboriginal self-government. It allows the Aboriginal peoples of Canada, including the First Nations, to govern themselves.

A.   Circle the correct words. Put "+" for pros and "-" for cons. Then answer the question.

Aboriginal self-government is a form of government that was granted by the **federal / municipal** government to the Aboriginal communities (including the First Nations). It **allows / prevents** the First Nations to exercise their freedom, make decisions, and form solutions that make sense for their **leaders / communities** . Even though the First Nations govern themselves in some areas, many issues are still handled by the **federal / municipal** government.

Pros and Cons from the Perspective of the First Nations

> Before the status was granted, there was a lot of debate within the First Nations on its pros and cons.

1. pay fewer taxes

2. might make mistakes and then our children will suffer

3. have control of our land and freedom to make decisions ourselves

4. not ready to govern ourselves because we do not have the expertise

5. can attract private investment and develop our lands the way we want

6. If you were a member of the First Nations, would you vote for or against the status? Explain.

_____

_____

ISBN: 978-1-77149-033-7

B. **Determine whether the roles below fall under federal jurisdiction (F) or Aboriginal self-government (A). Circle the correct letters.**

1. determining the tax rate on goods and services   F A

2. setting fishing and hunting laws   F A

3. setting guidelines for the First Nations Child and Family Services Program   F A

4. managing import and export activities in the territory   F A

5. licensing health and wellness programs   F A

6. overseeing international transportation   F A

C. **Read the quote and answer the questions.**

Cultural revival among aboriginal people is just one step toward regaining what has been lost. Self-government is the other key to the future of native people. When they are permitted to gain influence over the central institutions in their communities — the schools, the justice system, the child welfare system – Indian and Métis people have already demonstrated that they can repair the damage caused by centuries of racism and neglect.

Geoffrey York
Author of *The Dispossessed: Life and Death in Native Canada*

1. Why is Aboriginal self-government necessary according to Geoffrey York?

   _____

   _____

   _____

2. What does Geoffrey York mean when he says "centuries of racism and neglect"?

   _____

   _____

   _____

14

Traditional Ecological Knowledge

Traditional Ecological Knowledge (TEK) was built up in the daily interaction between the First Nations peoples and their natural environment. It has become an asset to their survival.

A. Fill in the blanks. Then check the correct sentence in each pair.

Traditional Ecological Knowledge (TEK) was gained through human interaction with 1._____ . The First Nations peoples used it on a daily basis and it was built up over a long period of time. TEK was a necessary tool for their 2._____ , and it allowed them to live sustainably using natural resources. Some First Nations communities living in reserves today still live with no 3._____ or running water. They continue to keep their 4._____ alive. Today, environmentalists are looking at the First Nations for ways to live 5._____ .

traditions
electricity
survival
nature
sustainably

How the First Nations Connect Themselves to Nature

(A) Mother Earth is a gift that can be used as one pleases.

(B) Mother Earth needs to be respected and used responsibly.

(A) Everyone needs to take care of only his or her own affairs.

(B) Sacrificing one's needs for the betterment of the community might be necessary.

(A) Every plant or animal, big or small, is connected in the circle of life.

(B) In the community, the rule of reciprocity can be ignored.

B. **Study the case below to see how TEK can help us understand more about nature. Complete the chart and answer the questions.**

An Example of the Use of TEK:
The Bowhead Whale Census

In 1977, scientists studied the bowhead whale population along the Beaufort Sea, a marginal sea of the Arctic Ocean. They found the whale population to be about 800 by observing the whale migration in open waters. However, through TEK, the Inuit estimated that the population should be about 7000. They indicated that the whales migrate not only in open waters, but also offshore and under the ice.

Later, new census methods were conducted and our population was estimated to be 8000.

1. Population of the Bowhead Whale in 1977

	a.	The Inuit
Method	scientific analysis	b.
Areas Observed	c.	d.
Population	e.	f.

2. According to the new census methods, what was the population of the bowhead whale? _____

3. Whose estimation in 1977 was more accurate? _____

4. From this example, do you agree that TEK is a valuable resource to scientists on environmental studies? Explain.

_____

_____

Rights and Responsibilities of a Canadian Citizen

Canada is a democratic country that provides many rights to its citizens. As a Canadian citizen, you have rights, but you also have to take on responsibilities.

A. Identify the rights.

The Canadian Charter of Rights and Freedoms

describes rights and freedoms that are guaranteed to every Canadian citizen.

Legal
Language
Democratic
Equality
Freedom
Mobility

1. _____ **Rights**

right to life; right not to receive cruel or unusual punishments

2. _____ **Rights**

right to speak with the government in English or French

3. _____ **Rights**

right to enter and leave Canada

4. _____ **Rights**

right to be treated and protected equally by laws

5. _____ **of Religion**

right to worship the religion of our choice

6. _____ **Rights**

right to vote and join political activities

ISBN: 978-1-77149-033-7

B.   Check the statements that identify the responsibilities of a good citizen.

The Responsibilities of a Good Citizen

Ⓐ to ignore environmental responsibilities

Ⓑ to disrespect people from other cultures

Ⓒ to follow rules in schools, in institutions, on roads, etc.

Ⓓ to advocate more assistance to the homeless and the less fortunate

To call for emergency when something is wrong, e.g. medical emergency, fire, or theft. Ⓔ

Every citizen should help make Canada the best country to live in.

C.   Study and analyze the cases. Identify the rights that are violated and give reasons.

Case 1

A store has refused to hire Peter as a cashier because he has a history of reckless driving.

Violation: _____

Reason: _____

_____

_____

Case 2

Farida is hired to work at a store with the condition that she removes her head scarf during work hours.

Violation: _____

Reason: _____

_____

_____

16

Levels of Government in Canada

There are three levels of government in Canada: Federal, Provincial/Territorial, and Municipal. Each level has its own responsibilities but they are all connected to almost everything that we do.

A.   Identify each level of government and circle the correct words. Fill in the blanks to show its responsibilities.

Federal Government

Provincial/Territorial Government

Municipal Government

The Three Levels of Government

1. _____ Government

- is headed by the Governor General of Canada on the advice of the **Queen / Prime Minister**

- looks after the entire country and **minor / international** issues that affect Canada

- makes decisions that affect **all / certain** parts of Canada

- is responsible for immigration, taxes, **national defence / policing** , and criminal laws

- Prime Minister of Canada:

  _____

Parliament Hill in Ottawa

Some of its Responsibilities

- setting a._____ safety regulations
  food/park

- setting the minimum b._____ for a Canadian soldier
  weight/age

- determining the criteria for the eligibility for c._____ insurance
  life/employment

ISBN: 978-1-77149-033-7

2. [   ] /Territorial Government

- is given authorities by the **federal / municipal** government

- is responsible for health care, education, and **office / road** regulations

- premier or commissioner of _____ : _____
  <small>your area</small>   <small>name</small>

Some of its Responsibilities

(A) issuing driver and vehicle licences

(B) providing national defence

(C) providing health care services

(D) setting school curriculum

Legislative Building in Ontario

3. [   ] Government

- governs cities, towns, and **provinces / districts**

- is responsible for libraries, parks, and local **airports / police**

- mayor of _____ : _____
  <small>your area</small>   <small>name</small>

Some of its Responsibilities

(A) arranging garbage disposals

(B) passing marriage laws

(C) building city parks

(D) providing water and sewage services

City Hall in Toronto

A law was passed to make a two-dollar coin. Which level of government was responsible for making this decision? Do some research to find out when the Toonie was introduced.

4. [   ] —government

5. [   ] —year

17

Health Care

Canada's health care system provides services on the basis of need rather than the ability to pay. Through taxes, the values of fairness and equity are demonstrated through sharing health care resources.

A.   Fill in the blanks to complete the paragraph.   Then put the letters in the circles under the correct levels of government.

The three levels of government work together to provide health care services for citizens. Most of the responsibility of providing health care services rests with the p_____ government. The f_____ government is responsible for delivering services to certain groups of people including the First Nations. The m_____ government shares responsibility in the areas of public health, sanitation, infectious diseases, and related education.

Health Care Services

Ⓐ *operating hospitals*

Ⓑ *supplying prescription drugs*

Ⓒ *providing emergency services*

Ⓓ *keeping immunization records*

Ⓔ *funding health research*

Ⓕ *managing medical clinics*

Ⓖ *providing long-term homes for the elderly*

Ⓗ *providing rehabilitation services for those in need*

Ⓘ *providing health care services for Canadian Forces, veterans, and refugees*

Ⓙ *publishing brochures on prevention and treatment of common diseases and injuries*

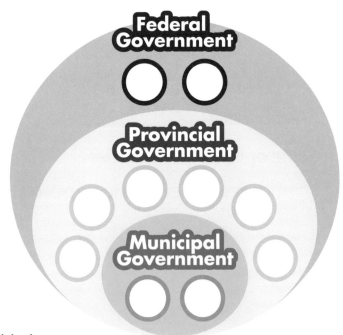

B. **Study the graphs about Canada's population and spending on health care. Then answer the questions.**

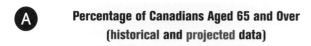

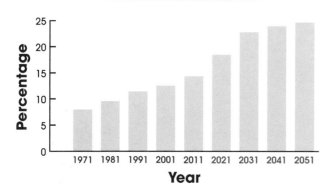

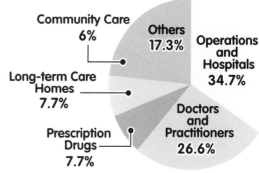

Graph A

1. Describe the trend for Canadians aged 65 and over.

   _____

2. How does this trend impact the spending on health care?

   _____

3. On which two categories does Ontario spend most?

   _____

Graph B

4. As the Canadian population ages, how will this category be affected? Explain.

   _____

   _____

5. *Make two suggestions to the government that support the health care needs for the aging population.*

   _____

   _____

Water Management

Canada is home to 7% of the globe's fresh water. Our landscape is defined by our lakes and rivers including the Great Lakes, the St. Lawrence River, and the Mackenzie River.

A. Fill in the blanks.

> *The responsibility for the provision of water and sanitation services is shared by the federal, provincial, and municipal governments. They jointly work to deliver clean water and resolve issues that would affect water quality.*

Federal Government

- 1._____ and protects water resources
- deals with water 2._____ shared with the U.S.
- leads 3._____ research
- allocates funds to the provincial and 4._____ governments
- monitors 5._____ and navigation

conserves
scientific
boundaries
fisheries
municipal

Provincial Government

- governs water 6._____ and sanitation
- takes action to resolve 7._____ issues
- regulates 8._____ and service quality

costs
ecosystems
quality

Municipal Government

- 9._____ safe drinking water
- collects and treats 10._____
- conducts water 11._____ tests

quality
waste water
delivers

Complete Canadian Curriculum • **Grade 5**

B. Study this bill that was presented to the Parliament of Canada. Then answer the questions.

Canada Water Preservation Act
Bill

Introductions:

first read to Parliament in September 2011 and again in March 2012

Description:

stating that Canada must protect the integrity of its ecosystems from the harmful impact of a large-scale removal of fresh water from the nation's major drainage basin

> *Before a bill becomes a law, it must get a majority vote in Parliament. Here are the arguments from each party.*

1. **Rate the arguments.**
   1 – most convincing
   4 – least convincing

   ◯ NDP   ◯ Green Party
   ◯ Liberal   ◯ Conservative

2. **If you were a Parliament member, would you vote for or against the bill? Explain.**

   _____

   _____

   _____

3. **Did the bill become a law?**
   (Do some research.)

   Yes / No

 NDP

I have seen other precious resources in our ground mined and exported with too little regard for Canadian priorities and needs. That must not happen with our water. We must pass this law to protect our waters from being exported to the U.S.

Liberal

The U.S. is at a crisis. They have 6% of the world's fresh water, but their population is nine times ours. At a conference, a U.S. government official was heard to say: "We don't have to worry about this (water shortage) because we'll just get the water from Canada." We need to protect our natural resource.

 **green** PARTY OF ONTARIO

This bill prohibits massive transfers of water. This bill needs to be legislated. We think we are a water-rich nation, but the reality is that we only have 9% of the world's renewable water. The U.S. has 6%. We are roughly in the same territory. If we allow a single transaction of the shipment of water in bulk from one drainage basin to another, we will have turned on the tap to impossible trade agreements with the U.S.

Conservative

The responsibility to manage natural resources has traditionally been at the provincial level. The federal government shares the responsibility when needed. Our provinces have put in place laws, regulations, or policies that prevent the transfer of water between basins or outside their boundaries. This bill does not need to become a law because it is duplicative.

Recycling and Waste Management

The responsibility for recycling and waste management is shared among the three levels of government. Their roles include imposing regulations and policies, collecting and transporting waste, and encouraging sustainable waste management practices.

A. **Fill in the blanks to learn the responsibilities of the three levels of government. Then identify and write the level of government that is responsible for each role.**

word bank: waste, recycles, homes, monitoring, manages, international

Federal Government

responsible for services on federal lands and resources; involved with interprovincial and 1._____ transport of 2._____ materials

Provincial Government

3._____ and sets policies for waste management including approving, licensing, and 4._____ of services

Municipal Government

collects, 5._____, and disposes of waste and recycle materials from 6._____, businesses, construction sites, and schools

7. collecting waste materials from construction sites _____

8. performing research and creating programs and practices that help reduce waste _____

9. passing legislation that defines hazardous materials _____

ISBN: 978-1-77149-033-7

B. **The graph displays how Ontarians' waste is managed, either disposed or diverted. Answer the questions about the graph.**

Every day, Ontario generates more than 33 000 tonnes of waste. This adds up to more than 12 million tonnes a year! Most of the waste is disposed in landfills while some of it is diverted (recycled, reused, or reduced).

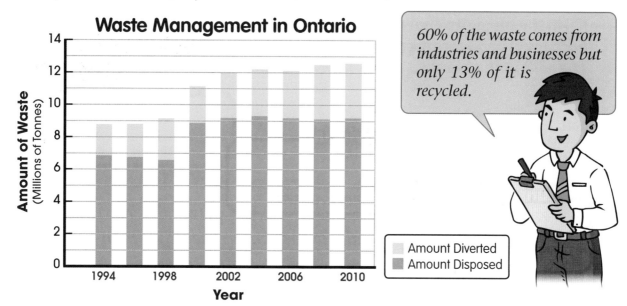

60% of the waste comes from industries and businesses but only 13% of it is recycled.

1. In 2010, about how much

    a. waste was disposed of?

    _____

    b. waste was diverted?

    _____

2. Describe the trend of the

    a. amount of total waste:

    _____

    b. amount of diverted waste:

    _____

3. Even though the amount of waste has stayed quite steady over the past decade, Ontarians are still generating a large amount of waste. What environmental problems will this cause?

    _____

    _____

4. Suggest two solutions to the problem.

    _____

    _____

20

Transportation

Transportation is a joint responsibility of all three levels of government. Traffic congestion is one of the major problems in big cities like Toronto.

A. **Fill in the blanks to show the responsibility of each level of government on transportation. Then fill in the blanks.**

Transportation in Canada

urban   intra-provincial
interprovincial

Municipal

_____
Transportation

Provincial

_____
Transportation

Federal

_____
Transportation

Over the last two decades, the federal government has been transferring some of its roles to private sectors and non-profit organizations.

Commercializing the Transportation System

more   expenditure   control   public
fewer   costs   benefits   investment

Advantages

• providing opportunities for company 1._____

• transportation users have 2._____ say

• reducing government 3._____

• 4._____ hurdles (e.g. getting consensus from the public to begin work)

Disadvantages

• higher 5._____ to the public (e.g. more toll roads)

• fewer government jobs and 6._____

• government has less 7._____ over developments

• may not meet the needs of the 8._____

ISBN: 978-1-77149-033-7

B. Look at the graphs and answer the questions.

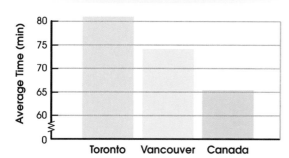

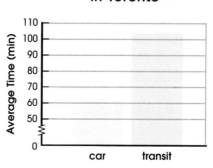

1. Compare the average commute time in Toronto with

    a. that of Vancouver. _____

    b. that of the whole country. _____

2. Compare the average commute time in Toronto between those who use cars and those who use transit.

    _____

3. Write two things indicated in the graphs about Toronto's transportation.

    _____

    _____

4. Make two suggestions to help Sally lower her transportation costs but still minimize the time she spends on the road.

    > *I live in Toronto and drive on Highway 407 for about 40 mins to go to work in Brampton. I pay $600 a month on toll. If I don't drive on the toll route, it will take me over 2 hours.*

    • _____

       _____

    • _____

       _____

Homelessness

In recent years, homelessness has become one of the major social issues in Canada, especially in cities such as Toronto and Vancouver. All three levels of government are looking for ways to solve this problem.

A. Fill in the blanks.

> There are different reasons for homelessness, but the inability to pay for living expenses is the main cause. The federal government is trying to reduce the homeless problem by funding different social programs and services. The provincial and municipal governments are responsible for the implementation of the programs.

Causes of Homelessness

- mental disorders
- inability to pay <u>1.   </u>
- escaping from <u>2.   </u> or abuse
- alcohol or <u>3.   </u> use problems
- exiting foster care or <u>4.   </u>
- low social assistance from the <u>5.   </u>

conflicts
drug
hospitalization
government
rent

federal   housing
affordable

Solutions from the Government

- In 1999, the National Homeless Initiative was created to fund <u>6.   </u> housing and support a range of services for the homeless.

- In 2007, the <u>7.   </u> government decided to spend $270 million between 2007 and 2009 to address homeless issues.

- In 2008, the Government of Canada announced that it would set aside $387.9 million per year for the next five years for <u>8.   </u> and homelessness programs.

ISBN: 978-1-77149-033-7

B.   Study the chart and answer the questions.

1.   Describe the changes in the population of people living

a.   outdoors:

_____

b.   in shelters:

_____

Homeless Population in Toronto

	2006	2013
Living Outdoors	735	447
Living in Shelters	3649	3970

2.   According to the data, do you think the government funding towards alleviating homelessness is effective?

_____

_____

3.   The demand for permanent housing among the homeless increased from 86% to 93% between 2006 and 2013. Check the possible solutions to help meet the demand. Then suggest one solution.

Ⓐ   provide funds for those in need of a home

Ⓑ   build more affordable housing

Ⓒ   shut down shelters to force the homeless to find housing

Ⓓ   subsidize rent based on income

✔   _____

4.   Solving the homeless problem helps build a better society. Check the positive outcomes it would bring about.

Ⓐ   lower crime rates

Ⓑ   reduced demand for health care services

Ⓒ   higher demand for police services

Ⓓ   improved overall make-up of the city

Taxation and Spending

All the services provided by the Canadian government come from taxation. There are many types of tax a taxpayer pays. In return, he or she can enjoy the public services the government provides.

A. Look at the chart. Fill in the blanks and answer the questions.

use   parks   value
facilities   sale   tax

Sources of Income
(City of Toronto)

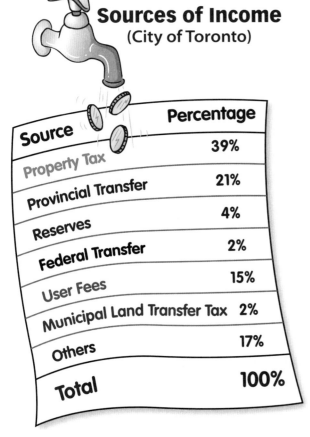

Source	Percentage
Property Tax	39%
Provincial Transfer	21%
Reserves	4%
Federal Transfer	2%
User Fees	15%
Municipal Land Transfer Tax	2%
Others	17%
Total	**100%**

Property Tax

amount of 1._____ is based on the value of land and its 2._____ (i.e. business or residential); the value is determined using market 3._____ standard

User Fees

payments for 4._____ including pools, skating rinks, and 5._____

Municipal Land Transfer Tax

one-time payment on 6._____ price of property (since 2006)

7. What are the three major sources of income?

    _____

8. If house prices increase, which two sources of income would change? Explain how.

    _____

    _____

ISBN: 978-1-77149-033-7

B.   Answer the questions by using the information from the graph.

Expenditure of City of Toronto

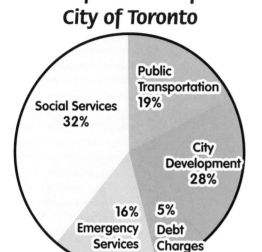

Toronto Transit Commission (TTC): 16%
Transportation Services: 3%

Public Libraries: 2%   Parks, Forestry, and Recreation: 4%
City Planning: 0.5%   Municipal Licensing and Standards: 1%
Economic Development and Culture: 0.5%   Others: 20%

Police Services: 10%   Fire Services: 4%
Medical Emergency Services: 2%

Shelter, Support, and Housing Administration: 9%
Children's Services: 4%   Long-term Care Homes: 2%
Public Health: 2%   Employment and Social Services: 15%

1.   Rank the types of expenditure of the City of Toronto (1 – least, 5 – most). Then identify the item in each type that incurs the most expenses.

(A)   Public Transportation: _____

(B)   City Development: _____

(C)   Emergency Services: _____

(D)   Social Services: _____

(E)   Debt Charges: N/A

2.   Below are some ways to reduce Toronto's debt. Pick one of them and describe what negative consequences it could bring to the city.

In 2012, Toronto's debt was $3.7 billion.

• increasing class size in schools
• charging fees for using libraries
• reducing government expenditure on police services

_____

_____

ISBN: 978-1-77149-033-7

Public Opinion

Canada has a democratic government system. As Canadian citizens, we have the means to work with the government in making the country the best it can be.

A. Fill in the blanks to show a citizen's participation in different government needs.

> In Canada, the general public elect the politicians who they think will represent them in their best interest. After elections, the public still have ways to share their opinions with government officials.

Municipal Level

- public can attend 1._____ to share concerns about their communities

- government makes decisions at 2._____

- public elect 3._____ from their ward (area) to represent them at these meetings

local councillors

town hall meetings

council meetings

Provincial Level

- public can attend the 4._____ and hear the proceedings

- government makes decisions at the 5._____

- public elect a Member of the 6._____ (MPP) to represent them at the Legislative Assembly

Provincial Legislative

Provincial Parliament

legislature

Federal Level

- government makes decisions in the 7._____ in Ottawa

- public elect a Member of the 8._____ (MP) to represent them at the House of Commons

House of Commons

Parliament

ISBN: 978-1-77149-033-7

B. **Circle the correct words to complete the report of the royal commission.**

*A **royal commission** is a public inquiry that is conducted by a team of experts appointed by the Governor General. Their goal is to make a detailed investigation into a national problem. A significant part of its research comes from public opinion. The reports would be sent to the Government of Canada for appropriate action.*

A Royal Commission Report: Future of Health Care in Canada

Roy Romanow
appointed to manage the Royal Commission on the Future of Health Care in Canada in 2001

less	equal	status	transparent
medical	healthiest	health care	

Observations

- We support the values of the health care system – _____ and timely access to medical services for all citizens, regardless of _____ and wealth.

- The federal government contributes _____ to health care than it did before the 1990s.

- There are inefficiencies between supply and demand, which have led to unacceptable wait times for some _____ procedures.

Recommendations

- We need to pay closer attention to where the _____ funding is going.

- We need a _____ health care system where information is shared with Canadians.

- We need to have a prevention and wellness strategy so that Canadians are the world's _____ people.

Result In 2004, the Government of Canada granted a transfer of an additional $41 billion over the next 10 years to support the health care system.

ISBN: 978-1-77149-033-7

Public Activism

Canadian citizens can take an active role in addressing environmental and social issues in their community. These actions are called public activism, which plays an important role in the government's decision-making.

A. Match each form of public activism with its description.

Public Activism is the use of direct actions in an effort to show one's opposition to a change or support of a cause.

boycott
rally
street march
strike
sit-in
hunger strike
writing letters to politicians

Over the last decade, using the Internet to initiate activism to address one's political concern has become increasingly popular.

1.

the most peaceful form of activism

2.

a mass group walking from one designated point to another

3.

withdrawal from commercial or social relations as a protest

4.

a group of participants fasts as an act of protest

Forms of Public Activism

5.

withdrawal of workers' services for the approval of workers' demands or in protest against terms imposed by an employer

6.

a large gathering of people for a protest or showing support for a cause

7.

one or more people occupying an area for a protest

ISBN: 978-1-77149-033-7

B. **Study the case below to see how public activism could make an impact. Do the matching and fill in the blanks.**

The Oak Ridge's Moraine is a largely undeveloped belt of hills, forests, and streams across the northern edge of Toronto. It acts as a natural filter for rainwater and snow melt, which flow to rivers and streams and into the lakes. In the late 1980s, public awareness was brought to conserve the moraine as land developers wanted to develop the area. Many people were opposing the idea of construction because they wanted to conserve the moraine.

Stakeholders' Views and Actions

Local Residents
◯ ◯

Naturalists
◯ ◯

Biologists
◯ ◯

Hydrologists
◯ ◯

Land Developers
◯ ◯

Views

Ⓐ It adds greenery.

Ⓑ It is inhabited by many species.

Ⓒ Developing it eases crowding in Toronto.

Ⓓ It serves to purify groundwater.

Ⓔ It is a diverse plant and animal habitat.

Actions

Ⓐ made a case against the threat to groundwater quality

Ⓑ hired scientists to argue that construction could be done without damaging the area

Ⓒ wrote to politicians to voice their concerns

Ⓓ made a case to protect over 900 species inhabiting the area

Ⓔ gathered 450 scientists to petition against developing the area

Outcome (Do some research.)

In 2001, a conservation plan was released. According to the plan, the moraine was to be divided into _____ zones with increasingly stringent controls on development in each. It limited the development to no more than _____ % of the land mass of the moraine.

ISBN: 978-1-77149-033-7 Complete Canadian Curriculum • **Grade 5**

Photo Credits:

Unit 16 p. 264 – Parliament Hill in Ottawa

"Centre Block - Parliament Hill" by Saffron Blaze - Own work. Licensed under Creative Commons Attribution-Share Alike 3.0 via Wikimedia Commons - http://commons. wikimedia.org/wiki/File:Centre_Block_-_Parliament_Hill.jpg#mediaviewer/File:Centre_ Block_-_Parliament_Hill.jpg

Unit 16 p. 265 – Legislative Building in Ontario

"Pink Palace Toronto 2010" by Benson Kua from Toronto, Canada - The Pink PalaceUploaded by Skeezix1000. Licensed under Creative Commons Attribution-Share Alike 2.0 via Wikimedia Commons - http://commons.wikimedia.org/wiki/ File:Pink_Palace_Toronto_2010.jpg#mediaviewer/File:Pink_Palace_Toronto_2010.jpg

Unit 16 p. 265 – City Hall in Toronto

"City Hall, Toronto, Ontario" by Jerome Decq - originally posted to Flickr as Toronto City Hall. Licensed under Creative Commons Attribution 2.0 via Wikimedia Commons - http://commons.wikimedia.org/wiki/File:City_Hall,_Toronto,_Ontario. jpg#mediaviewer/File:City_Hall,_Toronto,_Ontario.jpg

ISBN: 978-1-77149-033-7

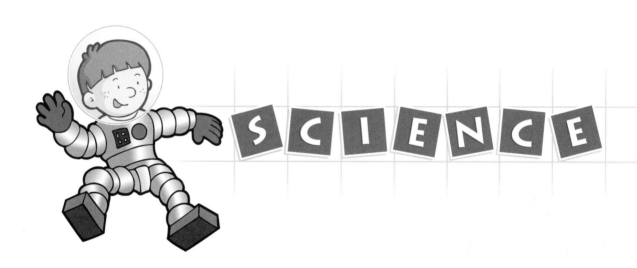

SCIENCE

Matter

Hm...this must be gas.

- Matter is anything that takes up space.
- Matter exists in three states – solid, liquid, and gas.

solid   liquid   gas

A.   Look at the picture. Check the things that are matter.

a cloud

sunlight ✓

a ball ✓

a game

a daydream

a beach umbrella

a sandcastle ✓

a shell ✓

a chat

water

front crawl

B. **Write "solid", "liquid", or "gas" for each description.**

1. My shape stays the same.

   Solid

2. My shape may change, and I can take up more space or less space, depending on the container I am in.

   gas

3. My shape may change, but I will take up the same amount of space.

   liquid

C. **What state of matter does each group of pictures show? Label the group. Then draw one more thing that belongs to each group.**

1. gas

2. Solid

3. liquid

 Science Fact

While most matter can exist in all three states, the only thing we commonly see in its three forms is water.

Water

Measures of Matter

- Mass measures the amount of matter in a substance.
- Density measures the amount of matter in a given space.
- Volume measures the amount of space matter takes up.

You are bigger than I, but we have the same weight.

A. **Read what Misha says. Circle the correct words to complete the sentences.**

Weight is the measure of the effect gravity has on mass. So if a force acts against gravity, or the amount of gravity changes, weight changes but mass does not.

1. Misha feels heavier / (lighter) in the water than he

    does on land even though his mass / (weight) has not changed.

2. Clark has the same weight / (mass) on the moon as he does on

    Earth even though he is (heavier) / lighter on Earth.

B.   Colour the matter with the greatest density.

1.

2.

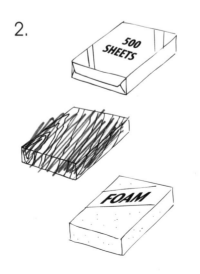

3.

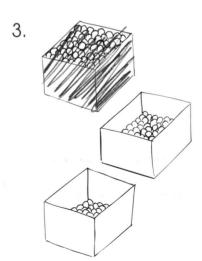

ISBN: 978-1-77149-033-7

C. Put the matter in order from the one with the least volume to the one with the greatest. Write 1 to 4 in the circles.

1.

2.

D. Play "I spy". Find the answers.

I spy with my little eyes. I can see something that...

1. has a greater volume but less mass than the watermelon

beach ball

2. has a smaller volume and less mass than the book

crayon's box

3. is denser than but equal in volume to the sponge

Buney book

4. has about the same mass as but smaller volume than the beach ball

Watermelone

Science Fact

Because of all the salt in it, sea water has a higher density than fresh water. It is so dense that you actually float better in an ocean than in a lake.

Changing States of Matter

Abracadabra – liquid to gas!

- Matter can change from one state to another.
- Changes in matter can be reversible or irreversible.

A. Look at the pictures. Tell the states of the matter before and after the changes. Then fill in the blanks with the given words.

liquid   **condensed   melted   solidified   vapourized**

1.

   Change: from <u>Solidified</u> to ~~liquid~~ <u>Melted</u>

   The snowman has <u>Vapourized</u>

2.

   Change: from <u>liquid</u> to <u>Solidified</u>

   The cake batter has <u>Condensed</u> .

3.

   Change: from <u>Solidified</u> to <u>Melted</u>

   The water vapour has <u>Vapourized</u> .

4.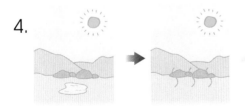

   Change: from <u>liquid</u> to <u>Vapourized</u>

   The puddle has <u>Vapourized</u> .

ISBN: 978-1-77149-033-7

B. Tell what must be done to the matter on the left to get the matter on the right. Fill in the blanks with "take away" or "give".

1. ice ➡ water   _____give_____ heat

2. ice cream ➡ melted ice cream   _____give_____ heat

3. raw egg ➡ cooked egg   _____give_____ heat

4. molten lava ➡ solid rock   _take away_ heat

5. melted butter ➡ butter   _takeaway_ heat

6. wax candle ➡ melted wax   _give_____ heat

C. Tell whether the changes in matter are reversible or irreversible. Write the letters.

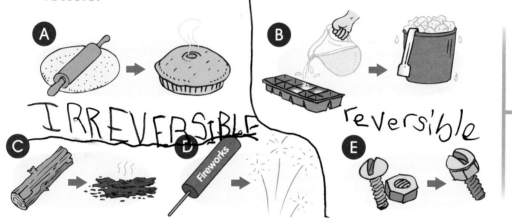

Reversible

Irreversible

IRREVERSIBLE

reversible

Experiment – Change the state of water!

- Pour cold water into a glass and let it sit in a warm room for a few minutes.

Why does water form on the outside of the glass? Where does it come from?

_____

Science Fact

Ice melts at a temperature of 1°C; steel needs a temperature of about 1500°C to melt.

Melting point
1500°C

steel

4

Properties of Matter

- We describe matter by its different properties.
- Properties of matter determine what we use the matter for.

A. Read the passage. Circle the eleven common properties of different materials.

Matter can be described by its properties. (Colour)(size)(hardness,) and (taste) are properties we think about every day. Matter can have other properties too. When we say a (cinnamon bun's) coating is ~~sticky~~ we are describing its viscosity. The (bun) itself has a smooth texture. The (knife) and (fork) we use to eat it have a shiny lustre, and have an opaque clarity, meaning we can't see through them.

We may want something sweet and in a liquid state for snack, like (lemonade.) We can't see or feel the (sugar) in our lemonade because it is dissolved; sugar has high solubility in (water.) The cook, making more cinnamon buns, is working with (dough) that has good malleability, changing from a round blob to a tasty, sticky, smooth spiral.

B. Look at the words you circled. Write the property that each word describes.

1. shiny   foar/knife
2. salty   gaughvsinominbun
3. large   siSe
4. brittle   hawdness
5. dissolves   Sugar
6. gas   Cawler

C. **Match each description with the correct picture. Then write another word that describes the matter.**

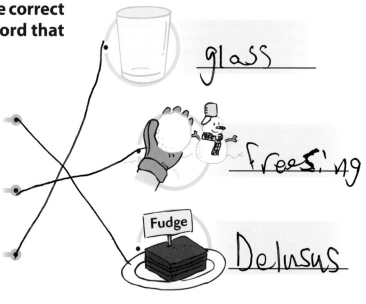

glass

1 I am a soft and sweet solid. You can't see through me because my clarity is opaque.

2 I am soft and smooth but very malleable. I'm cold and opaque.

freesing

3 I am transparent, smooth, and hard. You cannot change my shape because I am not malleable.

Fudge

Deluses

4 I taste good in soup, where I completely dissolve. Compared to most other things, I'm considered quite small.

SALT

grosc

D. **Circle the properties you would want your blanket to have.**

Making a blanket

Hardness: (soft as feathers) / hard as rock

Colour: brown / (orange) / (pink) / (yellow)

Size: large / small / (king-sized)

Texture: rough / prickly / (velvety)

🧪 **Science Fact**

Plastics are useful to us because we can base on their properties to make different things. A bike may have hard plastic parts, but polar fleece clothing is an example of soft plastic.

Weather and Climate

- Weather is what is going on in the air – temperature, moisture, and movement – at a certain place and time.
- Climate is a pattern of weather in large areas over a long period of time.

I like summer.

A. Read the sentences. Draw lines to tell whether they refer to weather or climate.

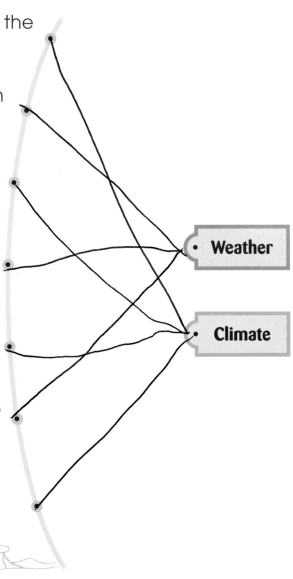

1. Areas near the equator receive the sun's rays most directly.

2. Large, dark clouds usually bring rain or snow.

3. Higher areas of land are not as warm as lower areas.

4. Storms and heavy snowfall sometimes close roads and schools.

5. Canadians often holiday in warmer parts of the world.

6. A hailstorm might ruin a whole crop of wheat.

7. Polar bears require cold winters and cool summers.

- Weather
- Climate

ISBN: 978-1-77149-033-7

B. Write "weather" or "climate". Then put the pictures in the circles in the correct groups. Write the letters.

Weather

B

Climate

A

A

Future site of the Summer Olympics

B

C. Match the descriptions with the correct climate words. Write the words on the lines.

~~desert~~   ~~mountain~~   ~~polar~~   ~~sub-polar~~
~~subtropical~~   ~~temperate~~   ~~tropical~~

1. always very hot, rain   tropical

2. very cold, frozen ground   Mountain

3. mild climate throughout the year   Sub-tropical

4. long winters, cool summers   Polar

5. very little moisture, hot in daytime, cold at night   desert

6. hot summers, mild winters, rain   temperate

7. higher ground makes it colder, fewer plants   Sub-Poaler

Science Fact

Climate change, caused in part by human activities, will change the weather patterns of different climates around the world.

ISBN: 978-1-77149-033-7

Temperature

- Air temperature, the amount of heat in the air, is measured with a thermometer.
- Many things we do are based on what the temperature is outside.

A. **Look at the record of the average monthly temperatures of Weatherton last year. Complete the broken-line graph and answer the questions.**

Jan	-8°C
Feb	-2°C
Mar	1°C
Apr	8°C
May	12°C
Jun	18°C
Jul	25°C
Aug	26°C
Sep	19°C
Oct	8°C
Nov	3°C
Dec	-4°C

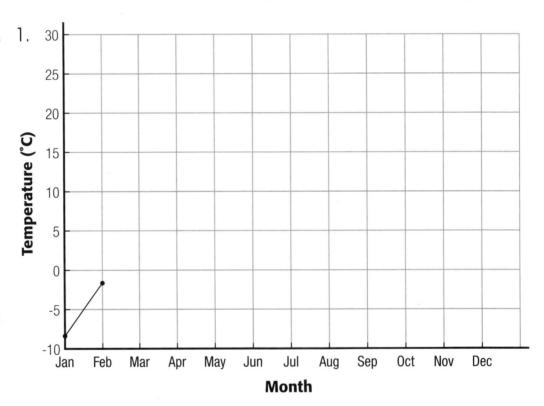

The Average Monthly Temperatures of Weatherton Last Year

1.

2. Which month has the highest average temperature? _____

3. Which month has the lowest average temperature? _____

4. If you want to go skating outside, the temperature must be below 0°C. During which month(s) would you go skating?

_____

B. **Look at the graph on the previous page again and the outfits below. Answer the question.**

These are the outfits I wore last year. In which months do you think I wore them?

1. _____

2. _____

3. _____

C. **Colour the thermometers to show the temperatures for the microclimates.**

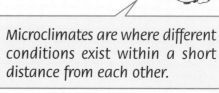

Microclimates are where different conditions exist within a short distance from each other.

Science Fact

One of the hottest places on Earth is Libya, where temperatures can reach nearly 60°C. Antarctica is the coldest, with temperatures as low as -89°C.

Antarctica
-89°C

Water Cycle

The Waters!

- All the water that is on Earth is the same as it always was and always will be. It goes round and round in the water cycle.

A. **Read the descriptions about the water cycle. Write the letters.**

A Water in the ocean evaporates into the air, becoming water vapour.

B Clouds form when water vapour joins with dust particles in the air.

C Rainwater soaks into the soil, and below that into the underground.

D The sun heats the air around the earth and oceans.

E An underground water spring flows into a stream, which joins with a river that leads to the ocean.

F Water droplets in clouds join together, getting so heavy they come down from the clouds as precipitation, usually as snow or rain.

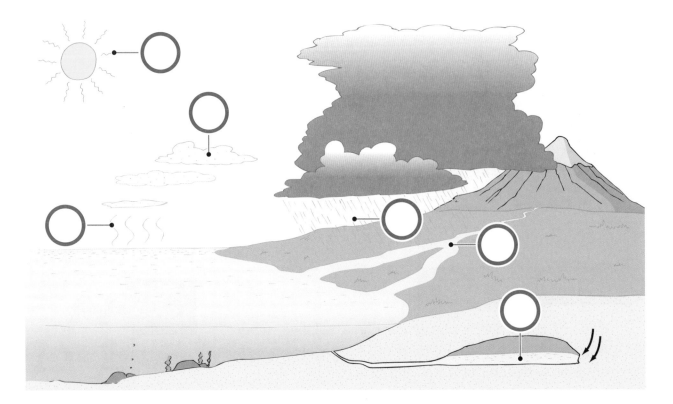

ISBN: 978-1-77149-033-7

B. Check the pictures of the water that may be the same as the water in your glass.

1.

2.

3.

4.

5.

C. Where is the Earth's water? Read what Dr. Green says. Check the correct graph.

Most of the water on Earth is in the oceans and is salty. Only a small portion of it is fresh water. The majority of fresh water is locked up in glaciers and ice caps. The rest is underground and in lakes.

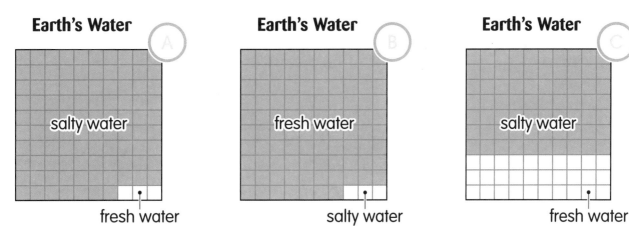

Earth's Water A

salty water

fresh water

Earth's Water B

fresh water

salty water

Earth's Water C

salty water

fresh water

Science Fact

The atmosphere has a very important role in the water cycle although it holds less than one thousandth of the entire world's water.

8

Clouds and Precipitation

- Clouds are named for their shapes and height in the sky.
- Not all clouds produce rain or snow, but all kinds of precipitation come from clouds.

A.   Read the rules to see how to name a cloud. Then name the clouds.

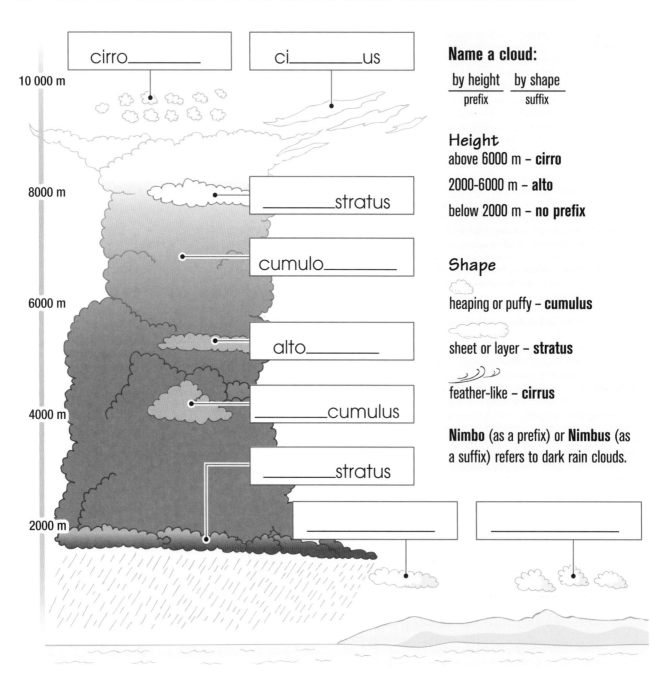

cirro_____

ci_____us

10 000 m

8000 m

_____stratus

cumulo_____

6000 m

alto_____

4000 m

_____cumulus

_____stratus

2000 m

Name a cloud:

by height	by shape
prefix	suffix

Height

above 6000 m – **cirro**

2000-6000 m – **alto**

below 2000 m – **no prefix**

Shape

heaping or puffy – **cumulus**

sheet or layer – **stratus**

feather-like – **cirrus**

Nimbo (as a prefix) or **Nimbus** (as a suffix) refers to dark rain clouds.

ISBN: 978-1-77149-033-7

B.   Fill in the blanks with the names of the clouds.

1.   Puffed up clouds 3 km above ground are _____ .

2.   A low sheet of cloud is _____ .

3.   A flat cloud at 8 km high is _____ .

4.   A cloud that spans all three layers of sky is _____ .

C.   Name the precipitation to complete the crossword puzzle.

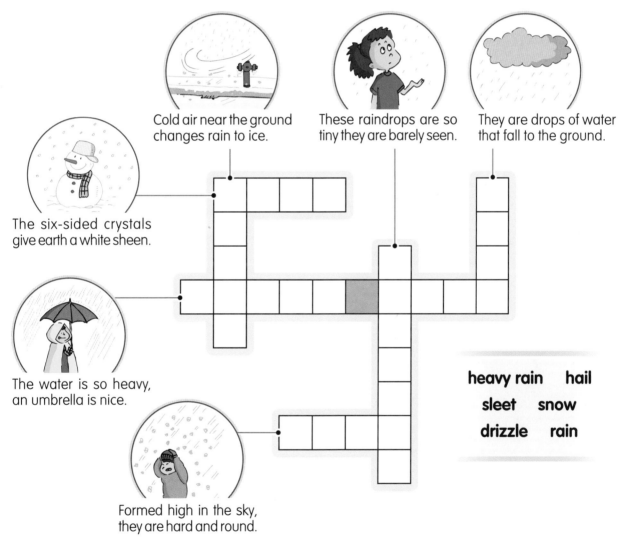

Cold air near the ground changes rain to ice.

These raindrops are so tiny they are barely seen.

They are drops of water that fall to the ground.

The six-sided crystals give earth a white sheen.

The water is so heavy, an umbrella is nice.

Formed high in the sky, they are hard and round.

heavy rain   hail

sleet   snow

drizzle   rain

Science Fact

Clouds are usually not just water droplets. Water vapour in the air condenses around dust and other tiny particles in the sky.

9

Wind

- Wind speed is numbered from 0 to 12 on the Beaufort Scale.
- Wind is very useful in nature and to us.
- Winds are named for the directions they are coming from.

A. **Look at the Beaufort Scale and each pair of pictures. Describe the wind in (A). Then give the wind in (B) a scale and description.**

1. (A) scale 4:

_____

(B) scale ____ :

_____

2. (A) scale 2:

_____

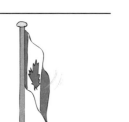

(B) scale ____ :

_____

3. (A) scale 11:

_____

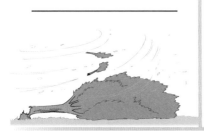

(B) scale ____ :

_____

Beaufort Scale

Rating	Description (speed in km/h)	
0	Calm	(<1.5)
1	Light air	(1.5 – 5)
2	Light breeze	(6 – 11)
3	Gentle breeze	(12 –19)
4	Moderate breeze	(20 – 30)
5	Fresh breeze	(31 – 40)
6	Strong breeze	(41 – 50)
7	Moderate gale	(51 – 60)
8	Fresh gale	(61 – 67)
9	Strong gale	(68 – 84)
10	Whole gale	(85 – 100)
11	Storm	(101 – 120)
12	Hurricane	(>120)

ISBN: 978-1-77149-033-7

B. **See how the winds are at work. Match the descriptions with the pictures and fill in the missing letters.**

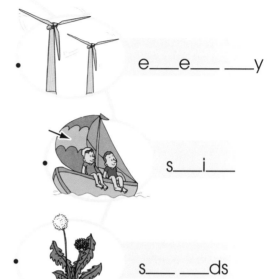

• e___e___ ___y

Wind helps them travel to
where they can grow. •

• s___i___

This part of the boat would •
not work without wind.

Wind moves the turbines •
to provide this for people.

• s___ ___ds

C. **Read what Timothy says. Tell the directions of the winds.**

The arrow of a wind vane points in the direction the wind comes from.
Winds are named for the direction they are coming from.

southerly   westerly   easterly   southeasterly   northwesterly

1.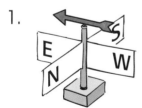

2.

3.

_____   _____   _____

Science Fact

The jet stream, a river of fast moving air in the sky, can make
a plane trip across Canada half an hour faster.

10

Extreme Weather

- *Storms, caused by turbulence in the atmosphere, come in different shapes and sizes.*
- *Sometimes when there is too much or too little precipitation, a number of disasters are possible.*

A. Match the descriptions with the words.

1. heavy rain •

2. a hurricane formed in the Indian Ocean •

3. snow and strong winds in cold temperatures •

4. a churning, spiral cloud formed over tropical oceans •

5. characterized by a funnel cloud with extremely strong winds •

6. electrically charged, billowing clouds, lightning and hard-driving rain •

7. a hurricane formed in the South China Sea •

8. heavy snowfall •

• **tornado**

• **cyclone**

Indian Ocean

• **blizzard**

• **hurricane**

• **thunderstorm**

• **rainstorm**

• **typhoon**

Hong Kong

• **snowstorm**

ISBN: 978-1-77149-033-7

B. Write whether the following happens due to "too much precipitation" or "too little precipitation".

1.

_____

2.

_____

3.

_____

4.

_____

Experiment – Take a closer look at snowflakes!

The snowflakes will hold their shapes longer than usual when they are on cold construction paper.

Things needed:
- a magnifying glass
- black construction paper
- a snowy day

Steps:

1. Put the black construction paper in the freezer for at least an hour before use.

2. When snow falls, catch some flakes on the frozen construction paper.

3. Examine the snowflakes with the magnifying glass.

How many sides does each snowflake have?

_____

Science Fact

Not all snowflakes are shaped like stars. There are columns, plates, columns with caps, and needles, too! Their only common feature is their six sides.

Weather Station

- Weather stations have special instruments for measuring and recording weather.
- Scientists who study the weather are meteorologists. They use information gathered at weather stations to predict future weather conditions.

A. Look at the function of each weather instrument. Name the instrument. Write the letters.

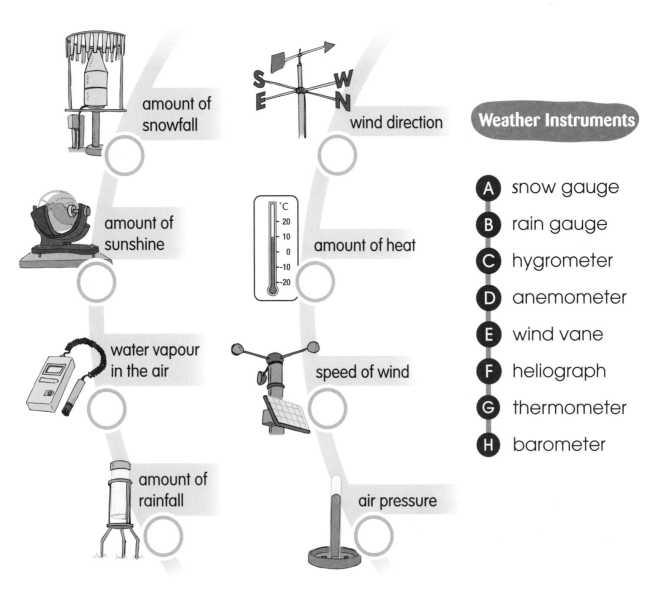

amount of snowfall

wind direction

Weather Instruments

amount of sunshine

amount of heat

- **A** snow gauge
- **B** rain gauge
- **C** hygrometer
- **D** anemometer
- **E** wind vane
- **F** heliograph
- **G** thermometer
- **H** barometer

water vapour in the air

speed of wind

amount of rainfall

air pressure

ISBN: 978-1-77149-033-7

B. **Read what the meteorologist says. Then tell who will be most affected by the information gathered at the weather station. Check the correct answers.**

> Dr. Smith, can you tell us what the weather will be like tomorrow?

1. Which sport teams will not practise tomorrow?

(A) Golf Grannies

(B) Serious Soccer Souls

> According to the information we collected, there will be a snowstorm tomorrow...

(C) Crazy Cross-Country Skiers

2. What does the store stock up on?

(A) umbrellas   (B) snow shovels   (C) boots

3. Who will stay home from work tomorrow?

(A) gardener   (B) veterinarian   (C) school bus driver

C. **Answer the questions.**

1. Give one reason why it is important to know what the weather conditions have been.

_____

_____

2. Give one reason why it is important to know what the weather conditions will be.

_____

_____

Science Fact

Weather stations keep their instruments far from the cover of buildings, trees, and hills. Shade and wind barriers will distort the results of some measurements.

12

Conservation of Energy

- The energy that we use comes from various places and is either renewable or non-renewable.
- Energy cannot be created or destroyed. Rather, it takes on other forms.

A. **Read what Nancy says. Match the pictures with the source of energy. Then tell whether each source of energy is renewable (R) or non-renewable (NR).**

Some sources of energy are good for future generations because they are renewable, which means they are always available for use. Other sources of energy, being non-renewable, take a very long time to accumulate, and cannot be replaced.

1. coal   ◯ : ____

2. biomass   ◯ : ____

3. oil   ◯ : ____

4. wind   ◯ : ____

5. solar   ◯ : ____

6. hydro   ◯ : ____

7. natural gas ◯ : ____

ISBN: 978-1-77149-033-7

B. See how the device or structure shows the law of the conservation of energy. Write the change of energy in each situation.

chemical   electrical   gravitational   heat   mechanical

1.

Energy change:

from _____ energy

to _____ energy

The Law of the Conservation of Energy

Not Created or Destroyed – Just Changed

2.

Energy change:

from _____ energy

to _____ energy

3.

In a car, _____ energy stored in the gasoline is changed into _____ energy that makes the wheels move. Thermal energy as heat is released as well.

C. Fill in the blanks with "kinetic" or "potential" to complete what Simon says.

The _____ energy in the stretched elastic is converted into _____ energy when it is "released".

Science Fact

Over half of the garbage that we throw away is organic, which means that it is stuff that came from living things. This ends up in our landfills and as it decays, it produces methane gas that, when collected, can be used to generate electricity.

13

The Wise Use of Energy

- We must use energy wisely, as our non-renewable sources, which we rely on so heavily, will not last forever.
- Everyone can do a little more to conserve energy.

A. Read what the people say. Tell whether each of them is a "wise energy user" or "unwise energy user".

1 I buy whatever is on sale. I don't even know what "watt" means; they are just light bulbs, after all.

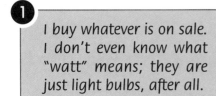

_____

2 I don't know what I'd do without my bike. I get a workout on my way to work, and I don't have to pay for parking.

_____

3 With this job, I found myself in a position of being able to choose my new vehicle, so I chose the most fuel efficient, environmentally friendly car that I could find.

_____

4 I have the money, but why should I spend it on an energy efficient refrigerator? This old one has been my parents' for 25 years, and it still works!

_____

5 We have tried to cut down on our meat consumption. We eat more vegetables, nuts, and fruit that we buy from local farmers.

_____

ISBN: 978-1-77149-033-7

B. Circle the correct words to complete the sentences.

Things to Do to Conserve Energy

1. Turn the thermostat up / down when everyone goes to bed in winter.

2. Use / Don't use blankets and socks to keep warm at night.

3. Find the cracks where the cold air is entering your house and let / seal them.

4. Connect all stereo and TV equipment to a power bar / separately so that all the parts of the systems will be easy to turn off.

5. If you must leave your computer on all the time, turn on / off the printer and the monitor.

6. Use natural / artificial light whenever you can.

7. Turn lights on / off when they are not being used.

8. Don't take long / short , hot showers.

C. Complete the chart to tell how to conserve energy.

Things I Do to Conserve Energy	Things I Could Do to Conserve Energy	Things I will Try to Do to Conserve Energy

Every spring, most Canadians set their clocks one hour ahead for daylight saving time. This extra daylight in the evening means less energy is used to light our homes.

14

Forces and Structures

This is compression!

- Many different types of forces act upon structures.
- Most structures must be able to withstand two common types of forces: compression and tension.

A. Dr. Shoes is doing a "boot test". Look at each picture. Name the force that acts upon the boot.

bending   sliding   squeezing   stretching   twisting

1. _____

2. _____

3. _____

4. _____

5. _____

B. Name the words that mean the same.

1. sliding force   _____

2. twisting force   _____

3. stretching force   _____

4. squeezing force   _____

5. bending force   _____

compression
shearing
tension
torsion
bending

C. Label each arrow with the right kind of force: tension or compression.

1.

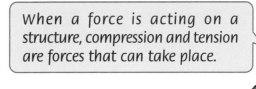

When a force is acting on a structure, compression and tension are forces that can take place.

compression ↓

2.

3.

4.

5.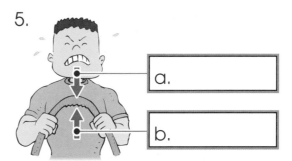

a.

b.

Experiment – Free-standing Structure

Using 50 straws and 2 metres of masking tape, make the tallest free-standing structure possible that will support a marble.

e.g.

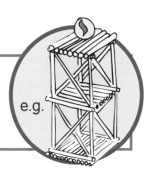

Science Fact

The arch bridge is one of the oldest types of bridges. It is very strong because it can change the downward force of its own weight, and any other weight pressing down on it, into an outward force towards its very strong sides and bases.

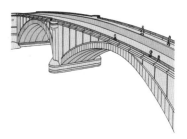

15

Forces and Mechanical Advantage

- Changing something in a simple machine can sometimes change the amount of force needed to move or lift an object.
- Mechanical advantage is a measurement of how this force is changed by using a simple machine of mechanism.

A. Look at the pictures in each pair. Check the one that requires less force to do the job.

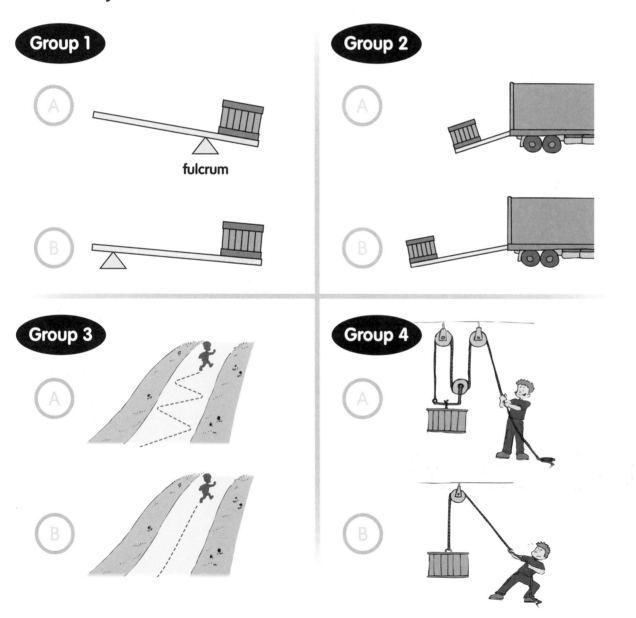

Group 1

Ⓐ

fulcrum

Ⓑ

Group 2

Ⓐ

Ⓑ

Group 3

Ⓐ

Ⓑ

Group 4

Ⓐ

Ⓑ

ISBN: 978-1-77149-033-7

B. **Look at each pair of pictures on the previous page again. Then fill in the blanks and answer the questions.**

1.

Group 1

a. Which picture shows the greater mechanical advantage?

_____

b. Moving the fulcrum closer to the load will _____
mechanical advantage.   gain/lose

2.

Group 2 What would you do to the ramp length to make the job of getting the object into the truck even easier?

_____

3.

Group 3 Which hiker is getting the better workout? Explain.

_____

4.

Group 4 In B, there is no mechanical advantage in using a single fixed pulley. Why use it then?

_____

C. **Find and circle eight words that are related to force.**

mechanical advantage   stop   rainfall

force   stretching   temperature   tension

torsion   bending   shearing   compression

Science Fact

Archimedes of Syracuse (287 BCE – 212 BCE) was a great mathematician who invented the compound pulley. He once used a pulley system to pull ships onto a position that had previously required a lot of manpower.

a pulley system →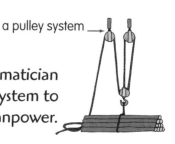

16

Cells

Hi! I'm one of your cells.

- Cells are the building blocks of all living things.
- Cells can be in different shapes and sizes, but almost all of them have the same parts.
- Animal cells of the same shape and size work together to make up larger body tissue.

A. **Fill in the missing letters to name the different parts of a cell. Then draw lines to match the parts with the descriptions and answer the questions.**

cell membrane   cytoplasm   nucleus   organelles

1.

A Cell

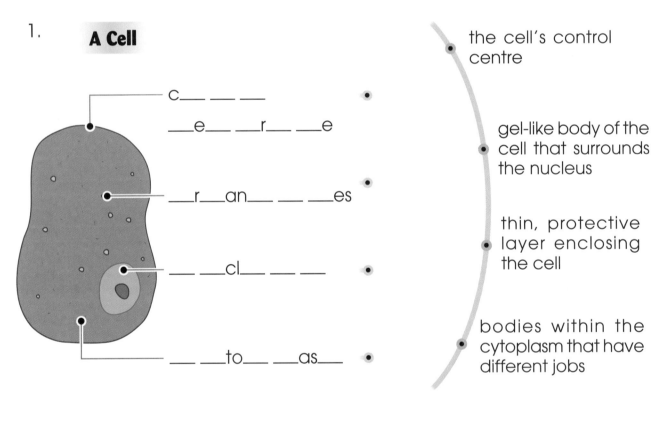

c__ __ __

__e__ __r__ __e

__r__an__ __ __es

__ __cl__ __ __

__ __to__ __as__

the cell's control centre

gel-like body of the cell that surrounds the nucleus

thin, protective layer enclosing the cell

bodies within the cytoplasm that have different jobs

2. Which part of the cell controls

a. the cell's function? _____

b. the amount of water entering and leaving the cell? _____

B. **Read what Dr. Stein says. Help him complete the drawing of the skin cells of an onion.**

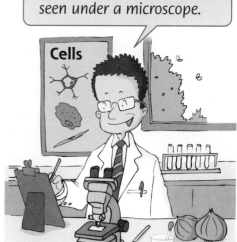

Cells of onion skin can be seen under a microscope.

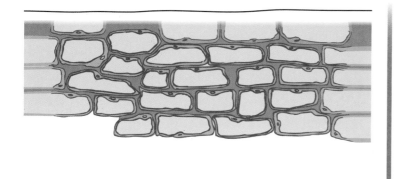

Cells of Onion Skin

C. **Read the following. Then tell what cell each picture shows. Fill in the blanks with the words in bold.**

Cells of the same shape and size make up a tissue. Tissues make up organs. **Skin** cells work together to form skin tissue. Longer **muscle** cells make up muscle tissue, and **nerve** cells build nervous tissue.

1.

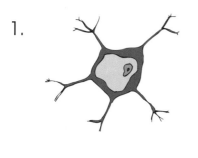

_____ cell

2.

_____ cell

3.

_____ cell

Science Fact

Humans and most other animals are made up of millions of cells, but some animals contain only one cell. Barely visible to the naked eye, one-celled protozoa are also the world's smallest animals.

17

Musculoskeletal System

My name's Skeleton.

- Bones hold our body up and protect our organs.
- Skeletal muscles work with the bones to let us move. This is our musculoskeletal system.
- Joints are where two bones connect. Different joints allow for different types of movement.

A. **Name the bones in the skeleton. Then draw lines to match them with the descriptions.**

| humerus | femur | vertebra | tibia | rib | mandible | patella | frontal bone |

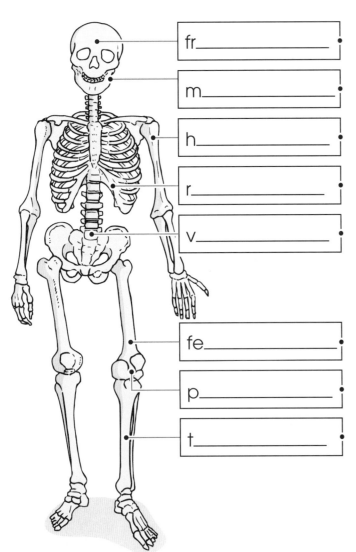

fr_____

m_____

h_____

r_____

v_____

fe_____

p_____

t_____

one of a set of bones protecting your heart, lungs, and liver

a long bone connected to the shoulder

a "cap" for a well-used joint

a part of your skull

the only movable bone in your head

the longest bone in your body

known as the shinbone

one of the 26 bones that make up your spine

ISBN: 978-1-77149-033-7

B. **Read what Susan says. Help her complete the puzzle by writing the names of the muscles.**

deltoid
pectorals
quadriceps
biceps
frontalis

Skeletal muscles stretch over joints to connect two bones. Together, muscles and bones allow our bodies to move.

muscle that moves the shoulder

upper arm muscle

muscle of the forehead

chest muscles

muscle on the front of the thigh

C. **Identify these types of joints.**

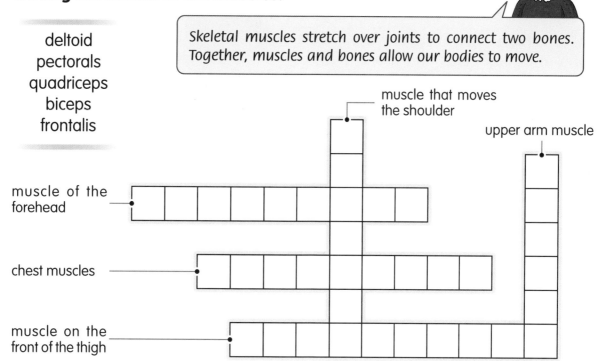

1.

2.

3.

4.

5.

Types of Joints

ball and socket
hinge
pivot

Science Fact

Facial muscles don't help us lift, walk, or do any kind of work, but they do help us communicate our feelings.

ISBN: 978-1-77149-033-7

Complete Canadian Curriculum • Grade 5

18

Nervous System

You have nerves in your tail.

- The nervous system is made up of the brain, spinal cord, and many, many nerves placed all over the body.

A. Read the passage. Label the parts of the nervous system with the words in bold.

Protected by the skull and a liquid membrane called the meninges, the brain is our body's control centre. It is made up of three main parts: the **brain stem**, the **cerebellum**, and the **cerebrum**. The brain stem connects the brain to the **spinal cord**. It makes us breathe and swallow, and do other things we need to do to live. Behind the brain stem, the cerebellum controls our balance and our muscle coordination. The largest part of our brain, the cerebrum, is the thinking part of our brain. Giving a speech, counting change, and planning a science experiment are all activities that begin with the cerebrum.

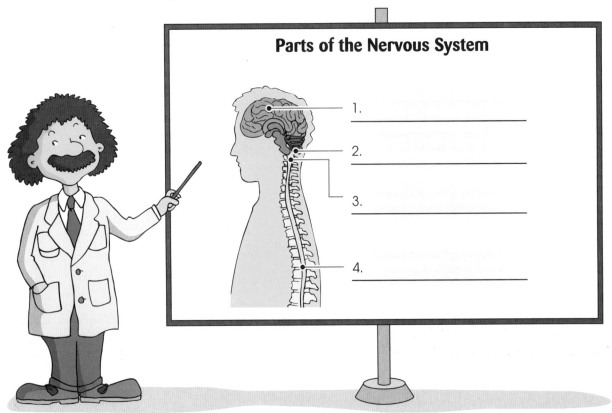

Parts of the Nervous System

1. _____
2. _____
3. _____
4. _____

B. Read the passage on the previous page again. Answer the questions.

1. Which part of the brain is responsible for

a. making your heart beat? _____

b. a daydream? _____

c. helping you walk along a narrow log? _____

2. Which two things protect our brain?

_____

3. What is our body's control centre?

_____

4. What is connected to the brain by the brain stem?

_____

C. Find and colour the nervous system words.

meninges		nerves		foot	
	kidney		skull		
heart		teeth		skin	
	cerebellum		spinal cord		
brain stem		nose		cerebrum	

Science Fact

In proportion to their body size, humans have the largest brain of all the animals.

19

Respiratory System

- All we do is breathe in and out, and the respiratory system does the job of getting oxygen to our blood cells, and releasing as waste the carbon dioxide we do not need.
- The respiratory system needs clean air to stay healthy.

A. Label the parts of the respiratory system. Then match the descriptions with the words in the diagram.

1.

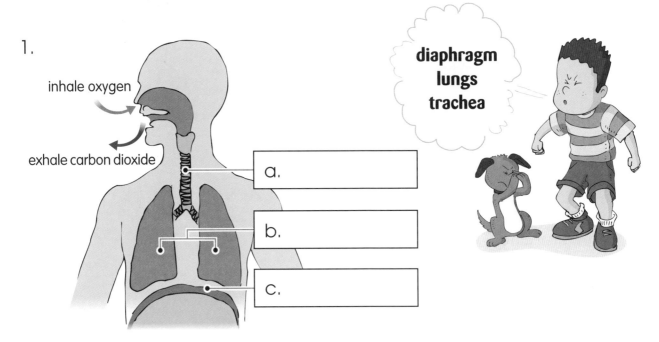

inhale oxygen

exhale carbon dioxide

a.

b.

c.

diaphragm
lungs
trachea

2. a gas that we breathe in _____

3. the tube that takes air from our mouth to our lungs _____

4. what we do to release carbon dioxide _____

5. breathe in _____

6. the waste gas we exhale _____

7. the muscle beneath our lungs that allows them to expand _____

ISBN: 978-1-77149-033-7

B. **Each picture shows something that affects our respiratory system. Unscramble the words to write what it is. Then put a check mark in the circle if it is good for us; otherwise, put a cross.**

1.

_____
g m **s** o ◯

2.

_____
g a **c** r e t i t e s ◯

3.

_____
a l **p** t n g i n ◯

4.

_____
n o l l o **p** i t u ◯

5.

_____
e m k **s** o ◯

6.

_____
n g o **j** g i g ◯

Science Fact

The diaphragm plays an important role in every breath we take, but it is barely noticeable to us – unless we have hiccups! Hiccups are caused by a spasm of the diaphragm.

20

Circulatory System

- The heart has a left side and a right side that work together to pump and receive blood.
- The rate at which our heart pumps blood varies according to our activities.

A. **Complete the labelling of the structure of a heart with the given words. Then fill in the blanks to complete the sequence of events in the circulatory system.**

The Structure of a Heart

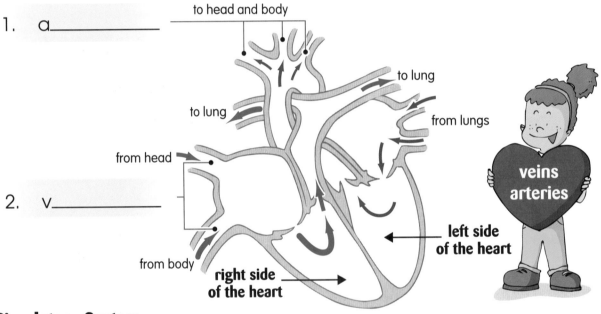

1. a_____

to head and body

to lung

to lung

from lungs

from head

2. v_____

from body

right side of the heart

left side of the heart

veins arteries

Circulatory System

veins   arteries   lungs   left

- The left side of the heart pumps oxygen-rich blood through the arteries.

- The 3._____ carry blood to vital organs, as well as every cell in our bodies.

- The 4._____ take the oxygen-depleted blood back to the right side of the heart.

- The right side of the heart sends blood to the 5._____ to receive oxygen.

- From the lungs, the blood goes back to the 6._____ side of the heart.

ISBN: 978-1-77149-033-7

B. **Match the heart rate with each activity.**

Heart rate (in beats per minute): 65   74   102   124

1.

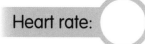 Heart rate: ◯

2.  Heart rate: ◯

3.  Heart rate: ◯

4.  Heart rate: ◯

Experiment – Take your own pulse.

Things needed:
- a clock with a second hand

Steps:

1. Rest for a few minutes before you start.
2. Place two fingers on the inside of your wrist, as pictured. You can feel an artery beating here with every pump of your heart.
3. Wait until the second hand of the clock reaches the 12. When it does, count the beats until the second hand gets to the 6.
4. Multiply the number you got by 2. That is your resting heart rate.

 **Science Fact**

Blood in the arteries is a brighter red than blood in the veins. The high oxygen level in arterial blood is responsible for its colour.

21

Digestive System

Hey! You have so much saliva.

- Food we eat travels through the body's digestive system, a group of organs that takes the nutrients and expels the waste.

A. **Name each part of the digestive system. Then draw lines to match the events of digestion with the correct digestive organs.**

mouth   *rectum*   *stomach*
colon   *esophagus*   *small intestine*

Digestive System

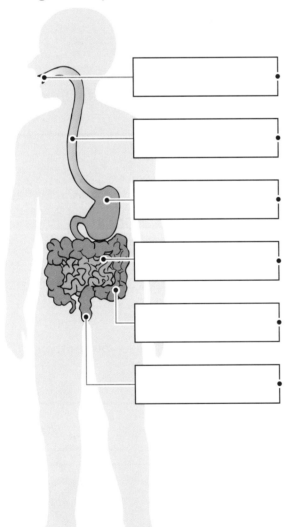

- Here, it is stored as waste before leaving the body.

- The body absorbs most nutrients when the food is here.

- This is where big pieces are broken down and saliva is added.

- This stretchy bag-like organ mixes the food up with gastric juices.

- Now called a bolus, the food enters the stomach through this tube.

- After the body has taken the nutrients, the food goes through this to have any extra water removed.

ISBN: 978-1-77149-033-7

B. Read the clues. Complete the crossword puzzle with the names of the digestive organs.

mouth esophagus
stomach gall bladder
rectum small intestine
pancreas colon liver

The pancreas, liver, and gall bladder contribute juices that aid in digestion.

absorbs nutrients into the bloodstream

a muscular tube pushing the food down into the stomach

removes water and pushes the rest out of our body as feces

stores the stool until evacuation happens

produces juices to digest oil

uses enzymes and juices to break down the food into smaller bits

chews and uses saliva and enzymes to break down the food

secretes bile to help digest fat

secretes hormones that affect the level of sugar in the blood

Science Fact

A flap of tissue, the epiglottis, stops food from going into the trachea when we swallow. This way, all food and liquid will go into the esophagus and stomach, instead of the lungs.

epiglottis

22

Excretory System

- The excretory system is a cleaning system. It cleans the blood and produces urine.

> Jane, I can't hold it anymore!

A. Fill in the blanks to complete the paragraph with the words given in the diagram.

Excretory System

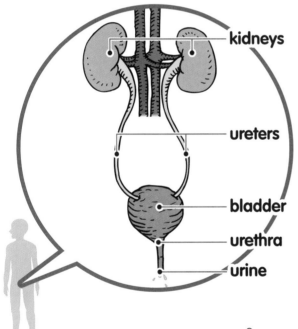

kidneys

ureters

bladder

urethra

urine

When cells in our bodies do work, they also make waste. The body has special organs that keep waste from building up. The 1._____ do the most waste removal work. They filter blood as it passes through them, sending clean blood out while keeping the waste behind. With extra water, the waste is now called 2._____ . Urine passes through the 3._____ and into the stretchy 4._____ where it is temporarily stored. When it is full, urine travels from the bladder, through the 5._____ , and out of the body.

ISBN: 978-1-77149-033-7

B. **Read the paragraph on the previous page again. Then match each part with its function.**

Kidneys •

Ureters •

Urethra •

Bladder •

• remove waste from blood, make urine

• passage for urine to exit body

• stores urine

• move urine from kidneys to bladder

C. **Write "true" or "false" for each sentence.**

1. The bladder is the last organ urine passes through before it leaves the body. _____

2. There are two ureters, one from each kidney. _____

3. The urethra is a passage that leads from one of the kidneys to the bladder. _____

4. Blood enters the kidneys to be cleaned, leaving behind waste that helps make urine. _____

5.

Kidneys filter the blood and remove waste materials in the form of urine.

_____

Science Fact

Other organs excrete waste too. When we sweat, we get rid of excess salt and water, and we breathe out carbon dioxide from our lungs.

oxygen

carbon dioxide

23

Nutrition

- Our bodies get nutrients from the food we eat.
- A healthful diet contains a variety of healthful food.
- Nutrition labels provide us with information to make good eating choices.

A. **Match the nutrients with the descriptions. Then tell which two food items are possible sources of each nutrient. Write the letters.**

fibre   vitamins   minerals   water
proteins   fats   carbohydrates

1. _____ ◯
give energy   ◯

2. _____ ◯
helps digestive process   ◯

3. _____ ◯
build tissues and muscles   ◯

4. _____ ◯
develop brain and nervous system   ◯

5. _____
controls body temperature, moves nutrients and waste   ◯
◯

6. _____ and 7. _____   ◯
help our bodies grow and stay healthy   ◯

ISBN: 978-1-77149-033-7

B.   Read the nutritional information labels. Then answer the questions.

Chocolate Chip Cookies

Nutrition Facts (serving size: 1 cookie)		
	Amount	% Daily Value
Calories	200	
Fat	9 g	14%
Saturated	0.4 g	2%
+ Trans	0.1 g	
Cholesterol	50 mg	17%
Sodium	140 mg	5%
Carbohydrate	26 g	9%
Fibre	2 g	4%
Sugars	14 g	
Protein	3 g	5%
Vitamin A 0%	Vitamin C 0%	
Calcium 0%	Iron 10%	

Banana Peach Muffins

Nutrition Facts (serving size: 1 muffin)		
	Amount	% Daily Value
Calories	260	
Fat	9 g	14%
Saturated	4.5 g	21%
+ Trans	0.5 g	
Cholesterol	90 mg	30%
Sodium	320 mg	11%
Carbohydrate	53 g	18%
Fibre	3 g	6%
Sugars	26 g	
Protein	8 g	14%
Vitamin A 0%	Vitamin C 3%	
Calcium 4%	Iron 20%	

1.   Which bakery item has more calories per serving?   _____

2.   Which bakery item has no vitamins?   _____

3.   How many milligrams of sodium (salt) does the muffin have?   _____

4.   Which bakery item is richer in minerals?   _____

C.   Look at the menu.   Add a food item to this meal to make it nutritionally balanced. Then explain your choice.

Tonight's Menu

• *Roast Beef and Gravy*
• *Bread*
• *Potatoes*

Food to add:

_____

_____

While fat is an essential nutrient, too much is unhealthful. Animal fats and trans fats should be especially avoided or limited.

Defence System

Huh...huh...
hut-chew!

- The body has different ways to defend itself against things that may make us ill.
- If the body's first defence fails, white blood cells can multiply and attack disease-causing microbes.

A.   Read the paragraph. Complete the diagram with the words in bold.

Some organisms are so small they can only be seen under a microscope. They are called **microbes**. **Viruses** and **bacteria** are two microbes that can cause illness if they enter our bodies.

small organism

small organisms that cause illness

B.   Match each body defence system with its description. Write the letter.

First Line of Defence

○ Skin

○ Mucus

○ Cilia

○ Earwax

○ Stomach acid

A These are tiny hair-like projections that move dirt and mucus out of the trachea.

B It wraps around the whole body, acting as a barrier between the inside and the outside.

C Produced only in our ears, this sticky substance traps dust and germs that may enter the ear canal.

D This slimy substance, produced by the body, catches intruders of the body's air passages.

E This juice, also called hydrochloric acid, kills germs that enter through our digestive system.

ISBN: 978-1-77149-033-7

C. Read what Dr. Howard says. Check the picture that shows the blood cells of a healthy person. Then colour the red blood cells red.

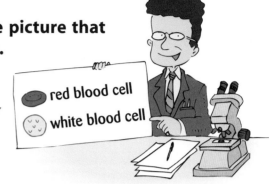

Blood is made up of red blood cells and white blood cells, with the red far outnumbering the white.

red blood cell
white blood cell

Blood

Blood

A

B

D. Circle the correct word to complete what Jason says. Then trace the dotted lines and continue the pattern to complete the next group of cells.

White / Red blood cells multiply themselves when dangerous microbes get past our first line of defence. They will start their job of attacking the intruders.

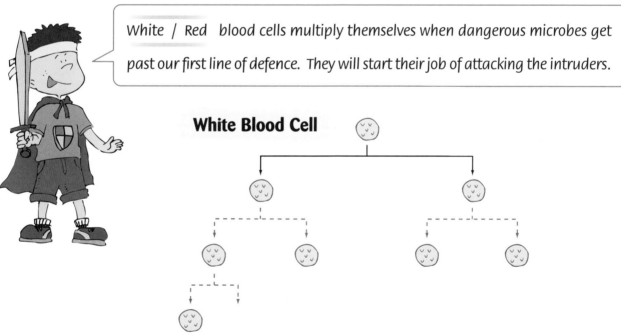

White Blood Cell

Science Fact

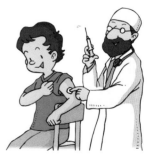

Another defence available to us is immunization. When we are immunized, our body makes antibodies to the disease we are immunized against.

ISBN: 978-1-77149-033-7

ANSWERS

ISBN: 978-1-77149-033-7 Complete Canadian Curriculum • **Grade 5** **333**

1 Numbers to 100 000 (1)

1. 3 ; 5 ; 2 ; 5 ; 35 025
2. 4 ; 2 ; 5 ; 7 ; 42 507
3. 5 ; 3 ; 6 ; 50 360
4. Thirty-six thousand four hundred fifty-three
5. Sixty-four thousand seventy-eight
6. Ninety thousand one hundred fifty-six
7. Twenty-eight thousand seven hundred fourteen
8. Fifty-nine thousand two hundred three
9. 30 000 + 4000 + 700 + 80 + 5
10. 70 000 + 6000 + 50 + 9
11. 50 000 + 2000 + 300 + 6
12. 80 000 + 500 + 40 + 8
13. 25 267   14. 41 058
15. 30 074   16. 58 962
17. 20 000 ; 7000 ; 800 ; 50 ; 4
18. 30 000 ; 6000 ; 800 ; 10 ; 9
19. 60 000 ; 5000 ; 900 ; 20 ; 3
20. 70 000 ; 5000 ; 100 ; 90 ; 6
21-22. (Suggested answers)
21. a. 51 234, 52 340
    b. 12 934, 23 945
22. 67 000, 87 000
23. <   24. >   25. <
26. <   27. >   28. >
29. <   30. <
31. 32 754, 37 254, 73 524, 75 324
32. 48 680, 48 060, 40 680, 40 068
33. 50 006, 50 060, 50 600, 56 000, 60 005, 60 050, 60 500, 65 000

2 Numbers to 100 000 (2)

1. 68 200 ; 68 250
2. 60 005 ; 70 005 ; 90 005
3. 80 250 ; 81 250 ; 82 250
4.

		96 118		50 118	49 118	48 118
	93 318	95 118				49 118
94 318	94 218	94 118	94 018			50 118
95 318		93 118				51 118
96 318		92 118	82 118	72 118	62 118	52 118
97 318		91 118				53 118
		90 118				
	89 218	89 118	89 018	88 918	88 818	88 718
		88 118				

5. 48 888   6. 93 645
7. 67 333   8. 58 604
9. 6 ; 79 998, 79 999, 80 000, 80 001, 80 002, 80 003

10. 55 555 ; Fifty-five thousand five hundred fifty-five
11-12. (Suggested answers)
11. 37 888 is 1000 more than 36 888.
    36 088 is 800 less than 36 888.
    37 888 is 80 more than 37 808.
12. 59 650 is 1000 less than 60 650.
    60 650 is 10 000 less than 70 650.
    59 650 is 100 more than 59 550.
13. 50 000   14. 20 000   15. 90 000
16. 90 000   17. 80 000   18. 60 000
19. 40 000   20. 40 000   21. 37 000
22. 47 000   23. 62 000   24. 99 000
25. 53 000   26. 73 000   27. 45 000
28. 11 000
29. a. 36 000   b. 14 000
    c. 12 000   d. 41 000
30. Exact: 36 418 ; About: 36 000
31. Exact: 89 705 ; About: 90 000
32. Exact: 21 516 ; About: 22 000
    Exact: 17 302 ; About: 17 000
33. a.

	Last Week	This Week
Exact	12 207 visitors	17 600 visitors
About	12 000 visitors	18 000 visitors

b. 30 000

3 Addition and Subtraction of 4-Digit Numbers

1. 5646   2. 3872   3. 7751
4. 6560   5. 6007   6. 5503
7. 4330   8. 3271   9. 7630
10. 5164   11. 4395   12. 6021
13.   14. 8267   15. 4647
16. 868   17. 1307   18. 427
19. 789   20. 4191   21. 1039
22. 424   23. 2038   24. 1678
25. 4252 ; 2778 g
    - 1474
    ───────
     2778
26. 6014 ; $767
    - 5247
    ───────
      767
27. 1500 ; 1225 mL
    - 275
    ───────
     1225
28. 2870 ; 1847 cm
    - 1023
    ───────
     1847
29. 4723 ; 1041 tickets
    - 3682
    ───────
     1041

30.
$$\begin{array}{r} 5657 \\ -2764 \\ \hline 2893 \end{array}$$; 2893 eggs

31. 6043 ;
$$\begin{array}{r} 3000 \\ +3000 \\ \hline 6000 \end{array}$$
32. 1409 ;
$$\begin{array}{r} 5000 \\ -4000 \\ \hline 1000 \end{array}$$

33. 5093 ;
$$\begin{array}{r} 2000 \\ +3000 \\ \hline 5000 \end{array}$$
34. 5073 ;
$$\begin{array}{r} 9000 \\ -4000 \\ \hline 5000 \end{array}$$

35. A: ✔ ;
$$\begin{array}{r} 4721 \\ -1464 \\ \hline 3257 \end{array}$$

   B: ✗ ; 7539 ;
$$\begin{array}{r} 8539 \\ + 477 \\ \hline 9016 \end{array}$$

   C: ✗ ; 4400 ;
$$\begin{array}{r} 4410 \\ -2806 \\ \hline 1604 \end{array}$$

   D: ✔ ;
$$\begin{array}{r} 2775 \\ +2478 \\ \hline 5253 \end{array}$$

   E: ✔ ;
$$\begin{array}{r} 4115 \\ +2885 \\ \hline 7000 \end{array}$$

   F: ✗ ; 5139 ;
$$\begin{array}{r} 5039 \\ -4193 \\ \hline 846 \end{array}$$

36. 4262 + 3788 ; 8050 ; 8050 people
37. 4262 – 3788 ; 474 ; 474 more
38. 4663 + 982 ; 5645 ; 5645 storybooks
39. 5645 – 3405 ; 2240 ; 2240 storybooks
40. 765 + 432 ; 1197 ; 1197 items

4   Multiplication

1.
$$\begin{array}{r} \overset{3}{3}4 \\ \times 28 \\ \hline 2 \end{array}$$
$$\begin{array}{r} \overset{3}{3}4 \\ \times 28 \\ \hline 272 \end{array}$$
$$\begin{array}{r} 34 \\ \times 28 \\ \hline 272 \\ 80 \end{array}$$
$$\begin{array}{r} 34 \\ \times 28 \\ \hline 272 \\ 680 \end{array}$$
$$\begin{array}{r} 34 \\ \times 28 \\ \hline 272 \\ 680 \\ \hline 952 \end{array}$$

952

2.
$$\begin{array}{r} \overset{2}{6}9 \\ \times 53 \\ \hline 7 \end{array}$$
$$\begin{array}{r} \overset{2}{6}9 \\ \times 53 \\ \hline 207 \end{array}$$
$$\begin{array}{r} \overset{4}{6}9 \\ \times 53 \\ \hline 207 \\ 50 \end{array}$$
$$\begin{array}{r} \overset{4}{6}9 \\ \times 53 \\ \hline 207 \\ 3450 \end{array}$$
$$\begin{array}{r} 69 \\ \times 53 \\ \hline 207 \\ 3450 \\ \hline 3657 \end{array}$$

3657

3.
$$\begin{array}{r} 27 \\ \times 14 \\ \hline 108 \\ 270 \\ \hline 378 \end{array}$$
4.
$$\begin{array}{r} 38 \\ \times 29 \\ \hline 342 \\ 760 \\ \hline 1102 \end{array}$$

5.
$$\begin{array}{r} 47 \\ \times 39 \\ \hline 423 \\ 1410 \\ \hline 1833 \end{array}$$
6.
$$\begin{array}{r} 34 \\ \times 22 \\ \hline 68 \\ 680 \\ \hline 748 \end{array}$$

7.
$$\begin{array}{r} 53 \\ \times 32 \\ \hline 106 \\ 1590 \\ \hline 1696 \end{array}$$
8.
$$\begin{array}{r} 68 \\ \times 45 \\ \hline 340 \\ 2720 \\ \hline 3060 \end{array}$$

9. 672
10. 481
11. 2745
12. 1870
13. 1679
14. 468
15. 988
16. 2401
17. 1206
18. 1272
19. 1680
20. 2214

21.
$$\begin{array}{r} 34 \\ \times 26 \\ \hline 204 \\ 680 \\ \hline 884 \end{array}$$
22.
$$\begin{array}{r} 59 \\ \times 47 \\ \hline 413 \\ 2360 \\ \hline 2773 \end{array}$$

23.

No. of Boxes	Chicken Burgers		Detergent	
	No. of Burgers	Cost	No. of Loads	Cost
15	180	$210	510	$195
29	348	$406	986	$377
47	564	$658	1598	$611
58	696	$812	1972	$754

24.

No. of Bags	Candies		Balloons	
	No. of Candies	Cost	No. of Balloons	Cost
18	936	$288	1296	$216
26	1352	$416	1872	$312
34	1768	$544	2448	$408
85	4420	$1360	6120	$1020

25. 16 x 34 ; 544 ; 544 loads
26. 42 x 72 ; 3024 ; 3024 balloons
27.
$$\begin{array}{r} 36 \\ \times 13 \\ \hline 108 \\ 360 \\ \hline 468 \end{array}$$
; 468 kg

28.
$$\begin{array}{r} 28 \\ \times 45 \\ \hline 140 \\ 1120 \\ \hline 1260 \end{array}$$
; They hold 1260 L in all.

29.
$$\begin{array}{r} 33 \\ \times 48 \\ \hline 264 \\ 1320 \\ \hline 1584 \end{array}$$
; The total length is 1584 cm.

30.
$$\begin{array}{r} 22 \\ \times 68 \\ \hline 176 \\ 1320 \\ \hline 1496 \end{array}$$
; There are 1496 pieces of dog treats.

5 Division (1)

1.
```
    1 8 4
  4)7 3 6
    4
    3 3
    3 2
      1 6
      1 6
```

2.
```
    1 2 1
  7)8 4 7
    7
    1 4
    1 4
      7
      7
```

3.
```
    1 2 4
  6)7 4 4
    6
    1 4
    1 2
      2 4
      2 4
```

4. 117
5. 214
6. 316
7. 117
8. 134
9. 128
10. 122
11. 255
12. a. 172   b. 119

13.
```
    7 2 R4
  7)5 0 8
    4 9
    1 8
    1 4
      4
```

14.
```
    2 8 7 R2
  3)8 6 3
    6
    2 6
    2 4
      2 3
      2 1
        2
```

15.
```
    1 2 5 R1
  6)7 5 1
    6
    1 5
    1 2
      3 1
      3 0
        1
```

16. ✔ ;
158 ; 3 ; 474 ;
474 ; 1 ; 475

17. ✗ ; 143R1 ;
144 ; 5 ; 720 ;
720 ; 4 ; 724

18. ✔ ;
161 ; 4 ; 644 ;
644 ; 3 ; 647

19. ✗ ; 154R3 ;
153 ; 6 ; 918 ;
918 ; 5 ; 923

20. Ribbon
```
    7 5
  7)5 2 5
    4 9
    3 5
    3 5
```
75

Flour
```
    9 1
  4)3 6 4
    3 6
      4
      4
```
91

Juice
```
    9 4 R1
  8)7 5 3
    7 2
    3 3
    3 2
      1
```
94 ; 1

Blocks
```
    5 1 R7
  9)4 6 6
    4 5
    1 6
      9
      7
```
51 ; 7

21. 78R4
22. 78R3
23. 62R6
24. 66R1
25. 27R3
26. 68R2
27. 83R2
28. 48R7
29. a. 162 ; 2   b. 69 ; 5
30. a. 188 ; 3   b. 125 ; 5
31. 413 ÷ 3 ; 137R2 ; 137 ; 2
32. 178 ÷ 8 ; 22R2 ; He needs to buy 23 bags of gumballs.
33. 125 ÷ 7 ; 17R6 ; She can get 17 lollipops. Her change is $6.

6 Division (2)

1.
```
    1 0 9
  4)4 3 6
    4
    3 6
    3 6
```

2.
```
    1 0 7 R5
  6)6 4 7
    6
    4 7
    4 2
      5
```

3.
```
    1 0 6 R2
  5)5 3 2
    5
    3 2
    3 0
      2
```

4.
```
    1 2 0 R2
  7)8 4 2
    7
    1 4
    1 4
      2
```

5.
```
    1 2 0 R5
  8)9 6 5
    8
    1 6
    1 6
      5
```

6.
```
    2 6 0 R1
  3)7 8 1
    6
    1 8
    1 8
      1
```

7.
```
    1 0 1
  5)5 0 5
    5
    5
    5
```

8.
```
    1 0 0 R6
  7)7 0 6
    7
    6
```

9.
```
    1 0 5
  6)6 3 0
    6
    3 0
    3 0
```

10.
```
    1 0 6 R4
  8)8 5 2
    8
    5 2
    4 8
      4
```

11.
```
    1 5 0 R1
  3)4 5 1
    3
    1 5
    1 5
      1
```

12.
```
    2 0 8 R2
  4)8 3 4
    8
    3 4
    3 2
      2
```

13. 120R5
14. 108R3
15. 180R2
16. 102R5
17. 107
18. 109
19. 104R6
20. 140R1
21. 120R4
22. 120R3
23. a. 822 ÷ 4 ; 205R2 ; 205 ; 2
    b. 822 ÷ 6 ; 137 ; 137 ; 0
24. 832 ÷ 4 ; 208 ; 208 g
25. 454 ÷ 5 ; 90R4 ; 90 g ; 4 g left
26. 100 ÷ 2 ; 50 ; 50 heads
27. 350 ÷ 5 ; 70 ; 70 loaves
28. 365 ÷ 9 ; 40R5 ; 41 loaves

29. 106 ; 1
30. There are 105 teaspoons of sugar in one bag. 7 g of sugar is left.
31. It lasts 125 days.
32. It takes Katie 15 months to save enough money.

29-32.
```
    106R1    105R7    125        15
  4)425    9)952    6)750    8)120
    4        9        6        8
    25       52       15       40
    24       45       12       40
     1        7       30
                      30
```

7 More about Multiplication and Division

1.
```
    36
  x 24
   144
   720
   864
```
2.
```
    79
  x 15
   395
   790
  1185
```
3.
```
    27
  x 48
   216
  1080
  1296
```

4.
```
    58R1
  9)523
    45
    73
    72
     1
```
5.
```
    112R2
  6)674
    6
    7
    6
    14
    12
     2
```

6.
```
    203R3
  4)815
    8
    15
    12
     3
```
7. 450

8. 1216   9. 91R2   10. 100R4
11. 151R4   12. 1148   13. 2211
14. 112R3
15. a. 945 ÷ 9 ; 105 ; 105 packs
    b. 15 x 76 ; 1140 ; 1140¢ or $11.40
    c. 31 x 2 ; 62 ; 62 packs
16. a. 321 ÷ 3 ; 107 ; 107 cm
    b. 18 x 32 ; 576 ; 576 kg
    c. 112 ÷ 7 ; 16 ; 16 minutes
17. 500 ; 4000 ; 4000 ; 20 000 ; 80 000 ; 25
18. 20 ; 10 sheets: 200 labels ;
    1 pack: 200 labels ;
    100 packs: 20 000 labels ;
    500 packs: 100 000 labels ; 500
19. 25 ; 16 packs: 400 markers ;
    1 box: 400 markers ;
    100 boxes: 40 000 markers ;
    500 boxes: 200 000 markers ; 500
20. 81 ÷ 3 = 27 ; 27 x 2 = 54 ; 54
21. 78 ÷ 6 = 13 ; 13 x 4 = 52 ; 52

22. 52 ÷ 4 = 13 ; 13 x 29 = 377 ; 377
23. 96 ÷ 4 = 24 ; 24 x 5 = 120 ; 120

8 Length, Distance, and Time

1. mm   2. dm   3. cm
4. km   5. m   6. m
7. cm   8. km
9. a. cm   b. m
10. 400   11. 8000   12. 60
13. 90   14. 8   15. 6
16. 7   17. 5
18. 7000 ; 7008   19. 90 ; 98
20. 50 ; 56   21. 400 ; 409
22. 4 km 20 m = 4020 m < 4150 m ;
    Circle C to D: 4150 m.
23. 1 m 15 cm = 115 cm ; 9 dm 8 cm = 98 cm ;
    Circle Sam's height: 1 m 15 cm.
24. Sally: 39   Frankie: 48
    Alexander: 26   Tiffany: 34
25. Frankie   26. Alexander
27. No
28. A: 3 h 42 min   B: 4 h 58 min
    C: 5 h 42 min   D: 4 h 47 min
29. A   30. 3 ; 13   31. 5 ; 35
32. 3 ; 13   33. 2 ; 24

9 Perimeter and Area (1)

1. A: 11.7 km   B: 14.2 m   C: 17.2 cm
   D: 11 mm   E: 8.8 km   F: 29.4 cm
   G: 22.5 m   H: 19.8 mm
2. A: about 18 cm²   B: about 19 cm²
   C: 12 cm²   D: 20 cm²   E: 20 cm²
   F: 15 cm²   G: 16 cm²   H: 10 cm²
3-4. (Suggested answers)
3.

4.

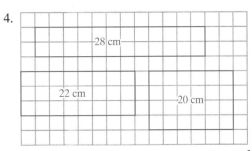

5. 24 cm   6. 52 cm   7. 1512 cm^2

8. 42 cm^2 9. 170 cm

10 Perimeter and Area (2)

1. 16 cm ; 10 cm ;
   16 ; 10 ; 26 ; 26 cm
2. 30 cm ; 20 cm ; 30 ; 20 ; 50 (cm)
3. 16 m ; 50 m ; 16 ; 50 ; 66 (m)
4. A: 2 x 16 + 2 x 8 ; 32 + 16 ; 48 (cm)
   B: 2 x 12 + 2 x 7 ; 24 + 14 ; 38 (m)
   C: 2 x 40 + 2 x 72 ; 80 + 144 ; 224 (cm)
   D: 2 x 13 + 2 x 18 ; 26 + 36 ; 62 (cm)
   E: 2 x 16 + 2 x 10 ; 32 + 20 ; 52 (cm)
   F: 2 x 32 + 2 x 30 ; 64 + 60 ; 124 (m)
5.

	Length	Width	Area	
			By counting	By using formula
Ⓐ	5 cm	3 cm	15 cm^2	5 x 3 = 15 (cm^2)
Ⓑ	2 cm	4 cm	8 cm^2	2 x 4 = 8 (cm^2)
Ⓒ	5 cm	6 cm	30 cm^2	5 x 6 = 30 (cm^2)
Ⓓ	5 cm	4 cm	20 cm^2	5 x 4 = 20 (cm^2)
Ⓔ	6 cm	2 cm	12 cm^2	6 x 2 = 12 (cm^2)

6. 153 ÷ 9 = 17 ; 17 cm
7. a. 48 + 10 = 58 ; 58 cm
   b. 2 x 58 + 2 x 48 = 116 + 96 = 212 ; 212 cm
8. a. 24 x 36 = 864 ; 864 cm^2
   b. 2 x 24 + 2 x 36 = 48 + 72 = 120 ; 120 cm
9. 118 – 32 – 32 = 54 ; 54 ÷ 2 = 27 ; 27 cm

11 Mass, Capacity, and Volume

1. t ; kg ; g ; mg
2. a. kg ; g ; mg ; kg ; g ; mg
   b. t ; g ; kg ; kg ; t ; g
3. mg   4. t   5. kg
6. g   7. mg   8. t
9. g   10. kg
11. Capacity: 35 ; 5 ; 175   Volume: 48 ; 6 ; 288
12. Capacity: 54 ; 4 ; 216   Volume: 77 ; 5 ; 385
13. 36 ; 5 ; 36 ; 5 ; 180
14. 50 ; 3 ; 50 ; 3 ; 150

15. A: 198 cm^3 B: 112 cm^3 C: 1792 cm^3
    D: 360 m^3 E: 288 m^3
16. Vol. of A: 48 ; 18 ; 864 ;
    Vol. of B: 32 ; 5 ; 160 ;
    Vol. of the solid: 864 ; 160 ; 1024
17. Vol. of A: 144 x 4 = 576 (cm^3) ;
    Vol. of B: 48 x 6 = 288 (cm^3)
    Vol. of the solid: 576 ; 288 ;
             864

18. Volume:
    Width: 16   Area: 30 ; 16 ; 480
    Height: 18   Volume: 480 ; 18 ; 8640
    Capacity:
    Width: 16 – 2 ; 14   Height: 18 – 1 ; 17
    Area: 28 ; 14 ; 392   Volume: 392 ; 17 ; 6664
    Capacity: 6664

12 Fractions

1. Proper fraction ; $\frac{3}{7}$, $\frac{5}{6}$, $\frac{2}{4}$

   Improper fraction ; $\frac{9}{5}$, $\frac{8}{7}$, $\frac{7}{5}$, $\frac{8}{8}$

   Mixed number ; $2\frac{3}{4}$, $1\frac{1}{5}$, $3\frac{4}{9}$, $1\frac{1}{3}$, $2\frac{7}{10}$

2. $\frac{3}{8}$ 3. $\frac{4}{6}$ 4. $\frac{7}{3}$
5. $\frac{34}{10}$ 6. $\frac{37}{8}$ 7. $\frac{15}{2}$
8. 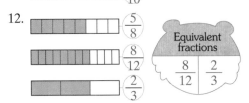   9.

10. A: $\frac{11}{2}$; $5\frac{1}{2}$ B: $\frac{14}{4}$; $3\frac{2}{4}$

11.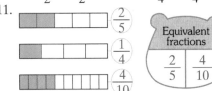

$\frac{2}{5}$

$\frac{1}{4}$

$\frac{4}{10}$

Equivalent fractions

| $\frac{2}{5}$ | $\frac{4}{10}$ |

12.

$\frac{5}{8}$

$\frac{8}{12}$

$\frac{2}{3}$

Equivalent fractions

| $\frac{8}{12}$ | $\frac{2}{3}$ |

13. $\frac{4}{7}$, $\frac{3}{5}$ 14. $\frac{3}{4}$, $\frac{5}{8}$ 15. $\frac{7}{10}$, $\frac{1}{3}$

16. $\frac{7}{9}$ 17. $3\frac{1}{5}$ 18. $\frac{11}{8}$

19. $3\frac{1}{7}$ 20. $4\frac{3}{6}$ 21. $\frac{20}{9}$

22. $2\frac{1}{5}$; $1\frac{3}{5}$; $\frac{4}{5}$ 23. $\frac{18}{12}$; $\frac{6}{12}$; $\frac{3}{12}$

24. $1\frac{3}{10}$; $1\frac{5}{10}$; $2\frac{1}{10}$ 25. $\frac{15}{4}$; $3\frac{1}{4}$; $2\frac{2}{4}$; Tim

13 Decimals (1)

1. A: 2.16 ; 2 ; 16
   B: 1.92 ; 1 and 92 hundredths
   C: 4.08 ; 4 and 8 hundredths
   D: 3.36 ; 3 and 36 hundredths
   E: 4.30 ; 4 and 30 hundredths or 4 and 3 tenths

2. 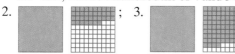 ; 3.

   1 and 37 hundredths   1 and 84 hundredths
4. 0.2   5. 3   6. 0.05
7. 0.09   8. 0.5   9. 0.08
10. 0.01   11. 8   12. 0.1
13. 4.27 ; 4.07   14. 6.16 ; 1.66
15. 3.11 ; 3.13   16. 18.09 ; 9.18
17. $\frac{15}{25}$;   ; 0.60

18. $\frac{4}{5}$;   ; 0.80

19. $\frac{12}{20}$;   ; 0.60

20. $\frac{2}{4}$;   ; 0.50

21. 0.40   22. 0.50   23. 0.60
24. 0.90   25. 0.20   26. 0.40
27. 5.92 ; 5.29 ; 2.95 ; 2.59
28. 3.66 ; 3.60 ; 3.06 ; 3.00
29. 2.40 ; 2.47 ; 2.70 ; 2.74
30. 6.68 ; 6.86 ; 6.88 ; 8.68
31. 9.30 ; 9.31 ; 9.32 ; 9.33
32. 6.17 ; 6.18 ; 6.20 ; 6.21
33. 8.09 ; 8.10 ; 8.11 ; 8.13
34. 3.98 ; 3.99 ; 4.00 ; 4.01
35. 9.97 ; 9.98 ; 9.99 ; 10.00
36. a.

   b. the bone at 5.96   c. the bone at 5.96

14 Decimals (2)

1. a.

   b. 4.1   c. 3.9
   d. 4.2   e. 4.0
2. a.

   b. 9.0   c. 9.1
   d. 9.1   e. 9.0
3. 5.6   4. 4.7   5. 6.2
6. 10.5   7. 15.8   8. 20.3
9. 10.0   10. 9.1   11. 15.2
12. 8.1   13. 3.4   14. 2.9
15. 62.5   16. 328
17. 4.060 x 1000 = 4060
18. 5.1300 x 10 000 = 51 300
19. 6.530 x 1 000 = 6530
20. 7.08 x 10 = 70.8
21. 8.6700 x 10 000 = 86 700
22. 9.62 x 100 = 962
23. a. 7.5   b. 7500
24. a. 85   b. 850
25. a. 1.3   b. 1300
26. 0.854   27. 0.067
28. 09.6 ÷ 100 = 0.096
29. 5.29 ÷ 10 = 0.529
30. 7.4 ÷ 10 = 0.74
31. 03.8 ÷ 100 = 0.038
32. 06.2 ÷ 100 = 0.062
33. 5.6 ÷ 10 = 0.56
34. 0.025 ; 0.08 ; B   35. 0.02 ; 0.021 ; B
36. 3.804 ; 3.804   37. 4.078 ; 4.078
38. 8.005 ; 8.005   39. 6.17 ; 6.17
40. 5.8 ; 5.8   41. 9.006 ; 9.006
42. A: 2.016   B: 2.061   C: 2.006 ;
    B
43. A: 8.9   B: 8.5   C: 8.8 ;
    A

15 Addition and Subtraction of Decimals

1. A: $\begin{array}{r} 2.68 \\ + 3.44 \\ \hline 6.12 \end{array}$ B: $\begin{array}{r} 5.14 \\ - 2.99 \\ \hline 2.15 \end{array}$ C: $\begin{array}{r} 4.67 \\ + 6.28 \\ \hline 10.95 \end{array}$ D: $\begin{array}{r} 8.07 \\ - 2.13 \\ \hline 5.94 \end{array}$

2. 9.02   3. 8.21   4. 1.63
5. 2.07   6. 5.71   7. 5.82

ISBN: 978-1-77149-033-7

8. 16.52　　9. 1.74　　10. 3.49

11. 16.51　　12. 12.79　　13. 12.95

14.
$$\frac{\begin{array}{r}4.79\\+\ 6.30\end{array}}{11.09}\ \bigg|\ \frac{\begin{array}{r}6.30\\-\ 4.79\end{array}}{1.51}$$
15.
$$\frac{\begin{array}{r}9.20\\+11.08\end{array}}{20.28}\ \bigg|\ \frac{\begin{array}{r}11.08\\-\ 9.20\end{array}}{1.88}$$

16.
$$\frac{\begin{array}{r}30.03\\+12.40\end{array}}{42.43}\ \bigg|\ \frac{\begin{array}{r}30.03\\-12.40\end{array}}{17.63}$$
17.
$$\frac{\begin{array}{r}5.86\\+20.50\end{array}}{26.36}\ \bigg|\ \frac{\begin{array}{r}20.50\\-\ 5.86\end{array}}{14.64}$$

18. a. 10.44　b. 1.16

19. a. 1.08　b. 1.36

20.
Estimate	Exact
3.0	3.02
+ 1.5	+ 1.46
4.5	4.48

a. 4.5
b. 4.48

21.
Estimate	Exact
8.7	8.73
+ 4.7	+ 4.65
13.4	13.38

a. 13.4
b. 13.38

22.
Estimate	Exact
50.8	50.76
− 36.3	− 36.25
14.5	14.51
7.2	7.18
+ 36.3	+ 36.25
43.5	43.43

a. 14.5
b. 14.51
c. 43.5
d. 43.43

23. 2.63 − 1.27 ; 1.36 ; 1.36 kg

24. 50 − 29.27 ; 20.73 ; $20.73

25. 1.08 + 1.08 ; 2.16 ; 2.16 kg

26. 3.64 − 1.85 ; 1.79 ; 1.79 m

27. 36.74 + 36.74 ; 73.48 ; $73.48

28. 4.26 − 2.78 ; 1.48 ; 1.48 kg

16　Money

1. (Individual estimates)
   Exact
   A: 307 ; 2 ; 307.02
   B: 271 dollars 10 cents or $271.10
   C: 252 dollars 50 cents or $252.50
   D: 106 dollars 31 cents or $106.31

2.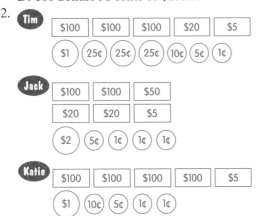

3. $623.99 ;
   $$\frac{\begin{array}{r}\$326.91\\+\ \$297.08\end{array}}{\$623.99}$$

4. $109.09 ;
   $$\frac{\begin{array}{r}\$406.17\\-\ \$297.08\end{array}}{\$109.09}$$

5. Armchair: $346.03 ; Task Chair: $115.79

6.

7.
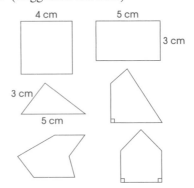

8. $115.79 + $115.79 ; $231.58 ; $231.58

9. $192.64 + $127.49 ; $320.13 ; $320.13

10. a. $259.52 ;
    $$\frac{\begin{array}{r}\$129.76\\+\ \$129.76\end{array}}{\$259.52}$$
    b. $70.24 ;
    $$\frac{\begin{array}{r}\$200.00\\-\ \$129.76\end{array}}{\$\ \ 70.24}$$

11. a. $130.61 ;
    $$\frac{\begin{array}{r}\$288.49\\-\ \$157.88\end{array}}{\$130.61}$$
    b. $912.84 ;
    $$\frac{\begin{array}{r}\$288.49\\+\ \$624.35\end{array}}{\$912.84}$$

12. $965.29 − $402.25 ; $563.04 ; $563.04

17　2-D Shapes

1. Colour the regular polygons: A, C, H, J, L
   A polygon with 5 or more sides: A, B, H, I, L
   Quadrilaterals: C, D, E, M
   Symmetrical shapes: A, B, C, D, F, G, H, J, K, L
   A polygon with 4 or fewer vertices: C, D, E, J, M

2. (Suggested answers)

3. A:  B:

C: D:

E:

4.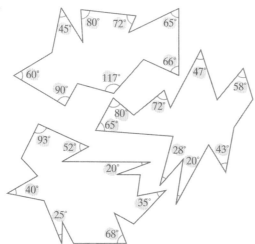

4 cm

5.

4 cm

14. (Suggested drawings)

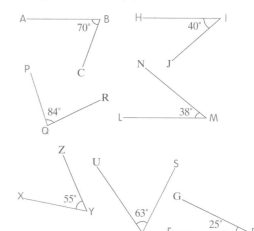

15.

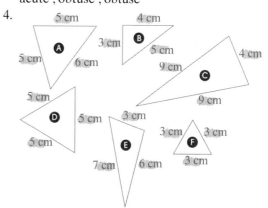

18 Angles

1. right ; 90°
2. straight ; 180°
3. one half ; 45°
4. one third ; 30°
5. one third ; 60°
6. ∠Q or ∠PQR ; a right angle
7. ∠M or ∠LMN ; an obtuse angle
8. ∠B or ∠ABC ; a straight angle
9. a. ∠Y or ∠XYZ ; an acute angle
   b. ∠Z or ∠XZY ; an acute angle
10. ∠F or∠EFG ; an acute angle
11. ∠K or∠JKL ; a right angle
12. ∠D or∠CDE ; a straight angle
13.

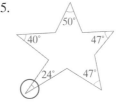

19 Triangles

1.

60°
80°   40°

acute ; acute

2.

52°
90° 38°

acute ; right ; right

3.

40° 110°
30°

acute ; obtuse ; obtuse

4.

A: isosceles
B: scalene triangle
C: isosceles triangle
D: equilateral triangle
E: scalene triangle
F: equilateral triangle

5-10. (Suggested drawings)

5.

6.

7.

8.

9.

10.

11. By Angles
Acute triangle: A, D ; Right triangle: B, E
Obtuse triangle: C

12. By Sides
Equilaterial triangle: A ; Isosceles triangle: B, D
Scalene triangle: C, E

13. (Suggested drawings)

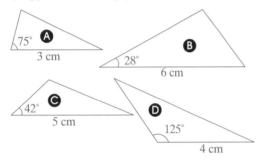

75° Ⓐ
3 cm

28° Ⓑ
6 cm

42° Ⓒ
5 cm

Ⓓ
125°
4 cm

20   3-D Figures

1. A, C
2. B, C
3. B, C
4. A, B
5. A, B
6. B, C
7. A, C
8. B, C
9. B

10. (Suggested drawings for the nets)

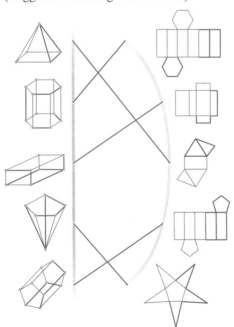

11.  ; hexagonal prism ; 6 ; 2

12. 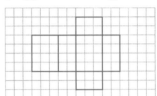 ;

triangular pyramid ; It has 4 triangular faces.

13. (Suggested drawing)

21   Transformations

1. does not change
2. B, C

3-7. (Suggested drawings)

3.

4.

5.

6.

7.

8. A, B, C, E, F, G, I, L

9.

22 Grids

1, 5-6.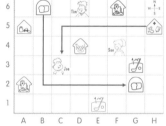

2.
3.
4. E3 and G1

5. 5 squares west and 2 squares south
6. She should go 4 squares south and 5 squares east.
7. He should go 1 square west and 2 squares south to find Joe. Then go 3 squares east and 1 square north to find Sue. Lastly, he should go 1 square west, 2 squares north, and 1 square west to go back home.
8. A3, C6, D1, I5, J9
9. A3, D1, E5, J9
10. (Suggested answer)
    He should start at G2, and then go 4 squares west, 3 squares north, and 1 square west to Monkey Kingdom.
11. Barnyard: 4 ; Reptile Garden: 7 ; Dino World: 9 ; Monkey Kingdom: 8 ; Cat Country: 4 ; Apple Orchard: 4
12. Dino World

13. Project 1: 12 square units
    Project 2: 4 square units
    (Suggested answer)
    Project 3: That can be done by including J3. The new area will be 8 square units.
14. (C3, C4), (D2, E2), and (F3, F4)

23 Patterning

1. add 6 ; 42 ; 48
2. divided by 2 ; 8 ; 4
3. subtract 25 ; 425 ; 400
4. multiply by 3 ; 2916 ; 8748
5. subtract 5 ; 142 ; 137

6. ; 43

Term number	Term
1	15
2	19
3	23
4	27
5	31
6	35

7. ; 11th

Term number	Term
1	20
2	18
3	16
4	14
5	12
6	10

8. ; 9th

Term number	Term
1	6561
2	2187
3	729
4	243
5	81
6	27

9. ; 1280

Term number	Term
1	5
2	10
3	20
4	40
5	80
6	160

10. ; A

Term number	Term
1	4
2	7
3	10
4	13

11. ; B

Term number	Term
1	21
2	17
3	13
4	9

12. ; A

Term number	Term
1	13
2	9
3	5
4	1

13. a.

b.

Tower	No. of Blocks
1st	3
2nd	6
3rd	9
4th	12
5th	15

c. 24 blocks

14. a.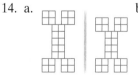

b.

Bone	No. of Square
1st	32
2nd	30
3rd	28
4th	26
5th	24

c. 20 squares

ISBN: 978-1-77149-033-7

24 Simple Equations

1. $C = 3 \times n$
2. $C = 6 \times n$; C ; n
3. $C = 2 \times n$; C ; n
4. $C = 9 \times n$; C ; n
5.

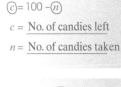
$c = 100 - n$
$c =$ No. of candies left
$n =$ No. of candies taken

$w = 100 \times$
$w =$ Total weight
= No. of boxes

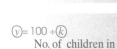
$y = 100 \div k$
$y =$ No. of children in each group
$k =$ No. of groups

$\triangle = 100 \div x$
$\triangle =$ Total cost
$x =$ Cost of the doll

6. A, B
7. A, D
8. B, C
9. C, D, F
10. 8
11. 16
12. 30
13. 16
14. 2
15. 18
16. 15
17. 192
18. 6
19. $m + 9 = 16$; $m = 7$
20. $b \div 4 = 6$; $b = 24$
21. $8 \times k = 48$; $k = 6$
22. $y - 16 = 45$; $y = 61$

25 Graphs (1)

1. 2 kinds
2. 100 boxes
3. 40 more
4. May
5. a. $425
   b. $560
   c. $475
6. Week 6
7. Week 10
8. a. 160 more
   b. 60 more
9. Weeks 4, 8, 9, and 10
10. 28 cm
11. 28 children
12. 8 children
13. 144 cm
14. 159 cm
15. 46 children
16. 12:00 noon
17. 300 km
18. 100 km
19. 200 km
20. He started driving back home at 8:00 a.m. and arrived home at 9:00 a.m.

26 Graphs (2)

1.
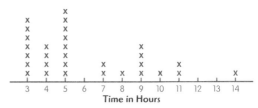

2. 11 children
3. (Suggested answer)
   Most of the children read 3 to 5 hours a week.
4.

No. of Orders		Sun	Mon	Tue	Wed	Thu	Fri	Sat
Combo 1	Actual	98	46	42	55	38	94	101
	Rounded	100	50	40	60	40	90	100
Combo 2	Actual	87	29	36	67	113	56	92
	Rounded	90	30	40	70	110	60	90

5.
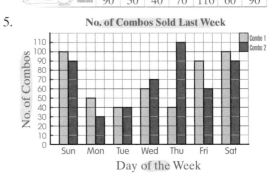

6. On Thursday, because the sales of combo 2 exceeded combo 1 by a large number.
7. (Suggested answer)
   The number of combos sold on Sunday, Friday, and Saturday was greater than on the other days.
8.
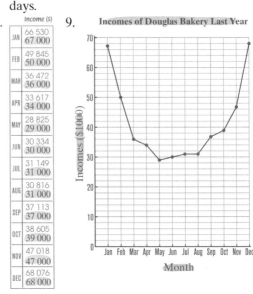

9.

10. March
11. January, December
12. $21 000
13. $154 000
14. $1000

15. a. December   b. May
16. 1000 cakes   17. $30 000
18. (Suggested answer)
    The bakery had better sales in wintertime.

Tina
Mean: 9 ; Median: 11 ; Mode: 14
Jimmy's data spread out evenly around the mean. Tina's data are mostly above the mean.

27 More about Graphs

1. 42 + 25 + 41 ; 144 ;
   144 ; 36 ; 36
2. 89 + 68 + 75 + 91 + 87 + 76 ; 486 ;
   486 ; 6 ; 81 ; 81 g
3. 750 + 600 + 850 + 750 + 750 + 850 + 680 + 650 ;
   5880 ;
   5880 ; 8 ; 735 ; 735 mL
4.

	Mean	Median	Mode
A	7 kg	7 kg	5 kg
B	43 muffins	35.5 muffins	29 muffins
C	$30	$27	$27
D	6 m	7 m	8 m
E	5°C	5°C	0°C

5.

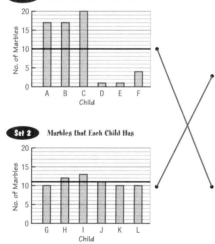

6. a. Mary
    Mean: 82 ; Median: 87 ; Mode: 87
    George
    Mean: 82 ; Median: 81 ; Mode: 80
  b. 82   c. 46 ; 87 ; above
  d. 23 ; should
7. Jimmy
   Mean: 8 ; Median: 9 ; Mode: 10

28 Probability

1. heads and tails
2. 1, 2, 3, 4, 5, and 6
3. A, B, C, and D
4. 2, 3, 4, 5, 6, 7, 8, 9, 10, 11, and 12
5. 4, 6, 8, 9, 12, 16, 24, 32, and 64
6. a. $\frac{4}{9}$ b. $\frac{3}{9}$ c. $\frac{1}{9}$
7. a. $\frac{6}{12}$ b. $\frac{2}{12}$ c. $\frac{4}{12}$
8. a. $\frac{1}{8}$ b. $\frac{4}{8}$ c. 0
  d. $\frac{2}{8}$ e. $\frac{1}{8}$
9.

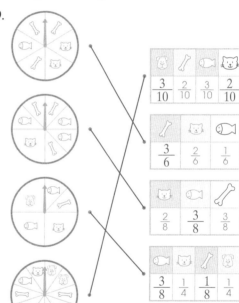

10. A: B:

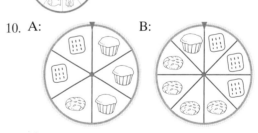

11. $\frac{2}{6}$ 12. $\frac{1}{8}$
13. A, because it has a greater probability to land on "muffin".
14. $\frac{3}{6}$

ISBN: 978-1-77149-033-7

1 European Microstates

A. 1. one of the world's oldest republics
2. world's smallest country
3. official language of Andorra
4. a mountain range
5. capital city of Italy

B. 1. It is a place ruled by a prince.
2. It is on the Mediterranean Sea along the coast of France, not far from the Italian border.
3. It is the world's most densely populated country.
4. (Suggested answer)
It is a small country with an appealing Mediterranean/moderate climate.
5. (Individual answer)

C. 1. country ; border
2. Monaco ; Monegasques
3. the Mediterranean Sea

D. 1. Many tourists visit Vatican City for its famous architecture.
2. The Pyrenees is the mountain range between France and Spain.
3. Besides tourism, things like banking, ceramics, clothing, wine, and cheese are also important to San Marino's economy.

E. 1. measured ; size
2. chose ; Monaco
3. visits ; Rome
4. sees ; the Pyrenees
5. learned ; German

F. 1. learn
2. paints
3. listens
4. sees
5. talks
6. (Individual writing)

2 Bluenose

A. Launch: 1921 ; Nova Scotia
Size: 49 ; 258
Mainmast: 38 ; 1036
Crew: officers ; deckhands ; cook

B. 1. It was built because the Canadians wanted to win back the trophy for the International Fishermen's Race from the United States.
2. It was sold to a company in the West Indies and became a tramp schooner.

3. They depicted Bluenose on a postage stamp and put it on the dime.

C. 1. Bluenose had a large mainsail.
2. Bluenose is Canada's national institution.
3. The game room is just right across from where we are.
4. Your timing was exact.
5. There were many crew members on board.

D.

E. 1. ADJ
2. ADV
3. ADV
4. ADJ
5. ADV

F. 1. We carefully built the ships.
2. The ship sails the sea calmly.
3. The cook skilfully chopped the onions.
4. The crew cheerfully greeted the kids.

3 Honeybees

A. 1. C   2. A
3. H   4. D
5. F   6. B
7. G   8. E

B. 1. T   2. F
3. T   4. F
5. T   6. F
7. F   8. T

C. 1. badly   2. near
3. good   4. good
5. nearly

D. My brother can get **real** distracted by the TV and does his homework **really bad**. He knows perfectly **good** that the TV often airs **badly** shows. That is why he only watches documentaries, which are stories about **real** people. But he can be **real** consumed by them. Maybe my brother should become a documentary filmmaker, so that his work will also be his play! That would be a **real** good idea!

1. really   2. badly
3. well   4. bad
5. really   6. really

E. 1. high ; ADV
    2. hard ; ADJ
    3. late ; ADV
    4. late ; ADJ
    5. high ; ADJ
    6. near ; ADV
    7. hard ; ADV
    8. near ; ADJ

F. (Individual writing)

4   Jess "n" Jacki Party Planners

A. 2 ; 6 ; 3 ; 5 ; 1 ; 4

B. 1. Before long, we were busy several times a week doing birthday parties, bar mitzvahs, and keeping children entertained during large family summer barbecues.
    2. Now we have our own website, and have decided to work throughout the year doing one party a week.
    3. Jess's uncle knows how to make balloon animals and taught us how. / We even came up with the idea of offering to supply cakes and snacks because my aunt is a pastry chef.

C. 1. most   2. more
    3. most   4. more

D. 1. This kid is smarter when he is outside the classroom.
    2. Sally is the funniest kid in class.
    3. Lizzy is the most beautiful of all the daughters.
    4. This story is more interesting than the other one.

E. 1. ✔
    2. ✘ ; Of these two restaurants, this one is better.
    3. ✘ ; Out of the whole class, Sarah got the least juice.
    4. ✔
    5. ✘ ; Is that the biggest one of this bunch?
    6. ✘ ; The kids built a smaller snowman today than yesterday.

5   The Superfoods

A.

B. (Individual answer)

C. 1. Beth | chews her food very carefully.
    2. Tom | likes spinach.
    3. Kiwis | contain a lot of vitamin C.
    4. The children | ate a variety of vegetables.
    5. Sally | added some walnuts to her tuna salad.
    6. Mom | makes a very healthful breakfast for us every day.

D. 1. Sara eats raw fruits and vegetables every day.
    2. My father bought milk containing soy.
    3. Yogourt becomes a treat when mixed with berries.

E. 1. ✔   2. ✔
    3.   4.
    5. ✔

F. (Individual writing)

6   The Halifax Explosion

A.

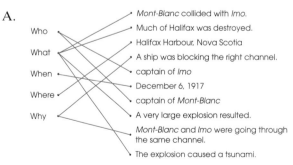

B. 1. World War I was going on.
    2. It became a fireball and vaporized.
    3. It led to medical advances in the treatment of eye injuries.

C. 1. has   2. is
    3. are   4. collide
    5. rises
D. 1. <u>occur</u> ; occurs
    2. <u>cause</u> ; causes
    3. <u>rise</u> ; rises
    4. <u>remain</u> ; remains
    5. <u>visits</u> ; visit
E. 1. The captains attempt a different course.
    2. Loads of munitions are on board.
    3. A/The tree snaps and a/the house is demolished.
    4. The family is devastated and refuses to believe it.
F. (Individual writing)

7 Cherry Blossom Time

A. 1. spring   2. islands
    3. south ; north   4. flower
    5. Vancouver
B.
    b l <u>o</u> ss <u>o</u> m s
    H <u>o</u> n s <u>h</u> u
    H o k k <u>a</u> i d o
    h o <u>n</u> o <u>o</u> u r a b l e
    m <u>o</u> u n t <u>a</u> i <u>n</u> s
    b l <u>o</u> o <u>m</u>
    p <u>i</u> c <u>n</u> i c s

    ohanami
C. 1. direct
    2. direct
    3. indirect
    4. direct
    5. direct
    6. indirect
D. 1. bracelet ; sister
    2. note ; Tom
    3. story ; Bill
    4. parcel ; cousin
    5. letter ; you
    6. project ; Tom
E. 1. the audience ; her painting
    2. the customers ; the menus
    3. the guests ; a video
    4. the children ; Christmas cards
F. (Individual writing)

8 Winter Camp at Lake Winnipeg

A.
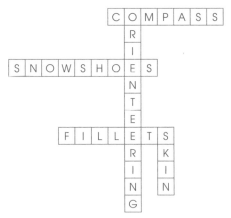

B. (Individual writing)
C. 1. She   2. us
    3. ours   4. his
D. 1. We told him that we wouldn't be long.
    2. Look! All of these are hers!
    3. Although it is still winter in Winnipeg, they don't mind the cold at all.
E. 1. We   2. me
    3. ours   4. me/us
    5. she/I   6. us/them
    7. we/they   8. it
    9. him   10. he
    11. us
F. (Suggested writing)
    1. a. Jenny wants us to go fishing with her.
       b. She wants my brother and me to go fishing with her.
    2. a. Uncle Max has always been good at it.
       b. He has always been good at ice fishing.
    3. a. "You should've asked if that marker was mine," said May.
       b. "You should've asked if it belonged to me," said May.
       c. "You should've asked if that marker belonged to me," she said.

9 Bethany Hamilton

A. (Suggested definitions and individual writing of sentences)
    1. ride the crest of a wave towards the shore on a surfboard
    2. the essence of a person ; the soul
    3. athlete who competes in three different sports
    4. device to stop bleeding

ISBN: 978-1-77149-033-7

B. (Individual writing)
C. 1. relative
    2. interrogative
    3. interrogative
    4. relative
    5. interrogative
    6. relative
D. 1. who
    2. which
    3. whom
    4. which
    5. whose
    6. what/who
    7. what
    8. who
E. (Individual writing)

10 The Inca

A. 1. fighters   2. ancient
    3. worshipped   4. Peru
    5. sure-footed   6. transport
    7. clothing   8. legends
B. 1. It was a large empire of 12 million people.
    2. They built it around the 16th century.
    3. They say that an enormous flood will overtake the land.
    4. (Individual writing)
C. 1. themselves
    2. myself
    3. herself
    4. one another
    5. himself
    6. each other
    7. itself
    8. yourselves
D. 1. each other
    2. one another / themselves
    3. yourselves
    4. ourselves
    5. themselves
    6. each other
E. (Individual writing)

11 The Hummingbird – a Unique Flyer

A.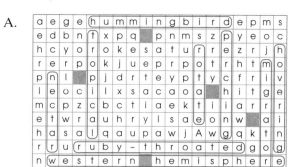
    1. rotate
    2. perching
    3. hummingbird
    4. hovering
    5. migratory
    6. nectar
B. 1. weighs
    2. consumes
    3. is leaving
    4. live
    5. feed
    6. is approaching
    7. are beating
    8. spend
C. 1. ✘ ; Ben and Jill give their dog a bath once every three weeks.
    2. ✘ ; Gwen dashes to the park after school every day.
    3. ✔
    4. ✔
D. (Individual writing)

12 A Letter from a New Pen Pal

A. 1. Rakesh   2. 11 years old
    3. India   4. Mumbai
    5. Bombay   6. 12 million
    7. biggest city   8. at a magazine
    9. as a computer programmer
    10. sister   11. five
    12. an aunt and an uncle
    13. Toronto, Canada

B.   (Individual writing)
C.   1. <u>was attending</u> ; attended
      2. <u>was spotting</u> ; spotted
      3. <u>was practising</u> ; practised
      4. <u>were arriving</u> ; arrived
      5. <u>planted</u> ; were planting
      6. <u>was asking</u> ; asked
      7. <u>was singing</u> ; sang
D.   1. was baking ; rang
      2. stayed ; enjoyed
      3. caught ; went
      4. were watching ; began ; left
      5. was pouring ; recognized ; walked
E.   (Individual writing)

13 Jeanne Mance

A.   1. founding fathers
      2. New France
      3. Aboriginal peoples
      4. Hôtel-Dieu de Montréal
      5. 1645
B.   1. a. brave
         b. debt
         c. soothe
         d. sufferer
      2. We have to-day a debt unpaid
         Should we now fail where you have laid
         Foundation on the rock of God
      3. O brave Jeanne Mance whose fame is ours
         As in a city's growth it flowers:
         The seeds you humbly helped to sow
         Give witness still and still they grow
C.   1. will be hosting
      2. will show
      3. will turn
      4. will be sharing
      5. will be snowing ; will read
      6. will arrive ; will be staying
D.   1. B
      2. A
      3. C
      4. D
E.   (Individual writing)

14 Canadian Sports

A.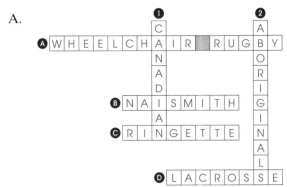

B.   1. T   2. F
      3. T   4. T
      5. F
C.   1. Mrs. Maple baked a pumpkin pie
      2. the ravine was explored by the nature-loving Aboriginal girl
      3. The diner around the corner was patroned by the basketball players
      4. Vikki and her teammates swam many lengths of the pool
D.   1. a. The colours create a spectacular light show.
         b. The curtains appear to be shielding the Earth.
      2. a. They are seen more often by people who live near the Arctic.
         b. But the occurrence of northern lights cannot be predicted.
      3. The Earth appears to be shielded by the curtains.
         People who live near the Arctic see them more often.
      4. They work better in their original voice because we should focus on "curtains" and "northern lights", respectively, to connect with the previous sentence in each case.

15 My Best Friend

A.   (Suggested writing of definition)
      using strength or power to make others scared or do what they do not want to do
      (Individual examples)
B.   (Individual writing)

ISBN: 978-1-77149-033-7

C.
1. have ; heard
2. Have ; rung
3. heard
4. has sung / has heard
5. sang
6. thought
7. has ; thought
8. rang

D.
1. ✔
2. ✗ ; Little Tim finished his homework at six o'clock today.
3. ✗ ; The teachers have not noticed anything wrong so far.
4. ✔
5. ✗ ; My brother threw one of his slippers out of the window a minute ago but luckily it didn't land on anyone's head!
6. ✔

E. (Individual writing)

16 The Skeleton Coast

A.
1. B
2. C
3. B
4. C
5. C
6. A

B. (Individual writing)

C.
1. The sand dunes of the Skeleton Coast can rise as high as 500 metres.
2. "The frequent fogs are the reason why this stretch of coastline is called the Skeleton Coast," Samuel quoted from his reading.
3. Of the elephant, springbok, brown hyena, and spiral-horned oryx antelope, which one would you want to see the most?
4. "Where do you want to visit next?" my father asked me.
5. Do you think the Skeleton Coast is really all that spooky?
6. "Yes, seal colonies can be found in Africa," said Tom matter-of-factly.
7. "What a wonderful example of life in extreme environments!" our teacher exclaimed in wonder.
8. Oh dear! Look at all these ship remains!
9. "You won't believe what my friend has done!" Amy said in anger.
10. "Sara, look at those seals over there," her mother said.

D.
1. When cold air mixes with hot air, moisture is produced(,)creating fog.
2. "I seem to hear voices speaking to me as the fog rolls(.)" Anna whispered to me.
3. (")The cold Benguela Current causes the sea breezes to be cold as well.(")
4. "From the shores of northwest Africa, can I see the Atlantic Ocean(?)" Bob asked.
5. "Maybe there were not that many sailors who perished here(!)" Marie tried to make her sister feel better in her calm voice.
6. "I can't take this anymore(,)" Fran called out in exasperation.

E. Lizzie and Paula go swimming every weekend. Lizzie is training to be a competitive swimmer, while Paula swims for fun. "Someday," Lizzie tells Paula, "I'm going to be an Olympic silver medalist!" A bit puzzled, Paula asks, "A silver medalist? Why don't you want to be a gold medalist?" Sounding matter-of-factly, Lizzie answers, "Silver is my favourite colour. Gold is a little too shiny for me. When I'm up on the podium, I want to be wearing my favourite colour!" Finding Lizzie's aspirations a little unusual, Paula is quiet and thinks to herself, "Sounds like Lizzie. Always making unpredictable choices."

17 The Story of K'iid K'iyass

A.
1. ecotourism
2. loggers
3. sacred
4. oral
5. misguided
6. conical
7. United

B.
1. A
2. C
3. B
4. D
5. B
6. C

C. Canada has produced some very talented people: writer Alice Munro; scientist David Suzuki; dancer Rex Harrington, and retired hockey player Mario Lemieux. A prolific writer, Munro's short stories always deal with the fascinating complexities of the human heart, winning international acclaim. Suzuki's charm and knack for public speaking make him a scholar and a great communicator: his show *The Nature of Things* draws the public's attention to the importance of protecting our environment. Harrington makes his ballet performances look so easy from his natural flare, you wouldn't have guessed how much hard work is required behind the scenes. Finally, Lemieux – whose name means "the best" in French – captained Team Canada into a gold medal at the 2002 Winter Olympic Games. Despite cancer and back pains, Lemieux never fails to play a good game, and is one of the NHL's greatest hockey players in history.

D. (Individual writing)

18 In Flanders Fields – a Poem of Remembrance

A. (Suggested definitions and individual writing of sentences)
1. small singing bird with brown feathers and long hind claws
2. something made or given as a gesture of respect, admiration, or affection for a person
3. an infection causing inflammation of the lungs
4. uselessness

B. (Suggested writing)
1. Not long ago, we lived and knew the beauty of dawn and of sunset.
2. The larks that are still bravely singing fly in the sky, but nobody hears them because of the noise of guns below them.
3. The poppies in Flanders Fields are blown in the wind, among the rows and rows of crosses where soldiers are buried.

C. 1. replace   2. impossible
    3. incomplete   4. unwilling
    5. regenerate   6. imprecise
    7. informal   8. indiscrete

D. careful ; care
insecurity ; secure
sincerity ; sincere
thoughtful ; thought
reunification ; unify

E. 1. breakable
2. provincial
3. Remembrance
4. publication

F. 1. review
2. discover
3. misplace
4. disorganized
(Individual writing of sentences)

19 The Seven Wonders of the Modern World

A.

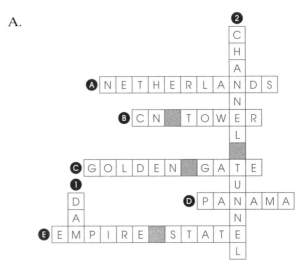

B. (Individual writing)
C. 1. subject
2. object
3. subject
4. complement
5. subject
6. complement
D. (Individual writing)
E. 1. photographed ; adjective
2. free-standing ; adjective
3. Digging ; moving ; noun
4. digging ; verb
5. resulting ; adjective
6. moving ; verb

ISBN: 978-1-77149-033-7

20 The Seven Natural Wonders of the World

A. 1. Nepal and Tibet
2. near Mexico
3. high latitudes
4. The United States
5. Australia
6. Africa
7. Brazil
B. (Individual writing)
C. 1. adjective
2. adverb
3. adjective
4. adverb
5. adverb
6. adverb
7. adjective
8. adjective
9. adverb
10. adjective
D. For adventure seekers looking for mountains to climb, Mount Everest is a <u>very popular</u> choice. With its summit at 8850 metres, it is <u>incredibly high</u>. To reach the summit of Everest is to reach the top of the world because it is the highest mountain on Earth. To some climbers, it is like conquering the impossible. But failing to reach the top does not necessarily mean failure. There are <u>really persistent</u> climbers who so desperately want to keep going, but whose bodies simply cannot withstand the lack of oxygen at <u>extremely high</u> altitudes. Knowing only too well that there have been deaths on this mountain in the past, these people have no choice but to turn back. In their case, nothing is <u>more sensible</u> than walking back down, which can save their lives.
E. (Individual writing)

21 A Letter from Sammy

A. 4 ; 1 ; 6 ; 3 ; 5 ; 7 ; 2
B. 1. Already I have eaten sushi, I have slept on the floor on tatami mats, and I have learned to compliment Kiyoka's mother for her good cooking.
2. Before long, I found myself in a Japanese home in the mountains, drinking green tea with Kiyoka and her grandparents.
3. We can't talk much but we laugh a lot together.
C. 1. so   2. when
3. but   4. as
5. and   6. before
7. where   8. Although
9. until   10. If
D. 1. whenever   2. where
3. while   4. since
5. unless
E. (Individual writing)

22 How Hurricanes Get Their Names

A. 1. The World Meteorological Organization maintains the lists of hurricanes.
2. They were named after saints. A hurricane on February 3 would be named Hurricane Blaise since February 3 is Saint Blaise's Day.
3. Every day is named after a saint.
4. Instead of using only women's names, both men's and women's names started to be used in alternate fashion.
5. It is retired.
B. (Individual writing)
C. 1. <u>A hurricane name is retired</u> if the hurricane is especially catastrophic.
2. <u>Names of saints had been used to name hurricanes</u> before men's and women's names were used.
3. "<u>I won't go out to the backyard</u> unless that skunk leaves the deck," my sister says.
4. "<u>I'm not coming out of my room</u> until it's dinnertime!" my little sister pouts.
5. We began using both men's and women's names for hurricanes <u>after we recognized how wrong it was to use only women's names</u>.
6. The practice of naming hurricanes with women's names became more common during World War II <u>when the United States also adopted this method</u>.
7. <u>Whenever there is a squirrel in the backyard,</u> my sister goes out to say hello.
8. "Why don't you help me wash the lettuce <u>while I cut the carrots</u>?" my mother asks.

D. (Check these sentences.)
1. There were hurricanes <u>whose names have been retired</u>.
4. This is the place <u>that Charlotte does not want to remember</u>.
6. It is fascinating <u>only because you like storms</u>.
8. <u>If there are more than 21 hurricanes in a given year</u>, the additional storms will be named after the letters of the Greek alphabet.
9. Ben thought of another way of naming hurricanes <u>while he was doing his math homework</u>.
E. (Individual writing)

23 Strange Names

A.

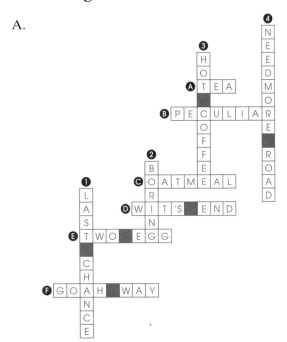

B. 1. compound
2. compound
3. complex
4. complex
5. complex
6. compound
7. complex
C. 1. a. It comes in many flavours and it comes in a variety of shapes.
b. The shape looks like a ring but it also resembles a nut.
2. a. There is the Dutchie which looks like a pillow.

b. Since this treat is made of dough, we decided to call it "doughnut".
D. (Individual writing)

24 Farewell, Kiribati

A. 1. D 2. B
3. C 4. G
5. F 6. A
7. E
B. 1. it has atolls that spread across the Pacific Ocean
2. tourism, coconut-processing, and fishing
3. it was the first to enter the new millennium, being the closest country to the International Date Line
4. it is a low-lying country, and so will be flooded by rising sea levels from global warming
C. 1. a. among
b. Between
c. between
d. among
2. a. less
b. fewer
c. less
d. fewer
3. a. number
b. number
c. amount
d. amount
D. 1. Among
2. number
3. between
4. less
5. fewer

25 Going Camping with a Rock Star

A.

Stone	Colour	Other Information
Amethyst	– violet	– a semi-precious stone
Granite	– many colours	– glints in the sun – some have other kinds of stone threaded within – a lot of it in Canadian Shield
Mica	– not very colourful	– cleaves into tiny sheets

ISBN: 978-1-77149-033-7

B. (Individual writing)
C. 1. anxiously
   2. easily
   3. always ; carefully
   4. slowly ; steadily
   5. massive ; broad
   6. fun-loving ; hilarious
D. 1. The Canadian Shield <u>makes up</u> half of Canada.
      The Canadian Shield <u>stretches across</u> half of Canada.
      – "Stretches across" is more visual than "makes up".
   2. Amethyst is a semi-precious stone.
      Amethyst is a semi-precious stone <u>that is violet in colour</u>.
      – A colour word is added to give a clearer picture.
   3. I love the way granite <u>looks</u> in the sun.
      I love the way granite <u>glints</u> in the sun.
      – "Glints" means "sparkles"; "looks" does not give that information.
   4. Different rocks <u>break</u> in different ways.
      Different rocks <u>cleave</u> in different ways.
      – "Cleave" means "cut along a line", which is more precise than "break".
E. (Individual writing)

26 The Long History of Extreme Sports

A. 1. T   2. T
   3. F   4. T
   5. T   6. T
   7. F   8. F
B. (Individual writing)
C. The comeback of surfing in Hawaii can be traced to the beginning of the 20th century. The missionaries' influence over the island had begun to decline by this time, which allowed the sport to regain its popularity. Along came a Hawaiian teenager named Duke Kahanamoku, who spent his days riding the waves. He and his buddies even created their own surfing club called "The Club of the Waves" and gave surfing a rebirth in Hawaii. Since then, the island has attracted scores of surfers – especially those from nearby California – and continues to be the destination for thrill seekers looking for some of the world's biggest waves.
D. (Individual writing)

27 Witch's Brew – or, "EEEEeeeeeew!"

A. (In any order)
   EEEEeeeeeew ; knew ; brew ; you ; too ; two ; clue ; threw ; glue ; chew ; flew ; spew
B. 1-2. (Individual writing)
   3. (Suggested writing)
      Each one gives additional information about the line that comes before it.
   4. The made-up words are "EEEEeeeeeew", "bluey", and "snoofed".
C. (Individual answers)
D. (Individual writing)
E. (Individual writing)

28 Folk Music Brings the World Together

A. (Suggested definitions, and individual synonyms and writing of sentences)
   1. tiring because of routine
   2. dull and gloomy
   3. cold or harsh
B. (Individual writing)
C. (Individual writing)
D. (Individual writing)

1 First Nations: Algonquin and Haudenosaunee (1)

A. Algonquin:
food ; beavers ; snowshoes
Haudenosaunee:
longhouses ; squash ; woman ; animals
B. Dwelling:
lived in wigwams ; lived in longhouses
Food:
fish, crops, and hunted animals ; fish, crops, and hunted animals
Roles of Men and Women:
men hunted and were leaders of families and women planted ; men hunted and women planted and headed their family or clan
Religion:
believed the spiritual world interacts with the physical world ; honoured the spirits who were believed to change the seasons and provide good crops and animals
C. 1. They were skilled at hunting because they migrated often and could not depend on farming for food source.
2. The Haudenosaunee women spent a lot of time planting and harvesting.

2 First Nations: Algonquin and Haudenosaunee (2)

A. 1.
2. Seneca ; Cayuga ; Onondaga ; Tuscarora ; Oneida ; Mohawk
3. B
4. B
5. Lake Ontario and the St. Lawrence River
6. They were located near water, and the easy access to water benefited them in farming.

7. The shortage of animals after hunting caused the Algonquins to migrate.
8. Unlike the Haudenosaunees who lived in permanent communities, the Algonquins migrated frequently, so they had less time to establish a more structured government system.

3 Haudenosaunee Confederacy

A. 1. Longhouse   2. Haudenosaunee
3. peaceful   4. Tuscarora
5. Mohawk ; Oneida ; Onondaga ; Cayuga ; Seneca ; Tuscarora
6. The Wendat had been at war with the Haudenosaunee nations.
B. 1. E
2. D
3. A
4. C
5. B
C. 1. council
2. chiefs
3. clan mothers
4. Grand Council
5. nations

4 European Explorers in Early Canada

A.

Newfoundland was the first destination the European explorers reached because it is the part of North America that is nearest to Europe.
B. 1. Vikings
2. overcrowding
3. North America
4. King Henry VII

5. Newfoundland
6. King Francis I
7. Asia
8. Atlantic
9. Jacques Cartier
10. St. Lawrence River
11. Quebec City

5 First Contact

A.

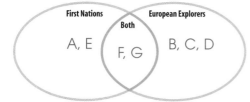

B. 1. a. They showed them new lands.
   b. They provided them with warm clothing and traditional nutritious foods like pemmican.
   c. They gave them fish and venison and taught them to make a herbal drink.
2. The First Nations considered it wrong to leave the Europeans suffering when they had means to ease their problems.
3. (Individual answer)

6 Benefits of Contact

A. First Nations to Europeans:
   A, C, F, G, H, J
   Europeans to First Nations:
   B, D, E, I, K, L, M
B. 1. metal
   2. hunt
   3. travel
   4. farm
   5. grains
   6. survival
   7. plants
   8. lands
   9. warm
   10. It strengthened the ties between the two groups and lessened the chances of conflict.

7 Negative Impacts on First Nations

A. 1. pelts
   2. decrease
   3. cleared
   4. waterways
   5. Wendats
   6. British
   7. conflicts
   8. influenza
   9. decreased
   10. alcohol
   11. Catholic
   12. parenting
   13. culture

B.

 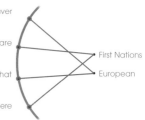

"They are sharing valuable beaver pelts with us for cheap axes."

"We like the metal tools they are sharing with us."

"The king will be happy with what we've established here."

"They are taking the best lands where we fish and hunt."

First Nations
European

8 New France

A. King:
   owner ; noblemen
   Seigneurs:
   large ; farmers ; church ; mill
   Habitants:
   seigneur ; harvest ; roads
B. 1. B
   2. (Individual answer)
C. 1. eastern
   2.

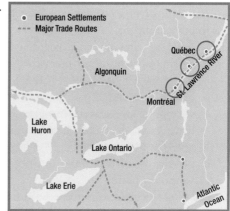

3. Goods were transported by canoes; settling close to waterways benefited the Europeans in trades.

3. They needed to be able to survive the hard work in New France and support their future husbands.

9 Jesuit Missionaries

A. 1. Colour the Jesuit's robe black.
    2. The king wanted to convert the First Nations peoples to Christianity so that New France would be like Europe.
    3. The Métis were the children born to First Nations and European parents.
B. 1. Sainte Marie
    2. priests
    3. traditions
    4. maps
    5. king
    6. trades
    7. convert
    8. Christianity
    9. They wanted to blend into their culture so they could convert the First Nations more successfully.
    10. The First Nations were interested in trading with the Europeans. By having the Jesuits trade with the First Nations, it increased their chance of converting the First Nations.

10 Filles du roi

A. 1. gain ; less
    2. fille du roi ; the king
    3. The king wanted to increase the French population by encouraging the French couples to have children.
B. 1. a. different parts of France including Paris and Normandy and other countries including Germany, England, and Portugal
       b. between 16 and 25
       c. very poor ; most were orphans and some were "spares" from large families ; low levels of literacy skills
       d. physically fit and have the potential to support a family
    2. Marriage ceremonies were held at church parishes and administered by priests.

11 People in the Fur Trade

A. 1. a. trading posts
       b. fur trade
       c. voyageurs
       d. coureurs des bois
    2. Before the fur trade, their purpose of hunting was food. Since the fur trade began, they hunted a lot more for animal pelts.
B. 1. spring
    2. furs
    3. stayed
    4. wives
    5. encouraged
    6. gain
    7. survival
    8.

sew clothing
carry heavy cargo
stitch moccasins for the team
set up tents and campfires
cook stew and prepare pemmican

12 Treaties and Land Claims

A. 1764:
    Niagara ; British ; First Nations ; to ensure that there would be fair and voluntary land dealings between the two parties
    1787:
    Gunshot ; British ; First Nations ; were offered some money, reserve lands, and annual gifts
    1871 to 1921:
    Numbered ; federal government ; First Nations ; received reserve lands and various forms of government assistance
B. 1. 1992   2. 1994
    3. 2005   4. 1993
    5. 2005   6. 2000
    7. 1978

ISBN: 978-1-77149-033-7

13 Aboriginal Self-Government

A. federal ; allows ; communities ; federal
   1. +
   2. -
   3. +
   4. -
   5. +
   6. (Individual answer)
B. 1. F
   2. A
   3. A
   4. F
   5. A
   6. F
C. 1. Aboriginal self-government would allow the First Nations to regain what they had lost after the Europeans arrived.
   2. (Individual answer)

14 Traditional Ecological Knowledge

A. 1. nature
   2. survival
   3. electricity
   4. traditions
   5. sustainably
   B ; B ; A
B. 1. a. Scientists
      b. TEK
      c. open waters
      d. open waters, offshore, and under the ice
      e. about 800
      f. about 7000
   2. about 8000
   3. the Inuit
   4. (Individual answer)

15 Rights and Responsibilities of a Canadian Citizen

A. 1. Legal
   2. Language
   3. Mobility
   4. Equality
   5. Freedom
   6. Democratic
B. C ; D ; E
C. Case 1:
   Equality Rights ; The job does not require driving. Peter is not treated equally as others.
   Case 2:
   Freedom of Religion ; Farida is being discriminated against practising her religion and is "forced" to abandon her religion to get employed.

16 Levels of Government in Canada

A. 1. Federal ; Prime Minister ; international ; all ; national defence ; (Individual answer)
      a. food
      b. age
      c. employment
   2. Provincial ; federal ; road ; (Individual answers)
      A ; C ; D
   3. Municipal ; districts ; police ; (Individual answers)
      A ; C ; D
   4. federal
   5. 1996

17 Health Care

A. provincial ; federal ; municipal
   Federal Government: E, I
   Provincial Government: A, B, C, F, G, H
   Municipal Government: D, J
B. 1. The elderly population has been increasing and is predicted to continue to increase.
   2. The expenses for long-term care homes and community care will go up. The cost to operate hospitals will also increase.
   3. Ontario spends most on "Operations and Hospitals" and "Doctors and Practitioners".
   4. As the population ages, more health problems will arise. To support the increasing demand, more doctors need to be hired, and more hospitals and medical centres need to be built.
   5. (Individual answers)

18 Water Management

A. 1. conserves
2. boundaries
3. scientific
4. municipal
5. fisheries
6. quality
7. ecosystems
8. costs
9. delivers
10. waste water
11. quality
B. 1-2. (Individual answers)
3. No

19 Recycling and Waste Management

A. 1. international
2. waste
3. manages
4. monitoring
5. recycles
6. homes
7. municipal government
8. federal government
9. provincial government
B. 1. a. 9.1 million tonnes
b. 3.4 million tonnes
2. a. increasing
b. increasing
3. (Suggested answer)
Landfills will eventually run out and burning garbage adds to greenhouse gases.
4. (Suggested answer)
Reduce waste and recycle materials.

20 Transportation

A. urban ; intra-provincial ; interprovincial
1. investment
2. more
3. expenditure
4. fewer
5. costs
6. benefits

7. control
8. public
B. 1. a. Toronto's average commute time is longer.
b. Toronto's average commute time is longer.
2. The average commute time of those who travel by transit is double that of those who drive.
3. Toronto has a longer commute time compared to other cities in Canada. The transit system needs to be improved.
4. (Suggested answers)
leave home earlier to avoid traffic on toll free roads ; live closer to her workplace

21 Homelessness

A. 1. rent
2. conflicts
3. drug
4. hospitalization
5. government
6. affordable
7. federal
8. housing
B. 1. a. decreased
b. increased
2. (Individual answer)
3. A, B, D
(Individual solution)
4. A, B, D

22 Taxation and Spending

A. 1. tax
2. use
3. value
4. facilities
5. parks
6. sale
7. property tax, provincial transfer, and others
8. Property tax and municipal land transfer tax would change because they are based on the market value of housing. As the price of housing increases, the income from the two sources will increase.
B. 1. A: 3 ; Toronto Transit Commission (TTC)
B: 4 ; others
C: 2 ; police services

D: 5 ; employment and social services
E: 1
2. (Individual answer)

23 Public Opinion

A. 1. council meetings
2. town hall meetings
3. local councillors
4. legislature
5. Provincial Legislative
6. Provincial Parliament
7. House of Commons
8. Parliament
B. Observations:
equal ; status ; less ; medical
Recommendations:
health care ; transparent ; healthiest

24 Public Activism

A. 1. writing letters to politicians
2. street march
3. boycott
4. hunger strike
5. strike
6. rally
7. sit-in
B. Local Residents: A ; C
Naturalists: E ; E
Biologists: B ; D
Hydrologists: D ; A
Land Developers: C ; B
Outcome: four ; 8

1 Matter

A. Check the following:
    a cloud, a ball, a beach umbrella, a sandcastle, a shell, water
B. 1. solid   2. gas
    3. liquid
C. (Individual drawings)
    1. gas   2. solid
    3. liquid

2 Measures of Matter

A. 1. lighter ; mass   2. mass ; heavier
B. 1.

2.

3.

C. 1.

2.

D. 1. the beach ball   2. the crayons
    3. the book   4. the sponge

3 Changing States of Matter

A. 1. solid ; liquid ; melted
    2. liquid ; solid ; solidified
    3. gas ; liquid ; condensed
    4. liquid ; gas ; vapourized
B. 1. give   2. give
    3. give   4. take away
    5. take away   6. give
C. Reversible: B, E
    Irreversible: A, C, D
Experiment: (Individual observation)
    Because the water in the air has condensed.

4 Properties of Matter

A. Circle the following words:
    Colour, size, hardness, taste, viscosity, texture, lustre, clarity, state, solubility, malleability
B. 1. lustre   2. taste
    3. size   4. hardness
    5. solubility   6. state
C. (Suggested descriptions)

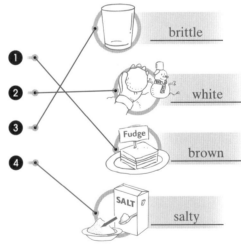

D. (Individual answers for colour and size)
    Hardness: soft as feathers
    Texture: velvety

ISBN: 978-1-77149-033-7

5 Weather and Climate

A.

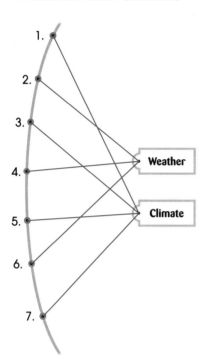

B.

weather · climate

C. 1. tropical   2. polar
3. temperate   4. sub-polar
5. desert   6. subtropical
7. mountain

6 Temperature

A. 1.

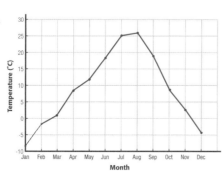

2. August
3. January
4. January, February, December

B. (Suggested answers)
1. July, August
2. January, February, December
3. April, May, October, November

C.

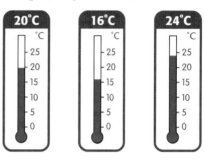

7 Water Cycle

A.

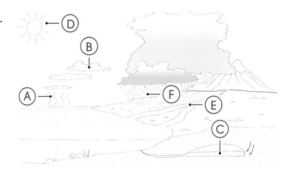

B. Check all pictures.
C. A

8 Clouds and Precipitation

A.

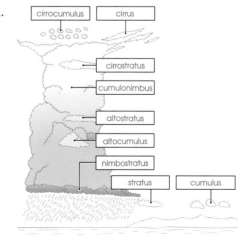

B. 1. altocumulus   2. stratus
    3. cirrostratus   4. cumulonimbus

C.

9   Wind

A. 1-3. (Suggested answers for B)
    1. A: moderate breeze
        B: 1 ; light air
    2. A: light breeze
        B: 6 ; strong breeze
    3. A: storm
        B: 8 ; fresh gale

B.
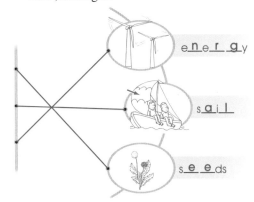

e n e r g y

s a i l

s e e ds

C. 1. easterly
    2. northwesterly
    3. westerly

10   Extreme Weather

A.
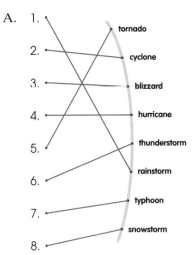

1.
2.
3.
4.
5.
6.
7.
8.

tornado
cyclone
blizzard
hurricane
thunderstorm
rainstorm
typhoon
snowstorm

B. 1. too little precipitation
    2. too much precipitation
    3. too little precipitation
    4. too little precipitation
Experiment: (Individual observation)
    6 sides

11   Weather Station

A.
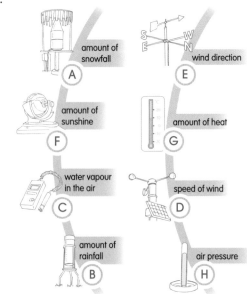

amount of snowfall   A
wind direction   E
amount of sunshine   F
amount of heat   G
water vapour in the air   C
speed of wind   D
amount of rainfall   B
air pressure   H

B. 1. A, B   2. B, C
    3. A, C

ISBN: 978-1-77149-033-7

C. (Suggested answers)
1. If rainfall has been low, there may be a high forest fire risk, or low water levels in reservoirs. If precipitation has been high, there may be a higher risk of flooding.
2. For safe travel, it is good to predict road conditions, flight conditions for airlines, space shuttle launchings, etc. It is also important for the construction industry to know when to work.

12 Conservation of Energy

A.
1. C ; NR
2. E ; NR
3. A ; NR
4. D ; R
5. G ; R
6. B ; R
7. F ; NR
B.
1. electrical ; heat
2. gravitational ; electrical
3. chemical ; mechanical
C. potential ; kinetic

13 The Wise Use of Energy

A.
1. unwise energy user
2. wise energy user
3. wise energy user
4. unwise energy user
5. wise energy user
B.
1. down
2. Use
3. seal
4. to a power bar
5. off
6. natural
7. off
8. long
C. (Individual answers)

14 Forces and Structures

A.
1. squeezing
2. stretching
3. twisting
4. bending
5. sliding
B.
1. shearing
2. torsion
3. tension
4. compression
5. bending
C.
1. tension
2. compression
3. compression
4. tension
5. a. tension
b. compression

15 Forces and Mechanical Advantage

A.
Group 1: A
Group 2: B
Group 3: A
Group 4: A
B.
1. a. A
b. gain
2. Make the ramp longer.
3. A – good for stamina ;
B – good for muscle strength
4. The weight of the puller helps move the object.
C. Circle the words:
mechanical advantage, force, stretching, tension, torsion, bending, shearing, compression

16 Cells

A.
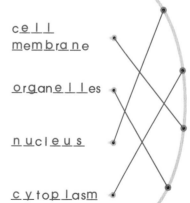
c e l l
m e m b r a n e

o r g a n e l l e s

n u c l e u s

c y t o p l a s m

2. nucleus
3. cell membrane

ISBN: 978-1-77149-033-7

B.

C. 1. nerve   2. skin   3. muscle

17 Musculoskeletal System

A.

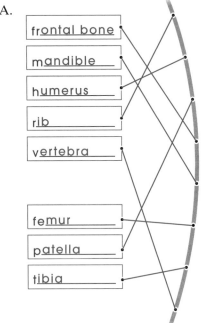

frontal bone

mandible

humerus

rib

vertebra

femur

patella

tibia

B.

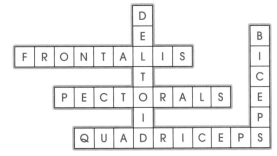

C. 1. pivot   2. ball and socket
   3. hinge   4. ball and socket
   5. hinge

18 Nervous System

A. 1. cerebrum   2. cerebellum
   3. brain stem   4. spinal cord
B. 1. a. brain stem   b. cerebrum
      c. cerebellum
   2. skull and meninges
   3. brain
   4. spinal cord
C. Colour the words:
   meninges, nerves, skull, cerebellum, spinal cord,
   brain stem, cerebrum

19 Respiratory System

A. 1. a. trachea
      b. lungs
      c. diaphragm
   2. oxygen   3. trachea
   4. exhale   5. inhale
   6. carbon dioxide 7. diaphragm
B. 1. smog ; ✘
   2. cigarettes ; ✘
   3. planting ; ✔
   4. pollution ; ✘
   5. smoke ; ✘
   6. jogging ; ✔

20 Circulatory System

A. 1. arteries   2. veins
   3. arteries   4. veins
   5. lungs   6. left
B. 1. 124   2. 65
   3. 102   4. 74

ISBN: 978-1-77149-033-7

21 Digestive System

A.

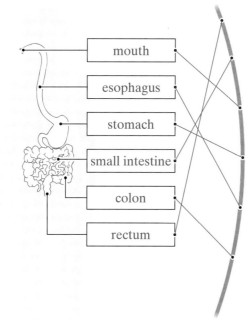

B.

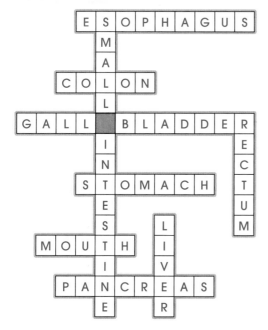

22 Excretory System

A. 1. kidneys
2. urine
3. ureters
4. bladder
5. urethra

B.

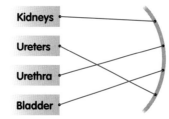

C. 1. false
2. true
3. false
4. true
5. true

23 Nutrition

A. (Suggested answers for the food items)
1. carbohydrates ; A, C
2. fibre ; C, F
3. proteins ; D, G
4. fats ; D, E
5. water ; B, F
6-7. minerals, vitamins ; D, F

B. 1. banana peach muffin
2. chocolate chip cookie
3. 320 mg
4. banana peach muffin

C. (Suggested answer)
Some vegetables for vitamins and fibre

24 Defence System

A. small organism: microbes
small organisms that cause illness: viruses, bacteria

B. Skin: B
Mucus: D
Cilia: A
Earwax: C
Stomach acid: E

C. **Blood**

ISBN: 978-1-77149-033-7

D.   White ;

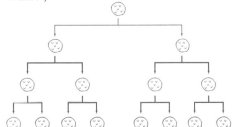

ISBN: 978-1-77149-033-7